Project
Change
Management

Other McGraw-Hill Books by H. James Harrington

- *The Improvement Process: How America's Leading Companies Improve Quality* (1987)
- *Business Process Improvement: The Breakthrough Strategy for Total Quality, Productivity, and Competitiveness* (1991)
- *Total Improvement Management: The Next Generation in Performance Improvement,* written with James S. Harrington (1995)
- *High Performance Benchmarking: 20 Steps to Success,* written with James S. Harrington (1996)
- *The Complete Benchmarking Implementation Guide: Total Benchmarking Management* (1996)
- *ISO 9000 and Beyond: From Compliance to Performance Improvement* (1997)
- *Business Process Improvement Workbook: Documentation, Analysis, Design and Management of Business Process Improvement,* written with Erik K.C. Esseling and Harm van Nimwegen (1997)
- *The Creativity Toolkit: Provoking Creativity in Individuals and Organizations,* with Glen D. Hoffherr and Robert P. Reid (1998)*
- *Statistical Analysis Simplified: The Easy-to-Understand Guide to SPC and Data Analysis,* written with Glen D. Hoffherr and Robert P. Reid (1998)*
- *Reliability Simplified: Going Beyond Quality to Keep Customers for Life,* written with Les Anderson (1998)*
- *Area Activity Analysis: Activities and Measurement to Enhance Business Performance,* written with Glen D. Hoffherr and Robert P. Reid (1998)*
- *ISO 14000 Implementation: Upgrading Your EMS Effectively,* written with Alan Knight (1999)*
- *Simulation Modeling Methods: To Reduce Risks and Increase Performance,* written with Kerim Tumay (1999)*
- *Performance Improvement Methods: Fighting the War on Waste,* written with Kenneth C. Lomax (1999)*

*Titles in the Harrington Performance Improvement Series

Project Change Management

Applying Change Management to Improvement Projects

H. James Harrington
International Quality Advisor
Ernst & Young LLP

Daryl R. Conner
Founder and CEO, ODR® Inc.

Nicholas L. Horney
Principal and Vice President, ODR® Inc.

McGraw-Hill

New York   San Francisco   Washington, D.C.   Auckland   Bogotá
Caracas   Lisbon   London   Madrid   Mexico City   Milan
Montreal   New Delhi   San Juan   Singapore
Sydney   Tokyo   Toronto

McGraw-Hill

*A Division of The **McGraw·Hill** Companies*

2 3 4 5 6 7 8 9 0 DOC   1 0 9 8 7 6

ISBN 0-07-027104-6

The sponsoring editor for this book was Catherine Schwent. Manuscript development and production by CWL Publishing Enterprises, Madison, WI, John A. Woods, President (www.execpc.com/cwlpubent).

Contents

About the Series

Project Change Management: Applying Change Management to Improvement Projects is one title in McGraw-Hill's Harrington's Performance Improvement Series. The series is designed to meet an organization's need to understand the most useful approaches now available to bring about improvements in organizational performance as measured by:

- Return on investment,
- Value-added per employee, and
- Customer satisfaction

Each title in the series is written in an easy-to-read, user-friendly style designed to reach employees at all levels of an organization. Our goal is to present complex methodologies in a way that is simple but not simplistic. The following are other subjects covered in the books in this series:

- Statistical process controls
- Process redesign
- Process reengineering
- Establishing a balanced scorecard
- Reliability analysis
- Fostering teamwork
- Environmental Management Systems ISO-14000
- Simulation modeling
- Rewards and recognition
- Performance improvement methods
- Creativity tools
- Statistical analysis simplified
- Area activity analysis

We believe that the books in this series will provide an effective way to learn about these practices as well as a training tool for use in any type of organization. In each title in the series, you'll find icons in the margins that call your attention to different points. Use these icons to guide your reading and study:

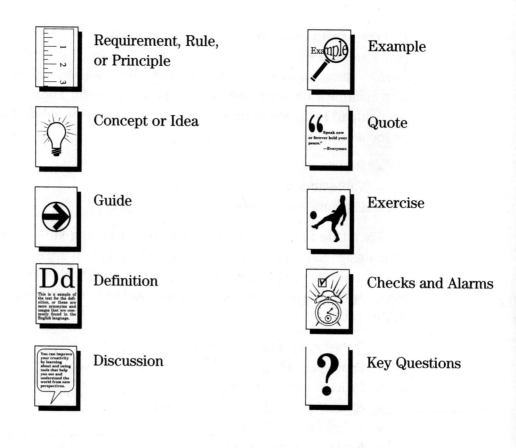

Requirement, Rule, or Principle

Example

Concept or Idea

Quote

Guide

Exercise

Definition

Checks and Alarms

Discussion

Key Questions

It is our hope that you will find this series of Performance Improvement books enjoyable and useful.

H. James Harrington
Principal, Ernst & Young LLP
International Quality Advisor

About the Authors

Dr. H. James Harrington is one of the world's leading process improvement gurus, with more than 45 years of experience. He has been involved in developing management systems in Europe, South America, North America, and Asia. He currently serves as principal with Ernst & Young LLP and as international quality advisor. He is also chairman of Emergency Technology Ltd., a high-tech software and hardware manufacturer and developer.

Before joining Ernst & Young LLP, he was president of the consulting firm Harrington, Hurd, and Rieker. He was a senior engineer and project manager for IBM and, for almost 40 years, he worked in IBM's quality function. He was chairman and president of the prestigious International Academy for Quality and the American Society for Quality. He has released a series of videos and CD-ROM programs that cover ISO 9000 and QS-9000. He has also authored a computer program on benchmarking, plus members' videotapes on performance improvement.

He has written 14 books on performance improvement and hundreds of technical reports. The Harrington/Ishikawa Medal was named after him in recognition of his support to developing nations in implementing quality systems. The Harrington/Neron Medal was also named after him to recognize his contribution to the quality movement in Canada. China named him its Honorary Quality Advisor, and he has been elected honorary member of eight quality professional societies and has received numerous awards and medals for his work. Recently, Dr. Harrington was elected into Singapore's Hall of Fame.

Daryl R. Conner is an internationally recognized expert in the field of change management and a well-known advisor to corporate leaders engaged in building nimble organizations. Mr. Conner is the founder and CEO of ODR® Inc., a research-based consulting firm that for the last 24 years has specialized in the human side of major organizational change. His experience in organizational consulting and his master's degree in behavioral psychology helped develop the foundation for his unique approach to optimizing organizational change initiatives. This approach is the Human Due Diligence™ methodology. Mr. Conner is the author of two books. His first, *Managing at the Speed of Change,* was published in 1993. His second, *Leading at the Edge of Chaos,* was published in 1998. ODR maintains offices throughout the United States and directs European operations from its UK office. In addition, ODR has offices in Switzerland and Mexico City.

Nicholas Horney is a principal and vice president of consulting services at ODR, Inc. in Atlanta, GA. In this capacity, he is a member of the firm's executive team. He has firm-wide responsibility for developing strategy, products, and teams to deliver change management consulting services. Dr. Horney acts as an advisor to senior management planning or undergoing major transformation. He also personally directs change implementation projects for clients (e.g., enterprise-wide IT implementation, mergers, corporate reorganizations, quality initiatives, process improvement, business process redesign). As an organizational psychologist with more than 20 years of experience, Dr. Horney has been able to identify and develop processes, products, and systems that initiate and sustain successful change. He was recognized for his work through his appointment by the Secretary of Commerce to the Board of Examiners for the Malcolm Baldrige National Quality Award and was sought by *USA Today* to help establish the RIT/USA Today Quality Cup award and serve as a judge since its inception in 1991.

Dedication

I dedicate this book to a close friend and a true professional Dave Farrell. Dave always takes time to challenge my thinking and wrote parts of Chapters 5 and 6. His thoughts on managing changes have had a big impact on my thinking.

—Daryl Conner

First and foremost, I dedicate this book to my wife, Rhonda, and my children, Amanda and Chandler, whose encouragement, support, and understanding were needed during the weekends and evenings of writing. Furthermore, the completion of this book would never have been possible without the skilled and persistent editorial support provided by Ern Clements of ODR, Inc. In addition, my thanks go to all of those who have made time in their busy schedules to provide comments and recommendations during our work on this book.

Jim, Daryl, and I have attempted to create a book that integrates the methodologies of project management and change management and applies the result to process improvement. Working with Jim and Daryl on this book has enabled us to expand our views about the other applications of the integration of project management and change management.

—Nick Horney

Preface

You are part of the change parade. It is up to you. Are you a bandleader? Or do you sweep up the horse droppings after the parade has passed?

~~Businesses are changing.~~ Everything is changing around the world at a pace that blurs everyone's vision. (See, things are changing so fast that I couldn't finish my first sentence before I needed to change it.) The good old days were last Friday, but now it's Monday and the rules have changed. If you have a good idea, act on it as soon as you get it. If you don't, someone else will. Organizations need to be immediately ready to pounce on every opportunity or they will be left at the starting gate.

Yesterday's competitors are today's partners. What was out of the question yesterday is practical today and obsolete tomorrow. If you feel comfortable with your business plan, you probably took too long developing it. In many organizations, by the time you have obtained all the approvals to buy the latest computer, the computer is obsolete. (I tried to donate a two-year-old computer to Goodwill Industries and they wouldn't even accept it.) The computer keyboard is almost obsolete as voice recognition systems come into their own. By 2004, people with typing skills will be as obsolete as buggy-whip makers.

Structures need to be fluid, allowing the organization to flow around obstacles, enveloping them and moving on as though they were not even there. We have evolved from organizations that depend upon capital to drive their success to organizations whose success is primarily dependent upon their knowledge.

This is an environment that is continuously changing. Things change so fast, you probably won't feel comfortable with one change before it is changed again. This means that you need to understand the big picture that defines the direction in which the organization is going and embrace each change as an opportunity. The winners look at each change as a steppingstone. Those who fight change soon find themselves as the foundation upon which someone else's stepping-stones are laid.

When it comes to change, people are a lot like electrical components. There are basically two types.

We have the resistors. In electronics, resistors are components that consume energy (watts) and get heated up. The more resistance there is in the circuit, the more force (current and voltage) is needed to get the job accomplished. In electronics a great deal of work has been directed at minimizing resistance in circuits to conserve energy and reduce heat. There are many people who resist change. In fact all of us have a tendency to resist change to some degree. Some of us are one-ohm resistors, while others are megaohm resistors. I don't mean to indicate that some level of resistance is not justified. We need to question each change, for some of the suggested changes may not be ethical, moral, or legal. But continuous resistance to change is a waste of energy, because things will change and you will be part of the parade. It's your choice whether you become a bandleader or come along after the parade has passed, sweeping up the horse droppings.

The other type of electrical component that is similar to the way people react to change is a capacitor. A capacitor stores up energy and releases it when it is needed. Likewise, people need to develop the capacity to store up additional energy and be able to release it when the pressure of change begins to impact them. This capacity to exist in changing environments and to seize the opportunity presented is called resilience. Building up your capacity to handle a continuous and never ending state of change is a key skill that is needed to survive in today's fast-moving environment. It is often as important to your future progress as a master's degree.

Now, as you think about how to handle change, there are two major considerations:

► What is the individual's responsibility related to how he or she handles change?

► What can the organization do to ensure that the projects that drive change are successfully implemented?

Although both are important and will be discussed briefly, the major focus of this book is what the organization needs to do to ensure the success of the projects that it is undertaking.

The difference between getting by and being great is not what you do, but how you manage the change process. In a 1997 survey of 410 executives from *Fortune* 1000 companies by Opinion Research Corporation International and Coopers & Lybrand, it was obvious that the difference between being really successful and just surviving is the way change was managed. You'll note in the following table that the most successful companies always had a heavier emphasis on managing the change process than the other companies.

	Most Successful	Other Organizations	SAP
Senior managers' behaviors support change	94%	76%	18%
Respected managers are advocates	87%	71%	16%
Organizational structure is effective	83%	59%	24%
Leaders of different units work together	70%	54%	16%
Leaders encourage open and honest communication	81%	71%	10%
Leaders issue frequent progress reports	66%	42%	24%
Leaders have effective communication strategy	64%	44%	20%
Employees' roles are aligned with goals and objectives	77%	47%	30%
Employees understand the mission and strategy	74%	44%	30%
Employees are rewarded for promoting innovation and change	68%	41%	27%
Employees believe daily activities are relevant	66%	43%	23%

Source: *Management Review* Magazine, May 1998, "Invigorating Change Initiatives" by Dick Smith, Partner, Coopers & Lybrand

The differences between getting by and being great

Everyone has two choices in life—you can choose to make the best of any situation or you can choose to let it get you down and act as a victim. The best thing to do is to treat it as a learning experience and better yourself.

PATTY A. HAWORTH, CELESTIAL SEASONING COMPANY, SOURCE: *QUALITY MAGAZINE*, AUGUST 1998

This book differs from other books on change because it first defines the change tools that need to be mastered in order to manage organizational change (Chapters 1, 2, 3, and 4) and then applies these tools to project management methodology, process redesign, and a typical SAP project (Chapters 5, 6, 7, and 8). The authors believe that this practical approach for implementing and managing organizational change in major projects will provide the reader with new insight related to what Managing Organizational Change (MOC) is all about. It will also provide a step-by-step approach for applying the MOC methodology to any project that the organization wishes to implement, thereby minimizing the chance of project cost overruns, missed schedules, and not producing the promised results.

▶ Chapter 1, Change and the New Millennium, shows the reader why it is important to step up to managing the changes that accompany most major projects.
▶ Chapter 2, Change Management: Strategic Risks to Successful Project Implementation, provides the reader with an understanding of the strategic risks that accompany change as well as an understanding of the Managing Organizational Change methodology.
▶ Chapter 3, Change Management: Tactical Risks to Successful Project Implementation, continues Chapter 2, providing the reader with an understanding of the tactical risks that accompany change, from the perspective of the Managing Organizational Change methodology.
▶ Chapter 4, Implementation Architecture, provides the reader with a road map that will help him or her implement MOC and

gives an understanding of the MOC assessments, surveys, and tools and when they should be used.

▶ Chapter 5, How MOC Fits into the Project Management Methodology, provides the reader with an understanding of how to integrate MOC into the way a project is managed.

▶ Chapter 6, Applying MOC to a Process Redesign Project— Phases I and II, defines how to integrate MOC into Phase I (Organizing for Improvement) and Phase II (Understanding the Process) of a process redesign project.

▶ Chapter 7, Applying MOC to a Process Redesign Project— Phases III and IV, defines how to integrate MOC into Phase III (Streamlining the Process) and Phase IV (Implementation) of a process redesign project.

▶ Chapter 8, Applying MOC to an SAP R/3 Project, defines how to integrate MOC into a major SAP project.

Note: Throughout this book are a number of terms, assessments, surveys, and tools whose names are copyrighted by ODR Inc. (A list of the assessments, surveys, and tools can be found on the CD-ROM.) Although the ODR names are used for most of the assessments, surveys, and tools, their purpose is defined in the book so that the reader can develop his or her own documents. If you would like to purchase copies of the documents, you can contact ODR in Atlanta, GA by calling 404 455-7145. Although Ernst & Young LLP has documents that serve the same purpose, the firm doesn't sell them to the public.

Our criminal system knows you cannot force anyone to change. All you can do is present them with the options so that they can set their own course.

Acknowledgments

We would particularly like to acknowledge the excellent work and effort of Steffy Hristova, who converted and edited endless hours of dictation into this final product. John Woods and Robert Magnan of CWL Publishing Enterprises have worked closely with us in giving the manuscript one final review and managing the production, turning it into the book you now hold. We would also like to acknowledge the efforts put forth by the personnel at SystemCorp in preparing the CD-ROM: Richard Rosenbloom, who brought the storyboard to life, and Ari Kugler, who provided the resources to create the CD-ROM free of charge. And last, but not least, Jaimie Benchimol, who managed and followed the process that created the CD-ROM.

A very special thanks is given to Dave Farrell of Ernst & Young LLP and Ernie Clements of ODR Inc., who prepared parts of the book and coordinated the book preparation between ODR Inc. and Ernst & Young LLP.

We would be remiss if we did not recognize our wives, who put up with us while we spent many nights preparing the manuscript. We love them for many reasons, one of which is for being so patient with us.

Most of the figures and many of the MOC assessments, surveys, and tools have already been trademarked by ODR Inc. or Ernst & Young LLP.

—H. James Harrington

1

Change and the New Millennium

It's not the strongest species that survive, or the most intelligent, but the most responsive to change.
—CHARLES DARWIN

Introduction to This Book

The challenges facing managers of business process improvement (BPI) projects are proportionate in difficulty to the increasing turbulence in today's market environment. Project-related work is becoming more critical to our organizations' success. We are asked to initiate and successfully complete more projects that are increasingly complex and interconnected in sometimes subtle and unexpected ways. The tolerance for failure is near to none; the cost of poor project implementation can easily run into the millions and derail an organization's successful track record. Speed to market is quickly becoming the banner of many projects that yield, at a minimum, a short-term advantage to those organizations that can effectively and efficiently implement projects faster than their competitors. A new approach to BPI project management is essential in facing these challenges.

Business Process Improvement (BPI)—The breakthrough methodologies used to improve individual processes, which include process redesign, process reengineering, benchmarking, restructuring, and major software projects like SAP.

Traditionally, project management has been defined in terms of the application of knowledge, skills, tools, and techniques to project activities in order to meet or exceed stakeholders' needs and expectations for the project.

Stakeholder—An individual or group of individuals or organizations with a common interest. Stakeholders of an organization typically are the customers, the owners, the employees, the employees' families, suppliers, management, and society. Stakeholders are sometimes called *interest partners* or *interested parties*.

Organization—Company, corporation, firm, enterprise, or association or any part thereof, whether incorporated or not, public or private, that has its own function and administration (source: ISO 8402:1994).

The emphasis of most project management activities, however, is on technical issues, with a significant lack of attention to the human aspects of the major change BPI projects. These human elements are addressed by another management discipline, known as "change management," that developed as a methodology for the most part independently of project management techniques and tools.

Major Change—A perceived departure from what was expected. Change is disruptive when a large gap exists between what was expected and what was experienced.

Change management refers to the application of behavioral science to the decision-making, planning, execution, and evaluation phases of the change process, all focused on the management of unnecessary disruption. (The process of change and related concepts will be further discussed in Chapter 2.)

Change management does not focus on *what* is to be changed (i.e., the BPI solution), but on *how* the solution is to be implemented. Its purpose is to substantially increase the likelihood of successful project implementation by addressing the human aspects of the change.

For years, many BPI managers "got by" adding only pieces and parts of change management methodologies, almost as an afterthought and with limited effect. Now, the true integration of our various business improvement techniques with a comprehensive change management methodology has become imperative to our success. We should no longer depend on "muscling our way" through projects. The careful attention the BPI project managers have traditionally given to the *technical* aspects of their projects must now be afforded to the *human* aspects, if the projects are to be successful in today's business environment. An integrated approach will help ensure an organization's success and, at the same time, shorten project implementation time and thereby cut the productivity costs associated with such projects (see Figure 1-1).

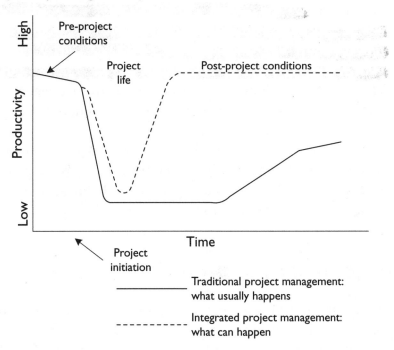

FIGURE 1-1. The benefits of integrated project management

We, the authors, have devoted substantial time to benchmarking successful and unsuccessful projects, both inside and outside our own organizations. Consulting firms, research organizations, conferences, books, and many other sources have provided a great deal of evidence to distinguish "the good, the bad, and the ugly" among attempted projects. From this, a disciplined approach to project management has formed that bridges and integrates the *what* aspect of the project with the *how* of change management. This integration is the subject of this book.

Introduction to This Chapter

Chapter 1 reviews the business environment we face today and what we believe will trend into the next century. We will discuss examples of some of the major problems and opportunities faced by most industry sectors that are now making our jobs challenging and will continue to do so. We will outline how it is possible to integrate project management with business process improvement and change management methodologies and how that integration will permit the wise use of your organization's human resources to serve strategic objectives. Later chapters will further explain key change management concepts and approaches, various business process improvement processes, and the integration of the two.

Our aim is to help you to be a successful project manager as you face more and increasingly unique initiatives. We cannot make your task simpler or less demanding; but with the ideas and tools presented here, we can help you to succeed.

Our Change Record to Date

There is no question about the need to be able to change rapidly to survive and thrive in today's world. The question is are we changing fast enough to survive and, if we are, is it costing us too much?

In 1997, organizations in the United States spent more than $250 billion on IT application development of approximately 175,000 projects. The average cost of a development project for a large organization is $2,322,000; for a medium organization, it is $1,331,000; and for a small organization, it is $434,000 (Standish Group, 1997). The Standish Group research reports that 31.1% of projects will be canceled before they ever get completed; 52.7% of projects will cost 189% of their original estimates.

William Schiemann, in his book, *Why Systems Fail* (1992), pointed out that fewer than half the changes undertaken by *Fortune* 500 companies are successful and that the chief reason for failure is resistance to the change.

Michael Hammer and James Champy point out in their book, *Reengineering the Corporation* (1994), that more than 50% of all the massive restructuring and reengineering projects fail.

The Standish Group report indicated that 91% of all the information technology projects undertaken in large corporations failed. Over 30% of the projects were canceled before completion.

In a study performed by MIT in 1992, researchers reported that the banking industry was more productive in 1981 than in 1991, despite the billions of dollars that companies spent on information technology. This was primarily because information technology was used as a *driver* rather than as an *enabler* and because the organizations were inadequately prepared to accept the new technology.

Numerous articles, in magazines such as *Fortune* and *Business Week*, point out that failures of TQM projects are extensive. The estimate of failed TQM projects runs between 60% and 75% of the total number of attempts.

L. Moran, J. Latham, J. Hogeveen, and D. Russ-Eft in *Winning Competitive Advantage* (1994) reported that 75% of the resistance to the quality improvement programs came from middle managers and 63% came from the first-line managers and supervisors.

You may not agree that we are as bad at managing change as these articles and reports indicate. But even if we were only one-half as bad or even one-fourth as bad, we would still be spending billions of dollars each year to bring about change that should have gone to the bottom line and, even more important, we would be moving ahead 25% faster. We cannot afford to continue wasting the effort and money we are now throwing at our improvement projects. We must reduce the failure rate of our projects, which currently is running over 50%, to less than 10% in the next two years and close to 0% by 2010. This demand for excellent implementation will not only continue into the foreseeable future, but significantly increase. The bar is being raised dramatically, and the already faltering techniques we use today will certainly fail tomorrow.

Another improvement project that failled

Business in the New Millennium

By all accounts, the 21st century is bringing rapid innovation driven by the continuing high-tech boom and expanding global markets from the last decade of the 20th century. The accelerating rate of change is and will continue to be driven principally by the exponential growth and global availability of information, technologies, and technology-based infrastructure, as well as the improving global transportation infrastructure. How well organizations are prepared to survive in this business climate is a fundamental issue. Part of the answer is that competitiveness and success will be earned through continually matching and re-matching products and services to what the customer will buy. They also will be earned through rapidly responding to abrupt changes driven by:

- Technology
- Knowledge management
- Growing population
- Global economy
- Geopolitics
- Culture
- Higher levels of education
- More brain power
- Increased capability
- Legislation
- Social pressures
- New markets

The successful enterprise in this environment will evolve, not through random mutation, but through purposeful strategies to effectively lead change initiatives that are predictable and respond effectively to unpredictable and shifting marketplace demands. Prosperous organizations will effectively:

- Strategize to fragment mass markets into niche markets.
- Compete on the basis of customer-perceived value.
- Produce multiple products and services in market-determined quantities.
- Design solutions interactively with customers.
- Organize for rapid response and proficiency at change.
- Manage through leadership, motivation, support, and trust.
- Fully exploit information and communication technologies.

- ▶ Leverage all capabilities, resources, and assets regardless of location.
- ▶ Partner with other companies as a strategy of choice, not of last resort.
- ▶ Adapt easily to changing customer expectations.
- ▶ Be highly creative in management style and products.
- ▶ Provide outstanding customer service.

The "good old days" when one organizational problem could be addressed in isolation of others will not return. For example, continuing to deploy legacy-based systems to generate financial reports is no longer tenable. These systems are not sophisticated enough or fast enough to meet today's organizational needs. Organizations depend upon the speed of computers and software that enable investment, operations, and sales decisions to be made "real time," not after a report can be generated, analyzed, and then faxed to the corporate CFO. Competitive advantage is measured by the speed and accuracy of solution. Companies are now regularly experiencing the futility of treating one problem as independent of others and—at least those that have survived—recognizing the need to consider the simultaneous interaction of many business challenges at once. Compounding the difficulty in meeting these kinds of challenges is that detailed, reliable forecasting over a long time horizon is impossible and cannot be used to build a long-term plan that will ensure a competitive position in the future.

Starting now, organizations will need to rethink old assumptions about organizational effectiveness in the new global marketplace. And they will have to do it "on the fly." There will be little time for discussion; decisions will be made rapidly. And those decisions will have to be made without relying on experience, as the nature of the business environment that unfolds before us will be, in large part, unique. The only thing we can depend on is a firm understanding of the professional methodologies we carry to the problem and the flexibility to meet these challenges. This is true for you as a project manager and for the people you will be asking to change the way they do business.

To get a better sense of what this turbulence means at "ground zero," let's look at two areas of organizational activity and how they may impact your performance as a project manager. The first is mergers and acquisitions, which is a challenge we have been facing for some years, but one that will increase in frequency and complexity as we enter the new century. The second is electronic commerce, a challenge with the potential for revolutionary consequences for companies on both the strategic and tactical levels.

Mergers and Acquisitions

The "merger-mania" of the mid-1980s has been surpassed by the vastly increased rate of organizational consolidation that has been taking place in the 1990s. Some 30,000 mergers and acquisitions have been completed in the United States this decade, at a cost of more than $1.5 trillion (Marks and Mirvis, 1998). Spurred by recent advances in technology, government deregulation, and the development of a global economy, companies are turning to mergers and acquisitions to achieve market advantages. For example, research has demonstrated that a dollar earned through growth is worth 30% to 50% more in the capital markets than the same dollar earned through cost cutting (Smith and Hershman, 1997). A recent survey of life and health insurance industries indicates that factors such as a heightened need to reduce costs, persistent stagnant growth, and the need to achieve economies of scale are driving mergers in those industries (Seifert, 1997). Although consolidation offers the potential for growth, increased capability, and a larger share of the market, consolidations often fail to achieve their corporate goals. Past results clearly show that the corporate merger and acquisition game is risky. Recent figures indicate that up to 70% of mergers and acquisitions undertaken over the past 20 years have failed to create any "synergistic value" (ICM Conferences, Inc., 1996). In fact, many efforts are abandoned before completion due to a lack of proper planning and management of the consolidation process.

Why do the majority of mergers and acquisitions fail to achieve their stated goals? A review of the literature indicates that, more than financial issues, the intangible human factors are cited consistently as being critical to the success or failure of a merger or acquisition effort. But how does this play out on the project management level? The answer to that has to do with the sheer complexity of the organizational processes involved. These processes are most often tangled by what we call "corporate culture."

Corporate Culture—The beliefs, behaviors, and assumptions shared by individuals within an organization. Includes such things as procedures, values, and unspoken norms.

To illustrate this point, we'll simplify the complexity of M&A and possibly bend U.S. banking regulations to clarify a few application issues. For this purpose, let's say two banks merge. One bank headquartered in the Midwest is very "old-fashioned," structured, inflexible. The other (ABC) is headquartered in Central America, very attuned to employee participation and empowerment, and very customer-focused. Both are successful. Now, as a start, let's look at some of the cultural issues over which you may have no control at an enterprise-wide level, but which will definitely influence the implementation of your projects:

- ▶ What are Company ABC's core competencies? Will the employees you inherit have the skills required to join the BPI team or, if not on the team, actually undertake the BPI solution in their day-to-day operations?
- ▶ What are Company ABC's corporate values? Do they value the kind of synergistic teamwork required to implement your project?
- ▶ What are the goals and objectives of Company ABC? Do their objectives align with yours? How might potentially disruptive gaps express themselves on an operational level, particularly in the areas related to your BPI project?
- ▶ How do decisions get made and by whom? Is there any confusion about who has the power to initiate and sustain your project?
- ▶ How do the leaders of Company ABC incorporate the company culture into their daily work, such as willingness to delegate? As project manager, what decisions are you allowed to make or not allowed to make? Will the team be empowered enough and have a level of authority appropriate to get the job done?

And what about these simple but potentially revealing situations?

- ▶ Your first BPI team meeting is teleconferenced. Some of your comrades in Latin American come on line 30 minutes after the start time. You next spend precious time establishing expectations about start time as 8:00, which means something different in Central America, where "8:00" may mean anything between 8:00 and 8:45. Some of the folks from the Midwest resist any flexibility around how to conduct meetings, to say nothing about customer service. Very strong beliefs and assumptions come into play. Which are right? How do you deal with the gap and get back on track and stay on plan?
- ▶ You suspect certain processes will be centralized. What about differences in language—a very basic behavior? The Midwest team assumes the primary language will be English. The other team is understandably concerned. Is there sponsorship for

bilingual training? If you don't sort out and manage the various prejudices around language, what sorts of resistance might you get from the Hispanic employees?

At least two issues that may confront you as a project manager now should be apparent.

First, the cultural resistance you will confront in such situations will arise apart from the particular BPI processes you deploy.

Dd

This is a sample of the text for the definition, or these are more synonyms and usages that are commonly found in the English language.

Resistance—Any thought or action directed against a change. Some level of resistance should be expected in any major change.

You can improve your creativity by learning about and using tools that help you see and understand the world from new perspectives.

That resistance (which is really resistance out of the clash of the two corporate cultures) will most likely be the harbinger of the resistance you'll find while implementing the BPI solution.

Second, and this is where the complexity comes in, while employees are resisting cultural changes, they will also resist the BPI solution. The pressure to more successfully achieve M&A revenue objectives will grow as management pushes to avoid the pain of missed opportunities through successful implementation. Management will continue to rely on a variety of business improvement process techniques to make that happen. The onus will continue to be on you and other project managers to produce the targeted results.

Perhaps less familiar to us than mergers and acquisitions are the ramifications of the revolution just beginning around how businesses use the Internet and, more specifically, electronic commerce. This technology and other new technologies that are just being born or are as yet unknown but "just around the corner" are certain to hold surprises that will affect strategic and operational aspects of most organizations, including how projects unfold.

Electronic Commerce

Adding to this swirl in organizational operations due to M&A, the changes brought about from electronic commerce are having a profound impact on individuals, teams, processes, organizations, suppliers, customers, supply chains, global commerce, and others yet to be envisioned. Organizational capability building for change is crucial for this new competitive and electronically global environment.

Organizations in virtually every sector of the economy are beginning to use the Internet to cut the cost of purchasing, manage supplier relationships, streamline logistics and inventory, plan production, and reach new and current customers more effectively. The effects of this development are being felt even at the project level—through such initiatives as enterprise-wide system implementation, business process redesign, and supply chain management deployment. Cost savings, improved cycle time, increased consumer choice, and improved consumer convenience are driving growth in the sale and delivery of goods and services via the Internet. Consider the following:

▶ Fewer than 40 million people around the world were connected to the Internet during 1996. By the end of 1997, more than 100 million people were using the Internet (NUA, 1997).

▶ Traffic on the Internet has been doubling every 100 days.

▶ Cisco Systems closed 1996 having booked just over $100 million in sales on the Internet. By the end of 1997, its Internet sales were running at a $3.2 billion annual rate.

▶ In 1996, Amazon.com, the first Internet bookstore, recorded sales of less than $16 million. In 1997, it sold $148 million worth of books to Internet customers. One of the nation's largest book retailers, Barnes & Noble, launched its own online bookstore in 1997 to compete with Amazon for this rapidly growing market.

▶ In January 1997, Dell Computers was selling less than $1 million of computers per day on the Internet. The company reported reaching daily sales of $6 million several times during the December 1997 holiday period.

The Internet's pace of adoption eclipses all other technologies that preceded it. Radio was in existence 38 years before 50 million people tuned in; TV took 13 years to reach that benchmark. 16 years after the first PC kit was introduced, 50 million people were using one (Meeker and Pearson, 1997). Once it was opened to the general public, the

Internet crossed that line in four years (Cerf, 1997). Internet commerce is growing fastest among businesses. It is used for coordination between the purchasing operations of an organization and its suppliers, the logistics planners in a organization and the transportation companies that warehouse and move its products, the sales organizations and the wholesalers or retailers that sell its products, and the customer service and maintenance operations and the organization's final customers.

Behind all of this upheaval, there is a logical explanation—Moore's Law. In 1965, Gordon Moore, one of the founders of Intel, predicted that the complexity of the integrated circuit would double every year. The prediction became known as Moore's Law. After a few years, the interval was changed from a year to 18 months. With that modification, the prediction has held true to present. In 1970, you could put about 1,000 transistors on a chip. The first Pentium chips had more than a million transistors. Today we can get nearly 10 million on a single chip. To help you visualize how big this change is, many of us wear more computing power on our wrists than there was in the whole world before 1961.

This is something dramatically new in human experience. When you double something every year, you're asking people inside and outside of organizations to handle a violent, continuous stream of turbulence. This represents a major turning point in how our world works. That's precisely the situation many organizations are in today. Making the changes required by this pace may begin with technology but it requires people with the capability and capacity to effectively implement the changes demanded.

What Do We Do?

Earlier, we discussed the business pressures facing project managers today, pressures that are likely to continue and increase as we move into the new millennium. These forces arise out of a turbulent market environment that is agitated by a host of changes in the global economy, including business strategies involving mergers and acquisitions and the advent of technologies such as electronic commerce. We believe that an increasingly important tool for you as project manager working in this environment is the integration of the tools of project management and change management. The pain of failure and the reward for success escalate proportionately as the stakes for rapid and full project implementation spiral for both you and your organization.

We will now take a look at how that integration can be achieved, starting with a simple review of how and why organizations initiate strategic activities and the role we, as project managers, play in that process.

The Realignment Process

A simple yet accurate way of trying to make sense of the complexity and turbulence we now face is to look at the relationship among shifting market demands, business strategies, and changes in strategic and operational success factors (i.e., the way we do business to achieve market success). Identifying the right success factors for a given market is a strategic imperative. Every organization strives to find the right formula to achieve and continue to repeat success for the life of the organization. This is its "success formula." Identifying the right success factors for a given market is a strategic imperative. Also, this formula is useful only when four conditions hold:

- when *quality* and *productivity standards* are maintained and
- when *customer demands* and *competitive pressures* remain stable.

It's rare for these conditions to remain the same for long. We can think of few if any examples. Even in the case of corn flakes, where manufacturing processes have remained essentially the same since the early part of this century, the means of selling and distributing (remember electronic commerce?) corn flakes and exploiting their expanding markets are ever-changing and highly sophisticated. The fact is, today's organizations' success formulas become obsolete more quickly than they did even a half-decade ago. That is why you will continue to be called upon to find and implement new and more appropriate processes (i.e., new success factors) before your latest solutions are thoroughly in place. The mechanics of this realignment process are outlined in Figure 1-2.

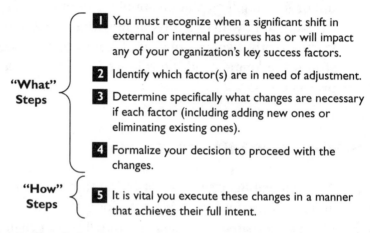

"What" Steps

1 You must recognize when a significant shift in external or internal pressures has or will impact any of your organization's key success factors.

2 Identify which factor(s) are in need of adjustment.

3 Determine specifically what changes are necessary if each factor (including adding new ones or eliminating existing ones).

4 Formalize your decision to proceed with the changes.

"How" Steps

5 It is vital you execute these changes in a manner that achieves their full intent.

FIGURE 1-2. The "what" and "how" of change

Step 1 of the alignment process involves senior management's recognition of trends and events it feels will influence the organization's future success. Step 2 entails the process of identifying the factor(s) most likely to help align the organization with the new requirements for success. For example, if you have identified that you are losing market share because your competition is able to redesign, retool, and launch a new model automobile in 17 or fewer months when it takes your organization up to three years, you may focus on your development process as the problem. Indeed, after initial analysis, you may actually determine (Step 3) that there are critical cycle-time problems around your roll-out procedures. Once this decision is made, Step 4 is to formalize the decision and complete the BPI process. Finally, Step 5 is the execution of your BPI solution.

Unless all steps are completed well, your organization cannot maintain its competitive position. As a project manager, your responsibilities are focused on Steps 2, 3, and 5. Unfortunately, Step 5 generally has been completed well technically, but with little success in addressing the human aspects of BPI projects. This has occurred for two reasons. First, in times when markets were less turbulent, there was a great deal more margin for error. If the human aspects of the project became a little "sticky," you might have nursed the project over a long enough period of time to achieve the desired results. This is no longer the case. By the time you start to get results on one project (however good or bad it may be), you must launch another. Second, those executives who sponsored your projects were often not willing to pay the price for better managing human resistance that often occurs.

What leaders typically didn't understand is that they are going to pay a price anyway. Either they invest the resources required to minimize resistance to projects as they are implemented or they pay an often greater price for "healing" from rampant resistance and poor results once the new process is in place. It is a lot like the oil commercial that stated, "Either you pay me now or pay more later."

Unfortunately, senior managers are trained to pay attention to ROI (return on investment). But these metrics, in the case of installing a

$$ROC_{hg} = \frac{\text{Yield from Effort}}{\text{Execution Cost}}$$

FIGURE 1-3. Calculating return on change

business process improvement, are usually focused on the costs related to employee involvement in the process, new hires, outplacement, new equipment, technical training, the outcomes of increased production, and reduced production costs. They ignore the savings associated with appropriate change management—or the costs associated with poor implementation. It is not a matter of neglect or stupidity that these executives ignore the costs and benefits of applying change management to their BPI projects; it is their lack of understanding. Business education has dropped the ball and, until recently, the human side of change simply wasn't "on the screen."

Return on Change

You can improve your creativity by learning about and using tools that help you see and understand the world from new perspectives.

Why, then, do you need to attend to the human costs of change? The answer is twofold. First, better understanding the basis and the costs of poor project implementation will make you a more effective project manager. Second, understanding the source of these costs will enable you to make the business case for applying the integrated approach to project management we present in this book.

Most major projects are launched to secure a competitive advantage. Because these efforts consume time, energy, and money with no guarantee of results, they should be seen as risky ventures that are subsidized by shareholders, owners, and other constituents. Attempts to implement major projects are no different from any other speculative exposure. Those taking the risk expect an adequate ROI to justify the gamble they take with their money. In today's uncertain markets, consistently strong return on change (ROChg) is becoming a prerequisite for attaining targeted ROI.

This is a sample of the text for the definition, or these are more synonyms and usages that are commonly found in the English language.

Return on Change (ROChg)—An objective measure of goal attainment, given the resources invested in your project activities. ROChg is derived by dividing the yield from a project by the implementation cost of that effort (see Figure 1-3).

Yield from Effort—A measurement of movement toward achieving the project's objectives. ("Movement" refers to the difference between the status of the organization before implementation of the initiative and its status after implementation.)

Execution Costs—The expense of identifying what to do—which you may figure into the cost associated with how the human aspects of change will be managed, the lost efficiency (productivity and quality) that typically occurs when resources are focused away from day-to-day operations to project implementation, and the price of any new infrastructure required to maintain the BPI solution (e.g., technology, people, and training).

What drives the equation into the red is this: the combined costs of determining what to do, lost efficiency, and any new infrastructure needed to succeed pale in comparison with the expense incurred when you do not adequately deal with the way employees react to your project. Unfortunately, many project managers and their sponsors fail to sufficiently prepare employees for the changes associated with BPI projects. This failure to act is so prevalent today that every organization should be asking the following questions:

► How can we better manage our organization's change adaptation resources? (These are the resources that enable an organization to successfully implement change without becoming dysfunctional.)

► How can we better prepare our organization to complete the alignment processes, including Step 5 (Execution/Implementation)?

► If we know what to change and we have the resources to build the necessary infrastructure, how do we develop an equal proficiency in how to orchestrate the human variables related to implementation?

▶ How can we improve our ROChg performance?

The answer to these key questions is twofold:

▶ *Raise* the organization's overall adaptation capacity to deal with any project that may be initiated.
▶ *Reduce demand* on the organization's adaptation capacity by implementing each major project with the appropriate mix of BPI techniques and a disciplined and structured change management methodology.

These activities are achieved through what we call the Human Due Diligence process.

Human Due Diligence

This is a sample of the text for the definition, or these are more synonyms and usages that are commonly found in the English language.

Human Due Diligence (HDD)™—Gathering information, planning, and engaging in actions related to the impact that change is having or will have on an organization's human capital.

You can improve your creativity by learning about and using tools that help you see and understand the world from new perspectives.

Successful executives in most organizations wouldn't consider entering into major initiatives without insisting on completing *financial* due diligence. *What are the costs? What are the risks? What is our potential return on investment? Can we afford to proceed? Can we afford to not proceed?* Decisions are based on financial data.

Few executives apply the equivalent *Human* Due Diligence (HDD) to the same decisions. Yet, the evidence is mounting that the human component of change implementation is the most significant risk factor. *What are the human costs? What are the human risks? What is our potential return on investment of the human resources involved? Do we have the human capacity to proceed with success? If we must proceed without the required adaptation capacity, how do we free it up or obtain it?*

In fact, this set of questions reflects only one component of HDD. As with its financial counterpart, HDD focuses on both: building reserves and managing demand. Reserves are built by increasing the organization's preparation for change; demand is managed through successful project implementation. Elsewhere, a comprehensive model has been presented for increasing an organization's capacity for implementing major change. The Board of Directors, the CEO, and his or her direct reports are typically involved in these organization-wide activities. In this book, we will take an in-depth look at how to best manage demand while undertaking the BPI process. Activities to manage demand are focused primarily on the project level.

Manage Demand

Managing the demands on your organization's adaptation capacity through successful change implementation requires that decision-makers within your organization make tough decisions and that those change initiatives selected then be effectively planned and implemented. There are three types of changes about which people in our organizations are deciding every day: bad ideas, good ideas, and business imperatives. Bad ideas cost more to implement than they are worth in return. Good ideas, conversely, produce positive business results, typically in the short term. Finally, business imperatives are critical to an organization's success. Business imperatives, unlike good ideas, must be implemented or the organization's competitive position may be placed at risk. It is possible, for example, that Barnes & Noble's decision to launch its online services was not a good idea, but—in the face of Amazon.com competition—it was a business imperative.

Most of us distinguish between bad ideas and good ideas. But even if the bad ideas are easy to reject, we still face the challenge of implementing the good ideas. Are you and your counterparts throughout the organization prepared to say no to an initiative that will delight the customer, face a positive reception among employees, and provide a return to shareholders? If it is a good idea, and not a business imperative, making that tough decision is critical to corporate success. Implementing good ideas may drain an organization's adaptation resources to such an extent that it is impossible to implement business imperatives. In these circumstances, even the best organization may lose its market position, or worse.

Executives need the skill to differentiate between good ideas and business imperatives. Good ideas must be put aside, no matter how favorably we first view them, until we are confident that we have the change adaptation capacity to successfully execute all of the business imperatives we are facing. The soundness of these choices is critical, first when you decide to initiate the BPI process and again when you decide to implement the solution identified by that process.

Poorly executed projects unnecessarily drain change adaptation capacity. Thus, once the tough decisions are made, HDD calls for thoughtfully architecting and executing change-implementation plans. For example:

- ► Roles must be explicitly identified, defined, and understood.
- ► Communicating strategies must be developed that focus your project in terms that those who will be affected can appreciate and understand quickly and easily.
- ► Change demand should be mapped against available capacity at the local-not organizational-level.
- ► Culture issues should be considered relative to the beliefs, behaviors, and assumptions required for the initiative to succeed.

The integration of HDD into the BPI project-management process for our organizations will help to ensure that these and other critical change management activities are effectively implemented each time.

Human Due Diligence: A Common Framework for Change Implementation

A common set of change management processes and tools with the expertise to use them—from the executive initiating the project, to the project manager, and down to the individuals of the project team-is critical to successful project implementation. Inability to use the available tools may introduce risk that can lead to major problems.

The following is a list of some of the change management processes that will be discussed in more detail in later chapters:

- ▶ Building implementation architecture
- ▶ Managing individual resistance to change
- ▶ Building individual commitment to change
- ▶ Managing the cultural aspects of a change
- ▶ Selecting and deploying change agents

The following is a list of some change management tools that will be discussed in more detail in later chapters:

- ▶ *Change Project Description Form*
- ▶ *Predicting the Impact of Change*
- ▶ *Change History Survey*
- ▶ *Role Map Application Tool*
- ▶ *Communicating Change: Announcement Plan*
- ▶ *Sponsor Evaluation*
- ▶ *Landscape Survey*
- ▶ *Change Resistance Scale*
- ▶ *Change Agent Evaluation*
- ▶ *Organizational Change Implementation Plan*

The following story illustrates the need to understand how to use the tools that are available to you.

There once was a foreman of a lumber camp who heard about a new tool that would supposedly greatly increase his crew's productivity. The foreman invited a salesman from the East Coast to demonstrate this marvelous invention. The salesman arrived on the next train to the lumber camp. He immediately made the bold statement that if a lumberjack used his new invention he could cut down twice the trees in half the time. The foreman was skeptical about the extraordinary claims but agreed to a test demonstration. The next morning the salesman showed up with a brand new, sharp, shiny, four-foot-long, 3-horsepower chain saw. The foreman gave the new saw to his best lumberjack and told him to put the new invention to the test.

After eight hours, the lumberjack returned absolutely exhausted and reported that the new tool was a terrible failure. Claiming he could normally cut 10 trees a day, he found the new chain saw heavier, harder to use, and much less efficient than the old, reliable six-foot cross-cut saw he was accustomed to using. The lumberjack reported, despite his best effort, that he was only able to cut down five trees that day. The salesman was heartbroken. He knew that his tool should work far better than a cross-cut saw and decided to see if the saw was running correctly; perhaps the carburetor needed to be adjusted or the chain needed sharpening. He called over the logger with the chain saw and he pulled on the starter. When the saw roared to life, the lumberjack jumped back, white as a ghost, and cried, "WHAT THE HECK IS THAT!?"

As this story suggests, having the change management tools and processes is only part of the solution. We need to know how to apply the tools in a project-management setting. Unless project managers and others involved in implementing a project understand when and how to apply the tools, small problems can turn into major cost overruns and schedule nightmares.

Summary

Drivers of change such as mergers and acquisitions and electronic commerce rewrote the tenets of business competition during the last decade. More companies are taking advantage of liberalized global trade conditions and a quickly developing competence in operating worldwide. This movement has not only brought a flood of new competition to most industries but also altered traditional economic models, supply chains, market gateways, and partnering needs. In almost every organization today, core assumptions about what makes for smart strategy have been turned upside-down.

Global competition has also forced many organizations to face the fact that they have been plagued by inefficiencies. Advances in enterprise-wide information technologies such as SAP, PeopleSoft, and Oracle have pushed process-reengineering initiatives to new heights. Huge capital investments have been made to change the way in which work is performed and information moves.

In this environment of dramatic change, both customers and investors are in the driver's seat. Customers today know to demand value for their money. Investors have shown that they won't tolerate poor performers in their portfolios. When disappointed, they look globally for better opportunities. Managers today are being forced to reconsider how they develop resources, compete for customers and capital, and deliver value to shareholders. The opportunities for companies that are efficient and nimble are enormous. A critical factor in successfully exploiting these opportunities is understanding the importance of their organizations' change adaptation resources and being willing to manage those resources wisely.

In Chapters 2 and 3 we will focus more closely on reducing the demand on adaptation capacity. We will address what we call the implementation risk areas, which will help you understand the fundamental concepts of change management. Finally, Chapter 4 describes a comprehensive "implementation architecture" with a focus on change management "to-do's."

A critical aspect of effective BPI project implementation is the disciplined application of a rigorous change management methodology.

References

Cerf, Vinton G. "The Internet Phenomenon." National Science Foundation Web site. http://www.cise.nsf.gov/general/compsci/net/cerf.html.

Conner, Daryl R., *Leading at the Edge of Chaos: How to Create the Nimble Organization* (New York: John Wiley & Sons, Inc., 1993).

Hammer, Michael, and James Champy, *Reengineering the Corporation: A Manifesto for Business Revolution* (New York: HarperCollins, 1994).

NUA Ltd. Internet Surveys, 1997. http://www.nua.ie/surveys.

Marks, Mitchell Lee, and Philip H. Mirvis, *Joining Forces: Making One Plus One Equal Three in Mergers, Acquisitions, and Alliances* (San Francisco: Jossey-Bass, 1998).

Meeker, Mary, and Sharon Pearson, *Morgan Stanley U.S. Investment Research: Internet Retail* (Morgan Stanley, May 28, 1997), pp. 2-2, 2-6.

Moran, L., J. Latham, J. Hogeveen, and D. Russ-Eft, *Winning Competitive Advantage* (San Jose: Zenger Miller, 1994).

Schiemann, William. "Why Change Fails." *Across The Board*, April 1992, pp. 53-54.

Seifert, C.A., "Insurance: Life and Health Industry Survey." *Standard & Poor's Industry Surveys*, 165 (No. 36, section 1), September 4, 1997.

Smith, Kenneth W., and Susan E. Hershman, "How M&A Fits Into a Real Growth Strategy." *Mergers & Acquisitions*, 32, September/October 1997, pp. 38-42.

Standish Group International, Inc., *Chaos* (Dennis, MA: The Standish Group International, 1997), http://www.standishgroup.com/chaos.html.

Note: For a more complete discussion of Human Due Diligence, see Daryl R. Conner's book, *Leading at the Edge of Chaos: How to Create the Nimble Organization* (1993).

2

Change Management: Strategic Risks to Successful Project Implementation

We cannot save ourselves without being changed.
—H.E. FOSDICK

Introduction: "So This Is the Project You Want Me to Manage?"

You have accepted the role of managing a large project that has the potential to contribute significantly to the organization's bottom line. Not only will the outcome of the project impact organization profitability, it will also impact the way business is conducted, the relationship with suppliers, overall customer satisfaction, and cycle time of core processes. Unfortunately, after several months of intense and often contentious work by you and many on your team, and the dysfunction associated with depleted adaptation resources (perhaps manifested in resistance, ranging from covert back stabbing to an outright refusal to cooperate), management significantly reduces the project's scope. What started with a lot of attention and great promise ends with just enough success for your sponsors to save face and for you to move on to another project.

Have you ever been a situation like this? Many projects start off with high outcome expectations, but somehow get off course, exceed the original scope, or do not deliver the expected results. What happened? The answer is often related to how the project was implemented, not the technical solution selected.

Project—A temporary endeavor undertaken to create a unique product or service.

Project Management—The application of knowledge, skills, tools, and techniques to project activities in order to meet or exceed stakeholders' needs and expectations for the project.

This chapter begins our focus on how to reduce the demand on adaptation resources as you manage the technical aspects of your BPI projects. The chapter summarizes some key facts about major change and the basic concepts and techniques of the MOC change-management methodology in terms of four strategic risk areas related to the probability of successful project implementation: resilience, change knowledge, decisions to initiate projects, and implementation architecture. Chapter 3 continues this discussion, focusing on four tactical risk areas: change agents, sponsorship, resistance, and organizational culture. This knowledge about the human dynamics of change will serve as the basis for your understanding and applying the implementation architecture discussed in Chapter 4.

The Basics of Change Management

First of all, it is important to understand organizations as complex systems of people, processes, technology, materials, procedures, and structures. Change in any area of an organization will create ripple effects in other areas, much like dropping a pebble in a bucket of water (see Figure 2-1). Often these ripple effects create unintended consequences that interfere with the implementation of a particular

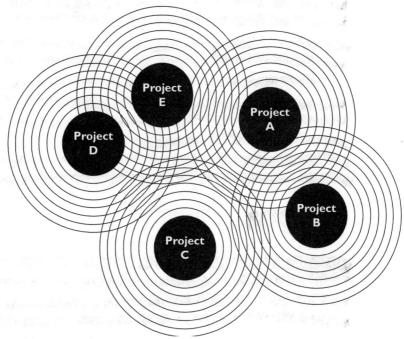

FIGURE 2-1. Overlapping projects

change initiative. This can become a serious problem as the simultaneous projects begin to increase and then interact.

For example, shortly after laboring over the planning stage of a new product development project, your organization decides that it should also implement a new supply chain management process during the same time frame. Both projects are seen as business imperatives, but run the risk of failing due to the amount of time and resources required by each to be successful. Often, the time and resources for projects of this magnitude come from the same departments, which are already stretched in dealing with the daily workload. As a result, many line managers impacted by these business imperatives find it more and more difficult to successfully implement these rapid-fire initiatives. The outcome generally will be reduced productivity among employees and managers as well as across departments, functions, and the enterprise as a whole. Therefore, your role as a project manager requires the conscious, deliberate management of change to account for these effects. The key for you as a project manager and the organization as a whole is to reduce the productivity losses by effectively managing the change in a disciplined, repeatable way. You might think of this process in terms of the "speed of change."

An organization's "speed of change" is not just the pace at which events are happening in a rapidly changing world, but the speed at which the organization can rebound from the disruption caused by major projects. When people impacted by a particular initiative are operating at their optimum speed of change, they are able to absorb a lot of fast, complex change with minimal loss of productivity and quality.

Resilience

In terms of increasing an organization's speed of change to support the implementation of a critical project, a crucial ingredient for you to consider as project manager is the degree to which key people are resilient, both those on the project team and those impacted by the project.

Dd.

This is a sample of the text for the definition, or these are more synonyms and usages that are commonly found in the English language.

Resilience—The ability to absorb high levels of disruptive change while displaying minimal dysfunctional behavior.

There are five characteristics of resilience: Positive, Focused, Flexible, Organized, and Proactive (see Figure 2-2). (We will discuss these characteristics later in the chapter.) The speed of change and resilience are directly related. The more resilient your organization's employees, the greater its speed of change.

Resilient people:

- Quickly regain their equilibrium after expectations are disrupted.
- Maintain a high level of productivity during periods of ambiguity.
- Remain physically and emotionally healthy while struggling with uncertainty.
- Avoid dysfunctional behaviors that impede the success of a project.
- Rebound from the demands of change even stronger than before.

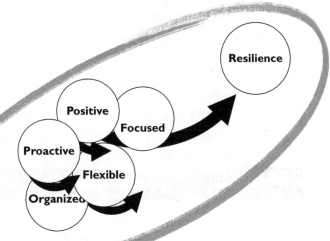

FIGURE 2-2. Characteristics of resilience

Resilience and Disruption

To understand the importance of resilience in your organization, it is first important to understand how a Business Process Improvement (BPI) project, which creates change, can cause dysfunction among employees and throughout an entire organization.

Dysfunction—Any change-related action or feeling that diverts resources away from meeting productivity and quality standards.

Most people deal with their change-related stress and anxiety by trying to maintain a sense of control over their lives.

Control—The extent to which individuals can direct or at least anticipate outcomes in a change process.

This feeling of control is achieved when people believe that they can foresee what will happen to them and influence the outcome of events. As a project manager, have you ever felt in control through the creation of a detailed project plan that defined such parameters as key milestones, resources, dependencies of tasks, and task assignments (see Figure 2-3), but lost your sense of predictability after meeting with senior management or maybe the targets being affected? How many times have you walked out of a meeting with the key sponsor, steering committee, or a group of disgruntled employees wondering how things could have become so confused? As project managers, we often feel somewhat in control by our ability to capture all of the technical aspects and events in a well-developed project plan. As many of us know who have been "run ragged" by the implementation process, projects that dramatically changed from the original plan can truly test our human and project-management need for control.

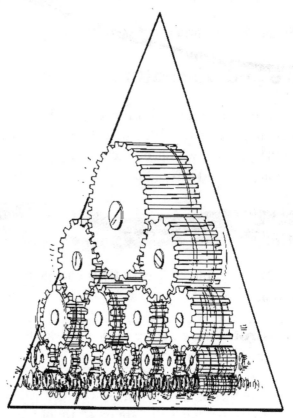

FIGURE 2-3. Project management!

Feeling in control, however, is something that is perceived from our mindset or frame of reference.

Frame of Reference (FOR)—A compatible set of ideas, theories, beliefs, feelings, values, and assumptions that allow meaning to be applied to a person's experience. FOR is an unconscious model for comprehending reality.

The frame of reference of a project stakeholder dictates how he or she selects what to perceive and how to interpret it. Frames of reference allow sponsors, project team members, and those impacted by the project to understand what to expect in the future. A person can reduce feelings of uncertainty and achieve a sense of control by accurately predicting and planning his or her future. Therefore, the ability to develop reliable expectations is fundamental to reducing uncertainty. (In Chapter 4 we will discuss how to reduce uncertainty to some degree through effectively communicating behavior changes.) Disrupting a person's expectation of the future derails this process, causing one of two basic psychological reactions.

If the change caused by the project is *minor*, the person will make easy adjustments to alter his or her expectations to adapt to the change. A minor change does not greatly threaten expectations. These shifts are so common that they often go unnoticed. In fact, they often leave the impression that a change has not even occurred.

If the change caused by the project is *major*, the person will feel uncertainty, fear, and disorientation and will experience dysfunction. A major change invalidates expectations. These feelings result from the contrast between what was anticipated and what is perceived. When this happens, the person no longer knows what to expect of himself or herself or of others. His or her frame of reference is disrupted.

Dysfunction, then, results from a breakdown in expectations. Whether change is positive or negative, planned or unplanned, if it results in a significant disruption of expectations it is *major* and always causes a certain level of dysfunction. As project manager, one of your most critical tasks is to recognize when and where the contributors to dysfunction—what we call "risk areas"—might arise as you implement your BPI projects.

Change Implementation Risk Areas

A primary role of a project manager is to help the project team and organization plan for this dysfunction, minimize it, and manage its impact to reduce the demand on its adaptation capacity. The way we generally approach change is in terms of identifying areas where risks may arise and undermine the implementation of your project and/or the identified solution. We call these *implementation risk areas*.

Risk Areas—Any class of activities or lack of activities that reduce the probability of successful project implementation. Examples include resistance, change knowledge, project overload, and implementation skills and techniques.

There are two types of risk areas:

▶ Strategic change risk areas
▶ Tactical change risk areas

There are four strategic and four tactical risk areas. Each of these represents an area of potential vulnerability: failure to address them can jeopardize the project's ability to survive during turbulence created by distractions and resistance to the project. We will discuss each of these risk areas in detail, focusing on the strategic areas in this chapter and the tactical areas in Chapter 3.

Strategic Change Risk Areas

Strategic Change—Any change that has a significant impact throughout an organization.

Under strategic change conditions, you should be concerned with four strategic risk areas:

1. **Resilience**—The ability of individuals and teams to absorb change. This includes the ability to absorb significant disruptive change while displaying minimal behaviors that distract from quality and productivity.
2. **Change Knowledge**—The working knowledge of change concepts. This includes the in-depth understanding of how change unfolds within an organization and among individuals.
3. **Managing Adaptation Resources**—The degree to which change decisions take into account the efficient use of typically scarce adaptation resources. This includes the alignment of an organization's changes, those planned and underway, with the resources available for implementing the change.
4. **Building Implementation Architecture**—The understanding of important leverage points in the implementation process. This includes the use of a structured yet flexible framework that uses concepts, techniques, and tools to address factors typically associated with change implementation.

First Strategic Risk Area: Resilience

The common source of implementation failure is low personal and/or team resilience. Resilient people and teams "bounce back" from major changes stronger and more capable than before.

For a number of years, ODR has used the *Personal Resilience Questionnaire* in research. This tool is designed to measure an individual's level of the specific characteristics that are linked to resilience. Feedback to individuals is given in the form of the *Personal Resilience Profile*. One aspect of resilience is the amount of energy (mental, physical, and emotional resources) we have available to recalibrate expectations after being disrupted by change. Some of this is determined by physical and psychological makeup (heredity). Some of it is related to the way we treat our bodies, such as the food we eat and the activities we choose. A third but equally important aspect of resilience is the way we use our mental, emotional, and physical resources in our daily lives. We have chosen to focus on how people use and manage their resources as they deal with the disruption of major change. The *Personal Resilience Profile* is based on our research in this area. The characteristics it measures involve areas of perception, thinking, and behavior that we believe to be related to resilience.

This research has identified the following characteristics as personal attributes that enable individual resilience during change:

- ► Positive: Resilient people display a sense of security and self-assurance that is based on their view of life as complex but filled with opportunity.
- ► Focused: Resilient people have a clear vision of what they want to achieve.
- ► Flexible: Resilient people demonstrate a special pliability in thinking and in working with others when responding to change.
- ► Organized: Resilient people are able to develop and find order in ambiguity.
- ► Proactive: Resilient people engage change rather than defend against it.

You can improve your creativity by learning about and using tools that help you see and understand the world from new perspectives.

Positive. There are two aspects to this characteristic: *world* and *yourself*. Let's look at *world* first.

Most situations and most people have both positive and negative aspects. Research shows that people differ in their tendency to focus on the positive or the negative elements. Those who tend to focus on the *positive* view their environment (i.e., the world) as complex and challenging. They are able to see opportunities and possibilities in situations that at first may look like problems. Those who focus primarily on the *negative* can get into cycles of anxiety and depression that prevent them from seeing value and opportunity in circumstances. Having a basically optimistic outlook is important, since it allows people to find ways to turn negative situations around. In addition, people who have a positive attitude toward their environment are better able to create situations that are positive.

Key Indicators. People who are *positive* about the *world*:

- Are generally upbeat about the future
- Find opportunities in times of turmoil
- Look for the good in situations that appear to be bad

Positive *self* refers to people who believe in themselves as being valuable and capable. This belief can be extremely powerful. People need a strong foundation from which to face uncertainty and stress in the world. They can develop this foundation by realistically assessing their capabilities and achieving self-acceptance while continuing to learn and grow. A person who feels capable of reaching his or her goals can take action confidently and weather failure without losing the feeling of self-worth. Also related to this positive view of self is the belief that we can influence the environment and what happens in our lives, rather than the belief that external forces determine our fate.

Key Indicators. People who are *positive* about *themselves*:

- Have high self-esteem
- Believe that their actions can influence situations and people
- Avoid feeling victimized by circumstances
- Believe in their abilities, have a "can-do" attitude

Focused. Because change is generally characterized by ambiguity and uncertainty, it should be no surprise that having a strong sense of goals and priorities is important to resilience. Having a sense of purpose and a focus in life is an advantage because, when goals and priorities are clear, it is easier to get back on course following major disruption. Research suggests that people who describe themselves as strongly committed to their goals or who see their lives as having meaning or purpose are better able to manage confusing situations. They can sort out the important issues, judge the relative worth of alternatives, and thus use their personal energy more efficiently. Without a sense of purpose and priorities, people are likely to use resources inefficiently, since every new situation would require them to determine what is important before taking action.

Key Indicators. People who are *focused*:

- Have a strong sense of purpose
- Are able to set goals and prioritize actions
- Can distinguish between critical and trivial objectives
- Use personal objectives to guide everyday actions and decisions

Flexible. There are two aspects to this characteristic: *thoughts* and *social*. Let's look at *thoughts* first.

Coping with the ambiguity that change presents is a critical skill for resilience. An important aspect of this type of coping is the ability and willingness to look at situations from multiple points of view, to suspend judgment while considering alternative perspectives, and to accept and live with paradoxes and contradictions as part of life. Many times, when a person is open-minded in finding different ways to view a situation, he or she will have a broader understanding of the problem and be able to form more creative, effective resolutions. Flexible thoughts increase the likelihood of finding these creative, effective ways to achieve goals. In contrast, people who would rather have immediate, straightforward solutions may draw conclusions so quickly that they miss information that could be useful.

Key Indicators. People who are *flexible* in their *thoughts*:

- Have high tolerance for ambiguity
- Feel comfortable dealing with paradoxes
- Are capable of seeing things from different perspectives, are open-minded
- Avoid "black or white" thinking

Flexible *social* refers to the ability to draw on the resources of others. Research indicates that highly resilient people recognize their interdependence with others. They are characterized by strong social bonds that they can rely on for support during difficult times. They are able to form and maintain close relationships, are willing to engage in the give-and-take of mutually supportive friendships, and can recognize ways in which other people's skills can complement their own. If this type of support is either not available or not sought, a person's capacity to deal with stress or uncertainty is decreased.

Key Indicators. People who are *flexible* in *social* aspects:

- ▶ Draw on external resources for assistance and support
- ▶ Value the ideas of others
- ▶ Recognize interdependence
- ▶ Are good "team players"

Organized. While flexibility is an asset in allowing people to see the possibilities in situations, another important element of resilience is the ability to organize and to find structure in ambiguity. This feature of resilience enables people to see the order in chaos and move beyond confusion toward action. It's important to have the discipline to face complex and convoluted situations, to assess the available information, to choose a direction in which to proceed, and to plan the steps needed to move forward. A person must set aside information that may be enticing but is not helpful at the moment, focus on the elements that are important, and logically structure them into a workable, understandable plan. Without the skill to organize chaotic situations, a person might waste a lot of resources trying one solution, then another, without making any real progress.

Key Indicators. People who are *organized*:

- ▶ Sort information quickly
- ▶ Build structure in chaos
- ▶ Plan action for maximum efficient use of resources
- ▶ Avoid acting on impulse

Proactive. The final characteristic linked to resilience is the willingness to act decisively in the midst of uncertainty, rather than becoming immobilized or simply reacting to circumstances. To be proactive, a person must be willing to take some risks and to endure some discomfort in the belief that positive outcomes (such as growth, personal development, and the achievement of important goals) will result. Proactive individuals seek challenges rather than avoid them and respond to disruption by investing energy in problem solving rather than withdrawing. In contrast, people who place an extremely high value on certainty, stability, and security may pass up valuable opportunities while waiting for a "sure thing" to come along.

Key Indicators. People who are *proactive*:

▶ Actively engage change
▶ Take reasonable risks
▶ Are willing to try new activities
▶ Don't continually strive for predictability and stability

Resilience Characteristics in Combination. The five characteristics of resilience are strongly interconnected. They reinforce and support one another in action. In addition, by focusing attention on improving areas of weakness in a particular characteristic, people appear to be able to increase their strength in other areas. For example, if someone has a particularly low score on both Positive and Focused, becoming more Focused can help the person become more Positive. If a person has low Organized and Flexible scores, raising the Flexible score may bring up the Organized score. Examples can be shown for any combination of resilience characteristics.

Project Team Resilience. We have identified several characteristics that describe the resilient project team. These, of course, echo the personal resilience characteristics:

▶ *Positive:* A resilient team is positive, both about the capability of each member to contribute to the team's work and about the team's ability to influence the organization during change.
▶ *Focused:* A resilient team is one in which individual energies are centered on the team's shared objectives during change, rather than toward multiple agendas, irrelevant discussions, or other off-task activities.
▶ *Flexible, Ideas:* A resilient team can incorporate a wide range of perspectives—from team members and from outside the team—into its approach to change, valuing varied ideas as contributing to effective solutions.

- *Flexible, Interpersonal:* A resilient team can elicit the open participation of team members. Each person recognizes that he or she cannot accomplish the team's task in isolation but benefits by drawing on the strength of others.
- *Organized:* A resilient team can translate the confusion that typically accompanies change into meaningful, patterned information by doing such things as evaluating relevance and setting priorities. This enables it to identify workable solutions for addressing change.
- *Proactive:* A resilient team engages action in the face of ambiguity, even when risk is involved, rather than waiting for stability. Because team members seek to learn from experience rather than merely to avoid failure at all costs, the team can change its plans when they are not effective.

Effective project teams must combine many factors, including a mission or goal, defined tasks, diverse but relevant skill sets, and processes that facilitate interaction. Although any of these factors alone might contribute to a project team's success, the impact is intensified if they are leveraged in a way that builds upon the team's strengths and offsets any potential weaknesses. We believe that the presence of these factors and the ability to leverage them depend on the team's resilience. Specifically, a resilient project team combines two factors—individual resilience and synergy. Each member of the project team possesses a specific complement of the five resilience characteristics—positive, focused, flexible, organized, and proactive. How the team uses these characteristics is determined by the level of synergy in the group.

Synergy—Individuals or groups working together in a manner that produces a greater total effect than the sum of their individual efforts, generates more benefits to the organization than the amount of resources consumed, promotes a higher future-shock threshold, and requires fewer adaptation resources to change.

This is a sample of the text for the definition, or these are more synonyms and usages that are commonly found in the English language.

Future Shock—The point at which no more change can be accommodated without the display of dysfunctional behaviors.

A high degree of synergy allows the team to leverage its strengths and guard against its weaknesses. For example, although not every member of a team may be highly flexible, a synergistic team can draw from those members who are flexible to maximize its performance. Not only does synergy leverage the group's resilience resources, but also, as commonly studied, it produces solutions that are better than and different from the original ideas of team members. As project managers, we have all experienced the creative results a project team can produce even with a reduction in an implementation budget.

Before synergy can be achieved, two prerequisites must be in place: willingness and ability. Willingness stems from the sharing of common goals and interdependence. Ability is a combination of empowerment and participatory management. Each of these prerequisites is briefly described below.

Prerequisites for Synergy

Willingness

- Common Goals—Team members understand and share a central purpose that drives their efforts.
- Interdependence—Team members recognize that they can achieve their shared purpose only through the collaborative efforts of all team members.

Ability

- Empowerment — Team members perceive themselves as valuable and influential in accomplishing the team's work.
- Participatory Management—The team structures mechanisms to elicit the input of individual team members.

You can improve your creativity by learning about and using tools that help you see and understand the world from new perspectives.

If a team has a *willingness* to engage in a synergistic interaction, its members share a purpose and realize their interdependence. If team members have the same goal, they strive for a unified objective.

The goal, therefore, has to be clearly articulated in a way that can be measured.

Interdependent project teams understand that every member adds value to the whole. Without each member, the team would be unable to achieve its shared purpose. A truly interdependent team would falter if any one member were removed. By necessity, interdependent teams are lean. A fundamental concept of a "lean manufacturing" project team is interdependence and representation from multiple functions within the organization.

If a team has an *ability* to engage in a synergistic interaction, its members are, because of their inherent value, able to influence the decisions of other members. In addition, the team structures processes and ground rules to foster this influence. Empowered individuals openly voice their ideas, thoughts, and beliefs to other members of the team. These individuals inherently believe their input can influence those around them. Empowerment is reciprocal. If team members are empowered, they not only are seeking to influence others, but also are open to being influenced. Project team meetings would therefore reflect a significant amount of two-way communication, as opposed to a one-way status update by the project manager.

Participatory management occurs when the team's sponsor, whether a participating member of the team or simply the person who sanctions its existence, is open to the input of the team as decisions are made. Participatory management is both a philosophy and a method for managing human resources in an environment in which employees are respected and their contributions valued and utilized. From a philosophical standpoint, participatory management centers on the belief that people at all levels of an organization can develop a genuine interest in its success and can do more than merely perform their *assigned* duties. This approach involves employees in sharing information, solving problems, making decisions, planning projects, and evaluating results.

Although participatory management encourages employee involvement in decisions affecting their work, this process can create problems if the nature of their involvement is not clearly defined. *Participatory* management should not be confused with *consensus* management. Inviting employee participation does not mean that management has relinquished its responsibility for final decisions. Management is instead *exercising its responsibility* by choosing to involve employees in reaching these decisions. Participatory management is not an abdication of management control but a *form* of management control.

And yet, participatory management maintains a balance of power. If managers want input from employees, they must deal with employees as if the employees had a true power base. Their power is in the value of their perspectives and knowledge. If managers and employees are truly in a foxhole together, both seek the same thing and believe they need each other to accomplish the task.

Today's workers want more information about the overall direction and goals of the organization, more input on the objectives of their own work, and a greater value placed on their ideas for doing this work more effectively. Management must remain ultimately responsible for all final decisions, but managers who use participatory techniques make their decisions with a much broader input base (which includes employee perspectives).

Give employees a view of what's going on

If an organization wants to be more effective during change, everyone in the organization must demonstrate a high level of commitment to the new initiatives. Organizational modifications can occur without commitment, but implementation will be difficult and costly in terms of lost production, absenteeism, turnover, alienation, and conflict. People are much more likely to support and take responsibility for projects they help create. Effectively using the participatory approach will help produce the necessary commitment for successful change projects.

Managers who use participatory techniques are not compelled to involve all their people in every decision all the time. Neither do all employees always have the same depth of involvement. Engaging employees in the change-related decisions affecting them is not a yes/no decision. Participatory management provides employees various degrees of involvement based on their familiarity with the task and the amount of flexibility that the situation allows for. Participatory management is an important prerequisite not only for synergy in context of team resilience. It is also an essential prerequisite to synergistic work among all role players during the change process.

Once the prerequisites are met, four additional and essential skills must be applied for synergy to occur. These skills are briefly outlined below:

- Interacting—Team members surface diverse ideas.
- Appreciative Understanding—Team members find value in the diverse ideas of their teammates.
- Integrating—Team members combine diverse ideas to generate creative solutions.
- Implementing—Team members effectively put their ideas into action.

Interacting. Synergy begins with interaction among project team members. To improve interaction, team members must learn to listen actively and communicate their ideas directly and clearly. Teams learn to recognize that members may vary widely in their communicating style preferences, that individuals may perceive facts, contexts, actions, and feelings very differently. The effective project manager has the obligation to create opportunities for significant team interaction.

Communicating Style—Manner or characteristic mode of interaction among people. A specific style suggests a frame of reference. The basic frames of reference are thinker, sensor, feeler, and intuitor.

Appreciative Understanding. As important as effective communication is to resilient teamwork, something more must occur. Project team members must learn to value and use their diversity. A basic condition for this to occur is an open climate where differences can be surfaced appropriately and different perspectives can be viewed as legitimate, though conflict may arise. When differences surface, the team is taught to address such issues in a timely and deliberate manner conducive to resolution, always with the goal to optimize the team's collective resilience. Project managers cannot allow differences to "go underground" and subvert the project's success.

Integrating. Although effective communication and valuing diverse perspectives are important to achieving team resilience, an important step toward achieving tangible results is integrating or merging diverse viewpoints and skills. Project team members must learn to step back from their ideas and evaluate all possibilities. They must also learn to identify issues or concepts that cannot or should not be integrated. The result is a team that can combine diverse ideas into mutually supported alternatives.

Implementing. Resilient teams are not easy to establish and maintain at productive levels. Teams must learn to harness the energies generated by their work and channel it toward a task. There are three conditions that must be considered:

▶ Team members must establish overall strategies and specific measurable goals and objectives regarding the project. These provide a blueprint for all goals and objectives that follow.

▶ Team members must monitor implementation progress and supply the necessary consequences to ensure success. The team learns the importance of follow-through and understands its impact on project implementation.

▶ Team members must modify the implementation plan when necessary to keep it relevant to current reality. In turbulent environments conditions are constantly changing. The team learns that it must respond to these shifts in reality in order to achieve its goals. As frustrating as it may be, the mechanics of project plan modification must be clearly articulated and followed.

Personal and team resilience potential can be fully realized when:

▶ Hiring and retention decisions are influenced by a person's baseline resilience.

▶ Resilience training is provided, followed by the appropriate coaching and rewards from management.

▶ Principles from the seven support patterns are applied to specific change projects.

▶ When a person's original level of resilience is raised through training, coaching, and rewards, it is referred to as raising "baseline" resilience to an "enhanced" level. When a person's enhanced level is raised even more by applying the appropriate resilience principles to a specific change project, it forms a temporary surge of resilience referred to as the "operating" level (see Figure 2-4).

Second Strategic Risk Area: Change Knowledge

A key indicator of how well projects will be managed is the knowledge people possess regarding the fundamental dynamics of project implementation. This kind of knowledge helps people respond quickly and effectively while implementing projects. Just as high levels of personal and team resilience increase the capacity of organizations to adapt to change and to prevent dysfunction, change knowledge further increases resilience by providing an inventory of concepts and techniques to

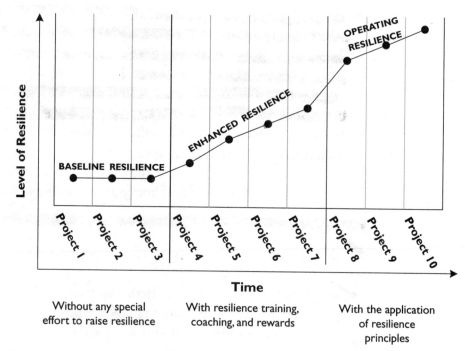

FIGURE 2-4. Maximizing resilience

more easily manage the project transition. The degree to which people have a practical understanding of the "structure of change" and can apply this information to maximize resilience for themselves and those they manage is second to importance only to personal resilience.

We refer to resilience as the primary element or pattern of the structure of change. Then follow the seven "support patterns" as shown in Figure 2-5. Each support pattern can serve as a source for strengthening the primary pattern by the application of the related skills and techniques of that support pattern. The result is to greatly increase the capacity to adapt to change.

The Nature of Change

As suggested earlier in this chapter, individuals enhance resilience when they realize that control is what we all seek in our lives and that the ambiguity caused by the disruption of expectations is what we fear

FIGURE **2-5. The support patterns**

and avoid. We are able to further increase resilience if we are afforded the opportunity to exercise some degree of direct or indirect control over what happens during the implementation of change. Figure 2-6 illustrates the relationship between control and expectations.

Direct Control—The ability to dictate outcomes.

Indirect Control—The ability to at least anticipate outcomes.

Not all people adapt to change at the same speed.

Adapt—To recover from a significant disruption in expectations. This is accomplished when new expectations are developed that allow people to succeed in an unfamiliar environment.

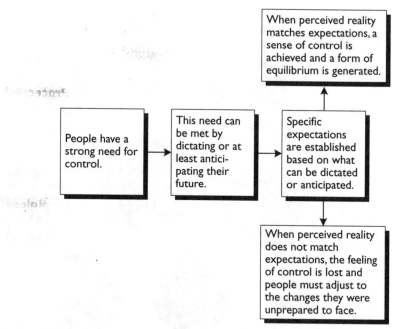

FIGURE 2-6. A summary of control needs

If we are able to adapt to change at a speed commensurate with the pace of events taking place around us, our resilience is adequate and maintains its current level or is even increased. If not, our resilience is drained.

To more fully appreciate how organizations respond to change, it is critical to first understand the micro implications. *Micro* change is when *I* must change, *organizational* change is when *we* must change, and *macro* change is when *everyone* must change. If we expect to manage major change in our lives effectively, our adaptation capacity must be able to meet the total adaptation demand from the micro, organizational, and macro transitions.

A key point here, as you work with targets related to your project, is that to motivate people to change, you must make your points relevant to them on a micro level first. People tend to begin more easily and go through the change process more quickly when they understand the costs and benefits to them personally. Once they understand these points at that micro level, you may also motivate them by explaining the costs and benefits on an organizational level, but not before the micro implications are clear, if you want to be effective.

The Process of Change

Change is an unfolding process, not a binary "either/or" event. This unfolding process is characterized by three states: present, transition, and the desired or "future state" (see Figure 2-7).

Present State—The status quo, the established patterns of expectations. It is characterized by relative stability and familiarity. It represents a dynamic equilibrium that continues indefinitely until a force disrupts it. As the rate of change increases, the present state shifts from stasis into fluidity.

Status Quo—Same as *present state*.

Transition State—The phase during which people no longer behave as they did in the past, but are not yet fully "set" in the new pattern. They disengage from the status quo. The dynamic equilibrium of the present state has been disrupted, but the desired or future state has not yet been reached completely.

During this period, people develop new attitudes or behaviors that lead to the desired future state. To attain what is wanted, people must pass through the uncertain, uncomfortable phase of the transition state. They disconnect from the current condition and begin moving toward the change. This is typically a time of great uncertainty and ambiguity. People may find the ambiguity too uncomfortable and so choose to remain tied to the status quo.

Desired Future State—This state results from vacating the current state and integrating the new behavior patterns required by a change. The desired future state represents full achievement of the objectives of the change.

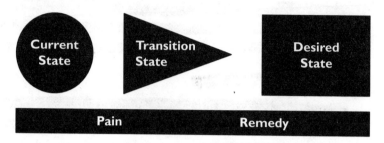

FIGURE 2-7. Change is a process

The strategies have been implemented and some immediate benefits have become clear. As the rate of change begins to increase, the desired future state becomes not so much a final stop, but a prelude to the next change.

To move from the present state to the desired future state, those people who must actually adopt the change must pass through the transition state, a period of high insecurity and ambiguity in which they are "thawed" from their current way of doing things and drawn to a new frame of reference.

Project managers and stakeholders are most successful when they accept that they will pay for getting what they want by managing the process of change or for not getting what they want, and that the payments may come early or late. They know that change is expensive and they will pay. The discomfort and ambiguity of the project-transition state are a natural reaction to the change process and far less expensive than the cost of staying in the present state (i.e., status quo).

Project managers can help people and organizations develop the resolve to change through recognizing that the change is truly a business imperative. Is the implementation of a new product-development process a business imperative or a good idea? In these situations, the issue is not *whether* the necessary commitment to act will be generated, but *when*, the timing of the resolve.

Pain and remedy are two prerequisites for successful organizational change that project managers can harness to their benefit.

Pain—A critical mass of uncomfortable information about staying in the status quo that justifies suffering through the transition state while moving toward the desired state.

Remedy—The actual behaviors needed to achieve the desired future state on time and within budget. A BPI solution is a good example.

The bond to the status quo is so strong that substantive change can occur only when people feel they have no choice. The tangible or emotional price for facing transition must be less than the "pain" people will endure if they remain in their current circumstances. A critical mass of current or anticipated pain related to unresolved problems or missed opportunities must be present to justify a person's breaking the inertia of the status quo. The remedy is an accessible and appealing solution to either a problem or an opportunity afforded by the situation. If there is only pain in moving from the present state and no remedy to cause movement to the desired future state, the change will not last. Selling the remedy provides the motivation to move to the desired future state. For major projects, pain and remedy must work together. Orchestrating pain messages throughout the organization is the first step in developing organizational commitment to change, but remedies must be available to overcome or avoid that pain and achieve the desired future state.

The Roles of Change

Another support pattern that helps explain change is the various roles that must be played in the organization for the change to gain full acceptance. Although there are a number of project-specific "jobs" (e.g., project manager), the change roles may fit into a number of different jobs. These roles are split into four general categories (see Figure 2-8):

► Sponsors
► Change Agents
► Targets
► Advocates

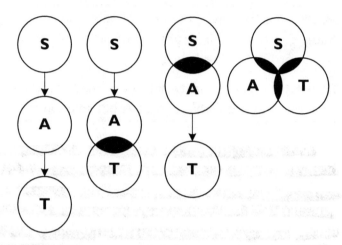

FIGURE 2-8. Role working relationships

Sponsor—The individual or group with the power to sanction or legitimize the project.

Sponsors create an environment that enables the changes caused by the project to be made on time and within budget. There are two types of sponsors: initiating and sustaining. An initiating sponsor is the person or group with the power and resources to start the change process. Sustaining sponsors use their logistics, their economic and/or political proximity to the targets (i.e., the people who actually have to change the way they work) to ensure that the initiating sponsor's directives are implemented.

Change Agents—The individuals or groups responsible for facilitating the implementation of the change.

The success of the agents depends on their ability to diagnose potential problems, develop a plan to deal with these problems, and manage human issues of the change process effectively.

Targets—The individuals or groups affected by the change.

Targets must be educated to understand the changes they are expected to accommodate and they must be involved appropriately in the implementation process.

Advocates—The individuals or groups that want to achieve a change, but lack the power to sanction it.

Change ideas can die an early death if those who generate the ideas do not have the skills to gain support from those who can approve them.

Role assignments for change projects seldom follow a linear path through an organization. Working relationships can be highly complex and convoluted, with people often playing more than one role and frequently shifting roles once a change is under way.

Let's say, for example, that you are a line worker in an auto plant. Obviously, your supervisor is your boss in most situations and you look to him or her to legitimize important changes before you act. But when a labor-management dispute causes the union to call a strike, it is your union shop steward who has the sanctioning power to get you to walk off the job. In this case, your supervisor has little influence on your decision to participate in the strike or not.

At different times and in the face of different challenges, you may play the role of sponsor, agent, target, and/or advocate. Many change projects require you to wear more than one hat. It is not unusual for people to say, "I'm an agent for my boss, but the sponsor to my people." The issue is not whether you are a sponsor or whether you are an agent, but in which type of situation you will be a sponsor and under what circumstances you will be an agent.

The configuration of role relationships in an organization can take one of three basic forms: linear, triangular, or square (see Figure 2-9). According to how they are managed, each of these structures can contribute to success or lead to dysfunctional behavior.

Linear relationships are represented by the usual management chain of command. The target reports to the agent and the agent reports to the sponsor. The sponsor delegates responsibility to the

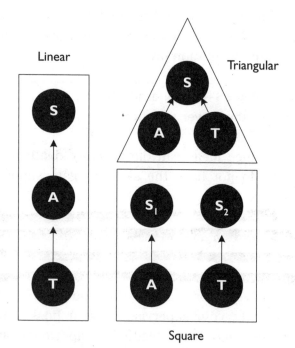

FIGURE 2-9. Key roles: three basic structures

agent, who in turn deals directly with the target to ensure that the change occurs. This is not necessarily a successful path to change, but it is easy to understand because it reflects the typical organizational hierarchy: senior managers tell their middle managers to get the employees who work for them to comply with a directive.

Triangular relationships are more complex and, in most situations, largely ineffectual. In the triangular configuration, the agent and the target work for a common sponsor, but the target does not report to the agent. A classic triangle is found when the sponsors are senior executives, the targets are line managers, and the agents work in a support function (such as human resources or information systems). Support-function relationships are not the only triangles, but they are simply good examples of the dynamics involved.

We have found that as much as 80% of the time organizations are not reaping the rewards they should from their triangular relationships. This poor record stems from sponsors attempting to delegate to their agents the power to authorize the change. That works fine when sponsors assign to an agent the responsibility for actually rolling up his or her sleeves and putting the change into effect; sponsors cannot pass on sanctioning power to people who do not hold that status with the targets.

Having agents tell targets who don't report to them what to do almost always fails. Such attempts to influence may work for minor changes, but rarely in major transitions. The inappropriate attempts by support staff to pressure line managers into complying with their wishes are at the heart of much of the line-versus-staff conflict so prevalent in today's organizations.

The true culprit in such situations is usually not the support staff, but the sponsors. Sponsors turn to their human resources director and say, "Go tell the line that they must use the new hiring procedure—that's what I pay you for." Or they say to the head of information services, "Force them to use the new system if you have to; that's your job." In effect, the mandate is "Tell people who don't report to you what they must do." Of course, when this message meets a brick wall, it is the agent who takes the heat for not doing his or her job.

Triangular configurations, however, are not the true source of the problem. Triangles are a natural formation in any organization. The problem is that too few people understand the dynamics that govern triangular relationships. You cannot manage such relationships if you do not understand and respect the mechanisms that guide their operation.

We spend a great deal of time advising sponsors and agents on how to succeed in triangular situations. To sponsors, we offer this guidance: always endorse the change project with the targets yourself *before* you have the agents actually implement the change. Once employees realize that the boss is supporting a particular change, they are much more likely to cooperate. To agents, we strongly suggest being wary of the risks involved in a project that calls for them to give orders to people who do not report directly to them. In such situations, they may be able to help *facilitate* change, but only after the targets' boss has informed them that he or she supports it.

In the square relationship structure, agents report to one sponsor and targets to another. These relationships are also usually dysfunctional in most organizations. The problems occur when Sponsor One directs his or her agent to bypass Sponsor Two and go directly to the target to gain compliance for a change. Targets rarely respond to major change directives unless these directives come from their sponsor, who controls the consequences applicable to them. In such situations, Sponsor One and the agent are actually advocates, because they have no power to sanction the change with the targets. We have found that unsuccessful advocates try to directly influence the targets, but usually fail because the targets' sponsor does not support the change. For an organization's vice president of budget and finance to send a financial officer to the marketing manager to insist on new cost-cutting procedures is not only ineffective but also counterproductive. The finance department's best strategy is for the vice president of budget and finance to send a financial officer to try to convince the vice president of sales and marketing that the measures are worthy so that the vice president will introduce the changes to his or her people.

Successful advocates spend their time with the sponsors of the targets, engaging in "remedy selling" and "pain management," which we discussed a few pages earlier in this chapter. They help the sponsors realize the importance of the desired change.

Resistance to Change

Resistance is a natural part of the change brought about by any project. It is the force that opposes any significant shift in the status quo. People do not resist change as much as its implications—the ambiguity that results when the familiar (what we know) ceases to be relevant. Some of the more common reasons employees resist change are:

- ▶ *Lack of vision.* When the corporate vision or specific organizational strategies are unclear, there may be confusion over how the changes should be interpreted.
- ▶ *Poor implementation history.* When an organization has a history of poorly implemented strategic plans, the members of that

organization tend to expect little of substance when new changes are announced.

▶ *Lack of middle-management support.* Middle managers often lack any feeling of the ownership and involvement necessary to enthusiastically support change.

▶ *Lack of understanding or belief.* Managers and supervisors will not be effective change agents or supportive sponsors if they do not understand or believe in the change themselves.

▶ *Low risk-taking.* A tendency to overly punish errors and reward the mere absence of mistakes promotes an environment of low risk-taking in which a "nothing ventured, nothing gained" attitude is more vice than virtue.

▶ *No consequence management.* When there are no positive or negative consequences for complying with a change objective, the targets of that change will likely ignore any new directives.

▶ *Lack of clear communications.* If information about a change is allowed to filter down the organization unmanaged, it becomes diffused and vague and it can be interpreted in arbitrary ways.

▶ *Lack of time.* If too little time is allotted for implementation, huge post-change maintenance costs will result. Time must be allowed for the targets to internalize or subconsciously adapt to the principles of the change.

▶ *Poor follow-through.* Many organizations launch major projects with great fanfare and reward those responsible for initiating the change, but then fail to follow through to see that the project achieves its stated goals.

▶ *Lack of synergy.* The various operations of an organization, even widely dispersed components, are to some degree interdependent. If this fundamental point is overlooked, a change that is initiated in one area may encounter enormous resistance in other areas because they are all part of the same system.

▶ *Rhetoric versus results.* Problems are sure to arise when senior managers say one thing about a change, but then behave in ways that send out opposite signals.

▶ *Poor management of resistance*. When resistance surfaces, it is often denied or suppressed. When overt resistance is not acknowledged and properly managed, it goes "underground," resulting in such covert activity as slowdowns, malicious compliance, or even outright sabotage. Overt resistance (e.g., memos, strikes, meetings, or other public exchanges) is the expression of open and honest opposition. Overt resistance should be encouraged because you can better manage resistance you can see. In contrast, covert resistance—opposition that is masked or concealed—can be very damaging. Covert resistance should not be tolerated.

It does not matter if the project is originally seen as good or bad; when people's expectations are disrupted, the end result is resistance.

The Seven Stages in the Perception of Change as Negative

There are seven main stages people pass through when they first perceive a change as negative—a change they don't want and can't control (see Figure 2-10):

Stage 1—Immobilization
Stage 2—Denial
Stage 3—Anger
Stage 4—Bargaining
Stage 5—Depression
Stage 6—Testing
Stage 7—Acceptance

Each stage calls for specific change agent activities to help the targets move successfully through the stages.

Stage 1: Immobilization. This stage is the initial reaction to a negatively perceived change—usually shock. Targets typically seem fearful, confused, and overwhelmed. At this point, agents should allow the targets to express their feelings and accept them as a normal part of the process.

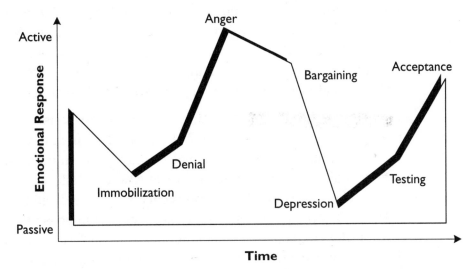

FIGURE 2-10. Emotional response to negatively perceived change

Stage 2: Denial. This stage is characterized by an inability to adapt to new information in the current frame of reference; this information is often rejected. Now the targets begin to defend against the change. The agents should begin cautious reality testing by encouraging the targets to look at the situation more objectively. The agents also should encourage the targets to ask questions about the change and should provide realistic answers while being careful not to be seen as threatening.

Stage 3: Anger. This stage involves frustration with the change and often irrational, indiscriminate lashing out. The targets want to regain control, but through reestablishing the status quo, not moving toward the desired future state. The agents should legitimize the targets' anger but not the motivation. The agents should also be careful not to personalize that anger.

Stage 4: Bargaining. In this stage, the targets resort to negotiating to avoid the negative impact of change, such as requesting delays or reassignments. The targets are beginning to see "the writing on the wall," but will try to minimize its impact. For instance, they may offer to take the new position, but try to continue reporting to the current supervisor, although that would be counterproductive to the change. The agents should be more direct in confronting the targets with the new reality: "I'm glad you are willing to try out the new job, but you know that you will also have to change supervisors. Let's take a look at that person and I think you'll find he has some real positives."

Stage 5: Depression. This stage is a normal response to major, negatively perceived change. The full extent of clinical depression, helplessness, and hopelessness is not usually found in organizational settings, but likely symptoms are resignation to failure, feeling victimized, a lack of emotional and physical energy, and disengagement from work. Now the targets start to understand the impossibility of remaining at the status quo; it's beginning to "sink in." The agents should be very supportive but, at the same time, should encourage the targets to take responsibility for themselves.

Stage 6: Testing. This stage helps people regain a sense of control and free themselves from feelings of victimization and depression. The targets begin practicing new alternatives. They may talk about what it would be like to be in the new position or actually go to the new work site and get a "feel for the job." The agents should help the targets explore realistic options and encourage further testing.

Stage 7: Acceptance. This stage involves a positive perception of the change, but that does not mean that the targets like it. The targets finally respond to the change realistically. The agents encourage this and acknowledge the targets' progress in adapting to the change and help them make plans for fully making the change.

It is important to note that a target may move back and forth between stages before he or she finally reaches acceptance. In such cases, the agent should be persistent in following guidelines for each stage. Should the target become significantly distressed and seemingly "stuck" in a particular stage (immobilization through depression), the sponsor should call in a specialist, such as a staff psychologist.

As project managers, we must be aware of these stages, understand their characteristics, and develop plans to address the behavior.

The Five Stages in the Perception of Change as Positive

The response to change perceived as positive develops differently and includes the following five stages (Figure 2-11):

Stage 1—Uninformed Optimism
Stage 2—Informed Pessimism
Stage 3—Hopeful Realism
Stage 4—Informed Optimism
Stage 5—Completion

Resistance still occurs, but typically at lower levels.

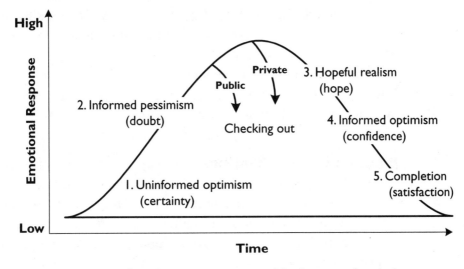

FIGURE 2-11. Emotional response to positively perceived change

Stage 1: Uninformed Optimism (Certainty). This stage is characterized by naive enthusiasm based on insufficient data. The targets typically hold positive feelings about the change and high self-confidence. The agents should reinforce that enthusiasm while preparing the targets for unforeseen difficulties (that will arise in Stage 2).

Stage 2: Informed Pessimism (Doubt). As major change unfolds, much of what we were promised does not come to pass and much of what begins to take place we are unprepared for. If Informed Pessimism is described as doubt, withdrawal from a change is called *checking out* (either privately or publicly). Now the targets begin experiencing negative feelings about the change and/or low self-confidence. What they first saw as a "piece of cake" becomes something of a "mixed message." The agents should legitimize the negative feelings as a sign of learning and provide encouragement and support for continued experimentation with adopting the change. If the targets show signs of public checking out at this point, the agents should develop a problem-solving climate where issues and concerns can be frankly addressed and where the target should find a rationale for continuing to adapt to the change. If the targets are privately checking out (covertly expressing their decision to not adopt the change), the agents should develop a safe climate in which the targets can express negative feelings and/or generate an expectation that the issues will be resolved. If the agents cannot reverse the targets' decision to check out, they should understand that the targets have looped into the model of negative perception of change discussed above and manage accordingly.

Stage 3: Hopeful Realism. This stage begins when the concerns of Informed Pessimism lessen. The targets begin to perceive the change project as achievable. Their negative feelings about the change will decrease and their self-confidence will increase. The agents should continue to build the targets' confidence by acknowledging the difficulty of what they have already accomplished and their ability to cope with any remaining problems.

Stage 4: Informed Optimism (Confidence). This stage begins as more and more issues are resolved. The targets become increasingly confident. They usually experience high levels of positive energy and greater self-confidence as the change approaches success. The agents should reinforce the targets' change-related competence while reminding them that it is important in this stage of the process to follow through.

Stage 5: Completion (Satisfaction). The targets either complete the change or begin the cycle again via another change. Finally, the targets strongly support the change and show a willingness to help others through the transition. The agents should reward the targets' achievement, help them identify important things learned, and prepare them for the next task.

Commitment to Change

This support pattern is about the resolve necessary to ensure project success. Most project failures trace back to some lack of commitment, either obvious (the sponsor cancels the project) or more subtle (stakeholder apathy). A project sponsor shows commitment to a specific outcome by the following behaviors:

- Investing resources (e.g., time, money, and staff) to ensure the desired outcome
- Consistently pursuing the goal, even when under stress and with the passage of time
- Rejecting ideas or action plans that promise short-term benefits but are inconsistent with the overall strategy for ultimate goal achievement
- Standing fast in the face of adversity, remaining focused in the quest for the desired goal
- Being creative, ingenious, and resourceful to resolve problems or issues that would otherwise block achievement of the goal.

Resilient organizations do not take project commitment for granted. They approach the development of project commitment as an understandable and manageable process. Six guidelines are crucial:

- People respond to change at different intellectual and emotional rates.
- Commitment is expensive; don't order it if you can't pay for it.
- Don't assume commitment will be generated without a plan of action. Plans for building commitment should include all parts of the organization that will be affected by the change.
- Keep in mind that building commitment is a developmental process. Simply announcing that a change is taking place starting now might work in the short term, but not in the long term.

► Either build commitment or prepare for the consequences. If you see the need for change, take immediate action, because the cost of failure will be greater than the cost to correct the problem.

► Slow down to increase the speed of progress.

Synergy and Change

Before you attempt to make a change, you must examine the relationships among the project's key sponsors, targets, agents, and advocates as indicated earlier in this chapter in our discussion of team resilience. These relationships can be viewed as *self-destructive, static*, or *synergistic*.

Self-destructive relationships require more energy to sustain than they produce and usually are full of miscommunication, defensiveness, and blaming. *Static* relationships have an even mix of negative, backstabbing behavior and productive, team-oriented behavior. People in this situation are as effective working together as they are working alone. The *synergistic* relationship, however, creates a sum that is greater than its parts. Each person willingly contributes a part of his or her expertise that is needed by the others; as a result, change is brought about quickly, and the team's productivity soars above what each member could have done alone.

Culture and Change

Culture is the frame of reference that helps distinguish one group of people from another and establishes a unique set of formal and informal ground rules for opinions and behavior. It seems that organizations have been recently seduced into thinking that changing their culture is a "quick fix." In reality, it is essential for a firm's very survival, but it is not quick in any way.

The following characteristics are crucial for understanding the relationship between culture and the success of a project:

► Culture is composed of the prevailing beliefs, behaviors, and assumptions of an organization. These components serve as a guide to what are considered appropriate or inappropriate actions for individuals and groups.

- Culture is shared. It provides cohesion throughout an organization.
- Culture is developed over time. An organization's culture is the product of beliefs, behaviors, and assumptions that have in the past contributed to success.
- Culture is nurtured in a self-fulfilling cycle. Culture provides a means of understanding strategic decisions. That understanding allows expectations to develop. Those expectations generate thoughts and emotions. Those reactions lead to decisions about implementation. Those decisions guide and justify activities that are supportive of the culture. This cycle is illustrated in Figure 2-12:

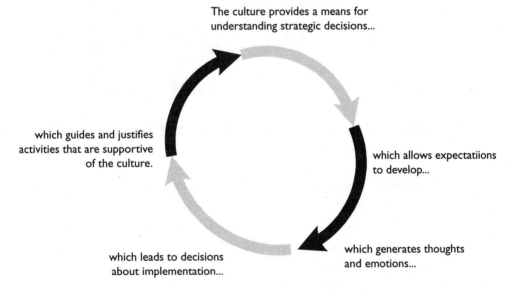

The culture provides a means for understanding strategic decisions...

which allows expectatiions to develop...

which generates thoughts and emotions...

which leads to decisions about implementation...

which guides and justifies activities that are supportive of the culture.

FIGURE 2-12. Self-fulfilling cycle

- Culture usually develops in one of two ways: evolutionary (reactive) and architectural (proactive, supportive of future strategy). As a project manager, the key element to enhancing project team resilience and minimizing the chance of dysfunctional behavior is the degree to which you can actively manage the culture. Whenever a discrepancy exists between the current culture and the objectives of your project, the culture always wins. The odds of implementing your project successfully grow as the similarity grows between the existing culture and the beliefs, behaviors, and assumptions required by the new initiative.

Third Strategic Risk Area: Managing Adaptation Resources

Resilience and the resulting increased capacity to adapt to change should be treated like any other strategic resource (e.g., capital and technology). It must not be wasted or misused. Instead, it is imperative that an organization's capacity to absorb change be skillfully developed and carefully protected. Decisions must be made in a manner that prevents the organization's capacity for adapting to change from dropping below the demands for change it faces.

To do this, key decisions involving major projects should be considered in light of the adaptation capacity. When the demands brought on by projects exceed an organization's capacity to adequately adapt to them, the changes may occur but they will be accompanied by costly dysfunctional behavior that reduces the value of the final results. As project managers, many of us have witnessed the implementation of a new information system while reports are still prepared and used "the old way." For example, we know of one organization that installed a new, automated expense-reporting system, only to discover that employees were still filling out all the old forms manually before entering the data into the system. Therefore as with many projects, the full projected benefit of the system was not realized.

When senior officers face critical decisions involving change, they must be in a position to determine if the proposed action would exceed the organization's adaptation capacity. If this should prove to be the case, one of the following actions is in order:

A. Reduce or delay the objectives of certain projects or terminate them altogether. (It is critical to discriminate between *good ideas* and *business imperatives*.)

B. Develop the organization's adaptation capacity to accommodate the additional demand by, for example, increasing the employees' resilience and change knowledge.

C. Both actions A and B.

Fourth Strategic Risk Area: Building Implementation Architecture

The MOC Implementation Architecture consists of a disciplined and structured approach to implementing major organizational change projects. It provides for the seven critical areas of application that are typically the sources of implementation failure when ignored or incompletely addressed:

► Clarify the parameters of a project.
► Communicate the project throughout the organization.
► Diagnose critical variables, such as sponsor commitment and target resistance.
► Plan the project based on the diagnostic results.
► Implement.
► Monitor implementation.
► Evaluate final results.

We will not discuss the details of the MOC Implementation Architecture here, as its application is the sole focus of Chapter 4. On a tactical level, the architecture specifically addresses problems and opportunities related to the risk areas discussed in Chapter 3.

Summary

This completes our discussion of the strategic risk areas. An important approach to increasing an organization's adaptation capacity and thereby increasing its overall probability for successfully implementing a project is careful attention to the four strategic risk areas discussed here.

When an organization launches a strategic initiative, it should bolster both individual and team resilience where needed. Second, these individuals and teams should be armed with a strong foundation in change knowledge so that they can better understand and manage the dynamics of change once implementation begins. Third, these employees' new baseline of adaptation capacity acquired through their enhanced resilience and learning should be drawn upon wisely. Senior management must make careful decisions about the changes it plans to initiate by always considering the demands on the employees' adaptation resources. Finally, management and employees need to be armed with a comprehensive methodology for project implementation. No matter how ready an organization may be in terms of training, education, and decision making, poor implementation will quickly tax even high levels of capacity.

We will now turn to the *tactical* risk areas associated with change. These areas are as important as the *strategic*, but focus more on the details involved in implementing a specific project.

See Daryl R. Conner's book, *Managing at the Speed of Change: How Resilient Managers Succeed and Prosper Where Others Fail* (New York: Villard Books, 1993), for a comprehensive discussion of the major concepts that support this methodology.

3

Change Management: Tactical Risks to Successful Project Implementation

It is easier to do a job right than to explain why you didn't.
—MARTIN VAN BUREN

Introduction

In Chapter 2, we reviewed the four *strategic* areas of risk: resilience, knowledge, adaptation resources, and implementation architecture. All four of the *tactical* areas of risk come from the last strategic area of risk, implementation architecture. The four tactical areas of risk in project implementation are:

- ▶ Building and sustaining commitment from those in a position to sponsor the project
- ▶ Achieving alignment between the culture and the project objectives
- ▶ Preparing and effectively utilizing the skills of change agents
- ▶ Managing the inevitable resistance of those who will be expected to change behaviors as a result of the project.

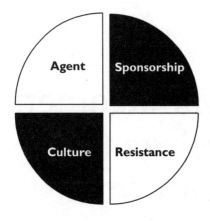

• **Sponsorship**–failure to have the initiating and sustaining sponsorship to appropriately sanction the change
• **Resistance**–the lack of understanding of how change unfolds within an organization and among individuals
• **Culture**–introducing a change that is inconsistent with the existing culture
• **Agents**–failure to have change agents who know how to diagnose transition problems, build implementation architecture, and assist others in the change process

FIGURE 3-1. Tactical risk areas

As you can see in Figure 3-1, much of the basic change knowledge represented in the various support patterns now comes into play in application, the tactical risk areas.

Tactical Areas of Risk in Project Implementation

First Tactical Risk Area: Sponsor Commitment

When project sponsors don't fully understand a project's implications or are unwilling or unable to take the necessary action, your role as a project manager will be to work as an advocate to convince the sponsors of the importance of the project or to be in a position to have the initiating sponsor replace them with people who will provide the needed support. Otherwise, you should prepare for the project to fail.

Without the appropriate project sponsor's attention, energy, action, and other resources, a major project will falter after it is announced. If a sponsor believes the project is a business imperative, he or she will probably be highly committed. If the project sponsor understands how the project will affect the organization, including both its short- and long-term consequences, and can empathize with those impacted directly by the project, he or she will likely sustain this commitment.

A committed project sponsor recognizes the demand that a change project makes on organizational resources, including knowledge, time, and money. The resolute sponsor will also publicly commit these resources while privately meeting with key individuals or groups to convey his or her resolve to see the project succeed. As a project manager, part of your role in managing the change required by the project will be to help a sponsor develop reward structures for those who support the implementation and enforce consequences for those who undermine it.

As a project manager, you can help a sponsor show that he or she means business by establishing procedures for tracking the progress and problems of a change project. A strong sponsor is aware that personal, political, or organizational costs always accompany major change, and he or she is willing to pay the price. A committed sponsor sacrifices other attractive opportunities if they pose a threat to the goal. The committed sponsor understands that follow-up is a crucial final step for any successful change project.

Your change management role as a project manager is to define and elicit effective sponsor characteristics and behaviors:

- *Power:* The organizational power to legitimize the change with those individuals whose behavior must change as a result of the project (targets)
- *Pain:* A level of discomfort with the status quo that makes change attractive
- *Vision:* A clear definition of what change must occur
- *Resources:* A thorough understanding of the organizational resources (e.g., time, money, and people) necessary for a successful project implementation and the ability and willingness to commit them
- *The Long View:* A total, in-depth understanding of the effect the project will have on the organization
- *Sensitivity:* The capacity to fully appreciate and empathize with the personal issues raised by major change

- *Scope:* The capacity to understand thoroughly the size of the group to be affected by the project
- *Public Role:* The ability and willingness to demonstrate the public support necessary to convey strong organizational commitment to the project
- *Private Role:* The ability and willingness to meet privately with key individuals or groups to convey strong personal support for the project
- *Consequence Management Techniques:* Being prepared to promptly reward those who facilitate acceptance of the project or express displeasure with those who inhibit it
- *Monitoring Plans:* The determination to ensure that monitoring procedures are established that will track both the transition's progress and problems
- *A Willingness to Sacrifice:* The commitment to pursue the transition, knowing that a price will most often accompany the project
- *Persistence:* The capacity to demonstrate consistent support for the project and reject any short-term action that is inconsistent with long-term project goals

Obviously, the demands of being a successful sponsor mean that no one can sponsor more than a few major change projects at a time. Yet poor sponsors often engage in far too many change initiatives, draining their time and energy to the point of being unable to adequately perform their duties. Your change role as a project manager is to advise the initiating sponsor of any risks you see in the identified list of cascading sponsors required to sustain the project implementation.

Resolve

The real challenge in maintaining the course of a project is the sponsors' resolve to persist with it. In your change role as a project manager, you can help sponsors understand and continue reminding them that the cost of the status quo is significantly higher than the cost of change.

Initiating sponsors are those with the power to break from the status quo and sanction a significant change. They are generally higher in the hierarchy than those who must perform the duties of the sustaining sponsors. *Sustaining sponsors* are the people close enough to the targets to maintain their focus and motivation on the change goals.

If an initiating sponsor assumes that a major change created by a project will sail through an organization without his or her continual guidance, that change is doomed. The project's initiating sponsor must be able to enlist the support of sustaining sponsors down in the organization or the change is certain to fail. Project managers can assist in this effort by collecting the data necessary to indicate the ongoing levels of commitment necessary to sustain the change and report the data throughout the life of the project in steering committee status reports.

Although it may not seem plausible for an employee to ignore a change directive from a senior officer of the organization, it occurs regularly in most organizations. It usually happens like this. The initiating sponsor of a change is a CEO who makes a videotape announcing the firm's new focus on customer service. The video is shown throughout the organization. Afterward, the local supervisor says, "Don't worry, it's just a bunch of hot air from the old man," or makes a less critical comment such as "That won't affect us, we are already customer-focused." The change is then poised on the edge of an abyss.

Anytime there's a gap between strategic rhetoric and local consequences, targets will always be more responsive to the consequences. When the rhetoric the targets hear from senior management is not consistent with the positive and negative consequences that they see coming from their supervisors, a corporate "black hole" forms.

Black Holes

Black hole—A condition where one or more managers fail to fulfill their sponsor responsibilities, such as by withholding or distorting information so that it doesn't get passed on to the rest of the organization.

The expression "black hole" is borrowed from the field of astrophysics, in which it applies to those areas in space that have a gravitational pull so strong that everything — including light — is drawn in. There are spots in the corporate universe that exert the same effect; it is common for management rhetoric to go into bureaucratic structures and then vanish without a trace. Like the black hole in space that captures everything that travels in its vicinity, various levels of management withhold or distort information so that it doesn't pass on to the rest of the organization. Without proper information, change will fail.

Black holes form where there are local or sustaining sponsors who do not adequately support an announced change (see Figure 3-2). This occurs because of unintentional confusion, covert sabotage, a lack of rewards, and pressures directly connected to the change. Regardless of the reason, when sponsors fail to display the proper commitment to a change, the targets below them will not fully support the transition.

Take, for example, a recent reengineering project that was announced to an organization. The initiating sponsor of the project was the president, who personally gave a presentation to the extended management team enlisting its support. Furthermore, the project team made numerous status updates to the steering committee and at open forums. However, there were still complaints and misunderstandings surrounding the level of commitment needed for the project. It was discovered that the majority of managers believed that, with the personal involvement of the president and ongoing communications from the project team, little was required of them. This became a "black hole"—until the project manager realized the impact of the lack of commitment and resolve by these sustaining sponsors, cascading their influence to their reports. Finally, in order to achieve the results expected by the project, the initiating sponsor established clear expectations of the sponsors and reinforced them with appropriate consequences.

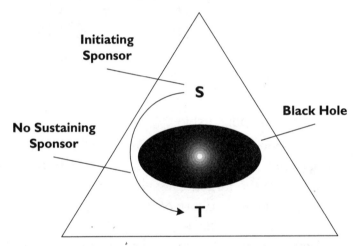

FIGURE 3-2. Black holes: typical ineffective sponsorship

It's important to realize that with all the downsizing, rightsizing, restructuring, reengineering, redesign, flattening of the organization, and self-managed work teams, middle and first-line managers have suffered a percentage of reduction more than double that of nonmanagement employees. Is it any wonder that they experience a level of disruption and therefore resist change far more than the employees? This resistance often results in the creation of "black holes" at many levels throughout the organization.

Black holes...

Cascading Sponsorship

Your remedy as a project manager to the black-hole phenomenon is cascading sponsorship, which begins with the initiating sponsor and ends with the target. Change expected from any project cannot succeed without a network of sustaining sponsorship that constantly reinforces the importance of a project as it moves through the organization (see Figure 3-3). With cascading sponsorship, initiating sponsors enlist the commitment of other key managers below them (treating them as targets, first) to support the change throughout the organization. These managers, in turn, do the same with those below them.

An effective network of cascading sponsorship minimizes logistic, economic, or political gaps that exist between layers of the organization, and it also produces the appropriate structure of rewards and punishments that promotes achievement. Reducing the gulf between the rhetoric of change and the incentives and pressures that guide employee behavior dissolves black holes. Continued attention is

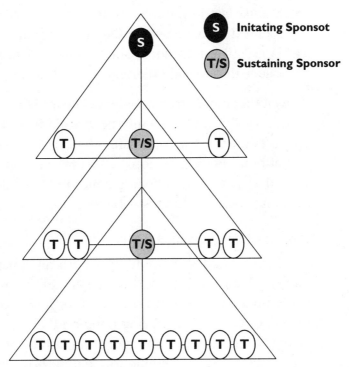

FIGURE 3-3. Cascading sponsorship

required to prevent new black holes from emerging throughout the life cycle of the project.

Second Tactical Risk Area: Target Resistance

As the work environment becomes more complex, organizational change demands more from targets than mere adjustment and compliance. Commitment to a specific outcome is evident when a target:

▶ Invests resources (e.g., time and energy) to ensure the desired outcome

▶ Consistently pursues the goal, even when under stress and with the passage of time

▶ Rejects ideas or action plans that promise shortcuts but are inconsistent with the overall strategy for ultimate goal achievement

▶ Stands fast in the face of adversity, remaining determined and focused in the quest for the desired goal

▶ Is creative, ingenious, and resourceful to resolve problems or issues that would otherwise block the achievement of the goal

Given that committed people will devote the time, endurance, persistence, loyalty, and ingenuity necessary, it is easy to see why commitment is critical for successful change. It is the glue that provides the vital bond between people and project goals. It is the source of energy that propels resilient people and organizations through the transition process at the fastest, most effective pace possible.

Stages of Change Commitment

Even though building commitment with all stakeholders is essential for major change, few project managers, in the role as change agents, seem to understand how to develop it or how easily it can be eroded. After many years of observing people in all kinds of projects either strongly commit to certain change initiatives or falter during implementation, we have been able to identify three specific phases in the commitment process:

Phase 1 — Preparation
Phase 2 — Acceptance
Phase 3 — Commitment

The vertical axis of the commitment model (see Figure 3-4) displays the degree of support for the project, and the horizontal axis shows the length of time someone has been exposed to the project. Each of the three phases—Preparation, Acceptance, and Commitment—represents a critical juncture in the commitment process. The model shows how the degree of support for a change project can progress or regress as time goes on. You can track the process of building commitment according to the points at which a project can be threatened (indicated by downward lines) or advanced to the next upward stage. Let's explore this model in more depth and understand the implications for any project.

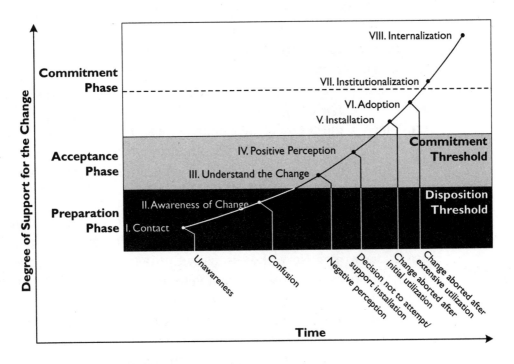

FIGURE 3-4. Stages of change commitment

Preparation Phase

The Preparation Phase of the commitment model consists of two stages:

▶ Stage 1—Contact
▶ Stage 2—Awareness

Stage 1—Contact

An employee's first encounter with imminent change varies according to how his or her job is related to the project. For example, if the change project is the development and implementation of a new product introduction strategy, the initiating sponsor (the business unit president) could have his initial exposure to the necessity of change while reviewing benchmark data regarding his business unit's time to market new products. The change agent (the project manager) might have first contact with the impending change through a meeting with the president. The targets (the Research and Development Department) will have their first contact with the change in the form of a staff meeting to discuss the formation of a project team to develop and implement a new product introduction process.

Contact efforts—whether in the form of meetings, speeches, or memos—do not always produce awareness. There are two possible outcomes of the contact stage: unawareness and awareness. Unawareness reduces the chances of adequate preparation for commitment. Awareness, of course, advances the preparation process.

Stage 2—Awareness

Employees pass into the awareness stage of the commitment process once they realize that modifications affecting their operations are in the works. Nevertheless, as with the contact stage, awareness does not necessarily mean a complete understanding of the change's full impact. In many cases, targets know that a change is coming but at the same time are confused as to the specific effect the change may have on them. They may be unclear about the scope, the nature, the depth, or even the basic rationale for the change.

The two possible outcomes for the awareness stage are confusion or understanding. Confusion reduces the likelihood of adequate preparation, whereas understanding advances the commitment to the second phase of the process—acceptance.

Acceptance Phase

The Acceptance Phase of the commitment model consists of two stages:

- ▶ Stage 3—Understanding
- ▶ Stage 4—Positive Perception

Stage 3—Understanding

Understanding the nature and intent of the project is the first portion of acceptance. People who are aware of and comprehend the change required by the project are now able to judge it. Nevertheless, the outcome of this judgment will be based on each person's view of reality, which varies according to his or her own intellectual and emotional viewpoints and values.

Once people begin to think and act in certain ways toward the change project, they have crossed the "disposition threshold." A positive perception of the change project signals progress into the Acceptance Phase. Negative perceptions indicate resistance to the project. Nothing is ever black and white, so change of any significance produces both positive and negative reactions. A change project may be perceived as negative from one aspect but still be accepted because of a stronger, more positive implication. For example, an employee may have a negative view of a new job that she will be doing as a result of an enterprise-wide system implementation. But she goes along with this change to achieve job security. She eventually accepts the new job as primarily positive, since she considers herself more marketable and has learned new skills, even though some negative perceptions may remain.

The development of a predominantly negative perception at this stage is the first opportunity in the commitment process for true target resistance. Failure to pass through the earlier stages may produce unawareness or confusion, but not resistance. Project managers often respond to unawareness or confusion as if they were symptoms of target resistance. These are signs of resistance only when they are feigned and thus part of a resister's strategy. Targets of the change project will engage in resistance actions (either covertly or overtly) only after they have formed a negative perception of the change required. For example, the illustration earlier about the reengineering project initially indicated target resistance by a significant group of the cascading sponsors. However, this was not resistance but was actually confusion about the level of commitment and actions required by cascading sponsors. Actual resistance develops only if the person has enough understanding to form a perception and judgment.

The possible outcomes for the understanding stage are *negative perception* and *positive perception*. A negative perception decreases support and provides an environment that may foster true resistance. Positive perception increases support and the likelihood of change acceptance.

Stage 4—Positive Perception

Once people perceive a change resulting from a project as positive, they must decide whether or not they are going to support it. It is one thing to view a new procedure as positive but quite another to decide on committing the necessary time, energy, and other resources to make it work. As a sponsor, you might view a prospective change as useful and still prefer not to implement it. In such a case, your positive perception would yield to the feeling that the potential return is too low compared with the high cost of implementation. For example, a recent time-reporting system was developed and introduced at a consulting company. Although the end result was to be useful information that would assist in the management of the organization, other immediate issues and concerns took higher priority.

Unlike sponsors, targets don't function as decision makers regarding change, but they do decide how much they will support a particular change. Most project managers have learned the hard way that reluctant change targets can stop right in its tracks a project that they do not fully support. Management-employee alienation, reduced productivity, decreased quality, absenteeism, grievances, and even overt sabotage are all possible symptoms of target resistance to change.

Once targets perceive a change project as positive, they are ready to move on to the Commitment Phase. Now targets support the project willingly and are involved in the steps necessary to fully carry it out. The two possible outcomes of the positive perception stage are either *a decision not to support implementation* or *a formal decision to initiate the change.*

Commitment Phase

The Commitment Phase of the commitment model consists of four stages:
- ▶ Stage 5—Installation
- ▶ Stage 6—Adoption
- ▶ Stage 7—Institutionalization
- ▶ Stage 8—Internalization

Stage 5—Installation

Once stakeholders decide to embrace the change project in some fashion, they have entered the fifth stage of the commitment process: installation. The project is now operational and a second milestone has been reached—the "commitment threshold." The installation stage is not only a pilot period in which the change is tested for the first time; it is where the first opportunity for true, committed action arises. This action requires consistency of purpose, an investment of resources, and the subordination of short-term objectives to long-range goals.

Given that this is a trial or pilot period for the change project, problems are inevitable and some degree of pessimism is unavoidable. Project managers can facilitate installation by helping cascading sponsors create a work environment that encourages the open discussion of concerns, which tends to solve problems and build commitment to action. As the difficulties are resolved, a more realistic level of conviction develops toward the change required by the project. This conviction is what allows commitment to advance to the adoption level. There are two possible outcomes for the installation stage. Either the change is *aborted* after initial implementation or it is *adopted* for longer-term testing.

Stage 6—Adoption

Though the dynamics of installation and adoption are similar, there are important differences between the two stages. Whereas installation is a preliminary test or pilot, focusing on start-up issues, adoption examines the extended implication of the change. It focuses on in-depth, long-term concerns. A considerable degree of commitment is necessary for organizations to reach the adoption stage. But a change project in this stage is still being evaluated—cancellation is an option. Typical reasons why change projects are aborted after extensive testing are:

▶ Logistic, economic, or political problems were found that could surface only after a significant testing period.

▶ The need that sparked the initial commitment no longer exists.

▶ The overall strategic goals of the organization have shifted and now do not include the change outcomes.

▶ People in key sponsorship or agent positions leave the organization or are not as active in the project as they once were.

There are two possible outcomes for the adoption stage. The change project can be *terminated* after extensive use Or the change can be *institutionalized* as standard operating procedure.

Stage 7—Institutionalization

Installation and adoption are short- and long-term test periods, respectively, in which turning back is still an option. Moving beyond the testing point means the question is not *whether* the change will be made, but *how*. Once the project has been institutionalized, targets no longer view the change as tentative. They expect to use it as a matter of routine. It is now the norm, no longer a deviation.

During institutionalization, the project manager will work with the initiating sponsor to alter the organizational structure to accommodate the change. Also, the project team will generally work with the human resources department to put rewards and punishments in place to maintain the change. What was once a project requiring substantial sponsor reinforcement becomes an integral facet of the operational system.

While institutionalization is indeed a positive development for many change projects, it can often contribute to problems. A theme that has become woven into the fiber of an organization can be extremely difficult to eliminate. If a change has been institutionalized, people may adhere to the procedures merely to comply with their bosses' wishes. For example, many change projects become institutionalized when targets are given the option to comply or face severe consequences. Despite their private beliefs about the change, the targets are motivated by reward or punishment to conform. When targets already have a negative perception of the effort, this strategy usually has little positive impact on their attitudes toward the change. In these situations, targets simply mimic acceptable behavior. They learn to say and do the "right" things. They are like the little boy whose parents demand that he eat his green beans: "You can make me eat 'em, but you can't make me like 'em."

Nevertheless, the success of the change project does not always depend on the targets' personal beliefs. Some projects require only that the new task be physically accomplished, with or without emotional support. But as the pace of change escalates and produces more disarray in the workplace, many project managers are reevaluating their beliefs that targets need not understand or emotionally support major organizational changes. Successful project managers have begun to realize that such an attitude typically results in half-hearted and inefficient implementation efforts that fail to produce a full return on investment. Institutionalization is powerful, but it only alters target behavior; it doesn't win their hearts. The outcome reflects bodies, not souls.

Stage 8—Internalization

When employees are highly committed to a change project because it reflects their personal interests, goals or values, the ultimate level of commitment forms—internalization. This is commitment that comes from the heart. For a change project to gain maximum support, employees must be driven by an internal motivation that reflects their own beliefs and desires as well as those of the organization. The organization may legislate the institutionalization of a change, but the targets control their own internalization.

When targets internalize a change, they "own" the change. They contribute deep-seated advocacy and take personal responsibility for the project's success. No organizational mandate could ever generate this sort of individual investment in a change. Enthusiasm, high-energy involvement, and persistence are the stuff of internalized commitment.

This behavior tends to be infectious. Usually, targets who have internalized a change are so devoted to a project that they engage others in the effort. This enthusiasm makes them hardly distinguishable from sponsors in terms of their emotional investment in the change.

Successful project managers have learned that the investment of time and energy in building commitment by the targets of the change project is well worth it in the early stages of the project. Otherwise, it's like the cost of quality: it costs much more to fix the errors than it does to prevent them. Usually, the "errors of commitment" are prevented through the effectiveness of the cascading sponsors and the degree to which the targets are involved in the changes that will directly impact them.

Third Tactical Risk Area: Cultural Alignment

An organization's cultural traits must be consistent with what is necessary for driving change initiatives or those initiatives may not be successfully implemented. But the overlap between the existing beliefs, behaviors, and assumptions and those required for a change to succeed may vary greatly.

If an organization's current culture and the change for which you are responsible as a project manager have little in common, your chances of successfully achieving that change are slim. The odds of implementing change successfully grow as the similarity grows between the existing culture and the beliefs, behaviors, and assumptions required by the new initiative (see Figure 3-5).

Because cultures are usually very highly resistant to major change, successfully alteration of a culture requires the investment of a great deal of time and resources. When you, as a project manager, are facing

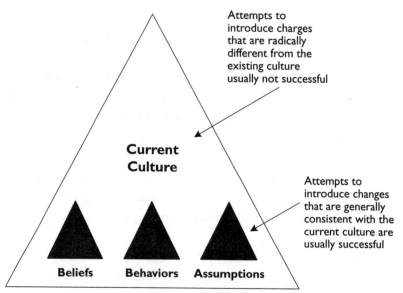

FIGURE 3-5. Introducing organizational change: two options

an organizational culture that may hinder a desired change, these are your options:

▶ Modify the change to be more in line with the existing beliefs, behaviors, and assumptions of your culture.

▶ Modify the beliefs, behaviors, and assumptions of the current culture to be more supportive of the change.

▶ Prepare for the change to fail.

For example, if an existing culture is authoritarian, but you are responsible for managing a reengineering project to decentralize decision making, you need to ensure that a culture change project is undertaken before or along with the reengineering project. Therefore, in cases where the failure of the change project is not an option, an audit of the existing culture is essential. This audit will identify consistencies and/or inconsistencies between the existing culture and the kind of culture required to drive the change, the strength of the existing culture, and the relationships between various work groups within the culture.

First, the audit surfaces employees' perceptions about what they consider to be key cultural gaps between the culture and the requirements of the change. For example, if the culture promotes an unspoken assumption that authority should never be questioned, yet the reengineering requires decision making (i.e., risk taking) down in the ranks, that gap must be identified and addressed.

Second, the audit identifies the strength of the existing culture. The strength of a culture reflects the degree of day-to-day influence it exerts on people and organizational operations. Strong cultures have a powerful impact on people's values, thoughts, feelings, and behaviors and are reflected in the organization's political, economical, and logistical decisions. Strong cultures are typically resistant to change, while weak cultures are more susceptible.

Finally, the audit assesses the influence of key work groups or "subcultures." It's possible that one or more of these subcultures are at variance with the change, even though the organization's overall culture is not. The subculture must be addressed if the change is to succeed. Also, the nature of the working relationships among work groups exerts a significant impact on the implementation of change. It is often the case that the relationship among key work groups is critical to the organization's future success. For example, the relationship between Marketing and Production could be essential if the implementation of new software designed to monitor sales and inventory is required. If members of each function do not cooperate in developing a shared data pool, the system may fail to work as planned.

Once functional recommendations have been approved at the appropriate level, senior managers combine the functional feedback into an enterprise perspective. They must then decide if the culture changes can be embedded in the original change project (such as our reengineering example) or be given the status of a separate change project that may need to precede the other project.

Fourth Tactical Risk Area: Change-Agent Skills

Being an agent of change is not an easy role to play. Your job may be that of a project manager; however, you are often filling the role of a change agent. Frequently, the agent acts as an intermediary between sponsor and target, monitoring sponsor commitment, conveying important information back and forth from target to sponsor and from sponsor to target, and remaining sensitive to the development of target resistance. The key attributes of an effective change agent include the following:

▶ Work within expectations set by the sponsor. The change agent is responsible for making the change happen. Still, the sponsor retains control of the initiative. It is imperative, then, that the agent clearly understand what course of action the sponsor desires.

▶ Apply in-depth understanding of how people and the organization react to the process of change. Agents must be well aware of the impact change has on people and organizations. The agent should be on the lookout for signs of dysfunction within the organization and be sensitive to subtle (or obvious) shifts in the corporate attitude. The agent must be prepared to take measures necessary to ensure that the change remains viable.

▶ Value the human as well as the technical aspects of change. It's crucial that agents understand the mechanics of change and it's just as important to understand the impact of change on targets. Change agents should be mindful that any change, whether perceived as good or bad, will be disruptive to the group it most directly affects. Without this empathetic view, the change is likely to be seen as one directed solely by mandate. If the targets perceive this to be the case, they will likely resist the change.

▶ Identify, relate to, and respect the different viewpoints of sponsors and agents. Agents should remember that, depending on an individual's frame of reference, he or she may view a change as either good or bad. Therefore, the agent should endeavor to address the concerns of sponsors and other agents from within that individual's particular frame of reference. Open resistance to a change should be encouraged and that resistance should be addressed from the individual's frame of reference. Maintaining this open and empathetic style is critical to achieving and sustaining a synergistic approach to managing change.

▶ Collect and appropriately use data regarding how and why people will resist the change. It's critical for agents of change to continuously seek new information that relates to how people respond during major change. Of course, gaining this knowledge is of little value if it is not applied. Therefore, agents must put what they learn to practical use to influence both targets and sponsors.

▶ Help build and maintain synergy among sponsors, agents, and targets. The probability that a major change will be sustained can be greatly enhanced if synergy is a key component of the organizational structure. If all the key players are working toward a common goal, the likelihood of reaching that objective is considerably higher. Because they are a strategic conduit between the sponsors and the targets, agents are powerfully positioned to foster a synergistic work environment, and it's incumbent upon them to do so.

► Communicate effectively with a broad range of people with differing communicating styles. A very important skill that change agents should work to develop and refine is the ability to identify and address the preferred communicating style of any individual involved in a change project. When dealing with a constituent one on one, agents should strive to identify the individual's preferred communicating style and use that style. When speaking to a group or conveying information and ideas in written form for general distribution, the agent should consider including language that will be meaningful to the group's communicating style. For example, a group of engineers may tend to be more responsive to concrete facts and figures, while marketing employees may be more interested in the "big picture."

► Help build and maintain appropriate levels of commitment to the change throughout the change-implementation process. A successful change initiative requires that key individuals maintain a degree of commitment in line with their particular role. For example, the person sponsoring a change should be highly committed to the project. Otherwise, the change will likely be abandoned. The change agent should be committed to the initiative, too, but only to the degree needed for him or her to sufficiently perform the duties required. The change agent may be as committed as the sponsor, but not necessarily. Conversely, those people whom the change will affect only a little (if at all) probably don't need to be as committed to the change.

► Use his or her power and influence to achieve the goals of the change. Agents are responsible for implementing the human aspects of the change. They are not responsible for the technical part of the change (although there may be some overlap of roles in certain situations). Although they do not wield the power of sponsorship, agents hold positions of considerable authority in the change process. Agents act as liaisons between sponsors and targets, giving feedback and direction concerning difficulties and developments. The agent sees to it that all potential problems are dealt with and that targets remain clear as to what is expected of them. The agent needs to pay particular attention to the sponsor's level of commitment throughout the project to determine whether he or she still considers the initiative a business imperative.

▶ Set aside personal agendas, desires, and biases that might hinder the success of the project. The agent must remember that his or her main concern is ensuring that the change initiative achieve its goals. The agent must be able to focus on what is in the best interest of the project and not allow personal preferences and prejudices to influence his or her actions in reference to the change.

▶ Agents should not work harder than their sponsors. If an agent gets involved in a change project that is poorly sponsored or lacks sponsorship altogether, that agent has taken "bad business." If this is the case and the initiative fails (which it will), the blame for that failure will fall directly on the agent. Because of that, the agent should be very sure that any change of which he or she is about to become part has a commitment of strong and consistent sponsorship. No matter how committed the change agent is to the change or how hard he or she may work at the change, it will not offset ineffective sponsorship.

Change is a process and it must be managed like any other process if organizations are going to survive.

Summary

In Chapters 2 and 3 we have emphasized the difference between a major and minor change as being the degree to which expectations are threatened. We have highlighted the dangers of disrupted expectations in terms of dysfunction and the resulting resistance to your projects. We have also emphasized that resilience is the key characteristic to help minimize this dysfunction. Finally, in these two chapters we have stressed the need to recognize and effectively manage the four strategic risk areas and four tactical risk areas in order to successfully implement the project. Hopefully, as a result of reading this material, you have begun the journey toward increased competence in managing the strategic and tactical risks you will confront in every major project in which you are involved. This journey, unfortunately, is not an easy one, as the challenges facing us in today's turbulent business environment require a sophisticated and comprehensive treatment of change management if we are to succeed in maintaining our strategic organizational objectives.

In Chapter 4 we discuss the actions you can take to limit the dysfunction caused by a major change, by applying the MOC implementation architecture. This architecture, when used appropriately, will help guide your actions as a project manager when planning, developing, and implementing your BPI initiatives.

A critical aspect of effective BPI project implementation is the disciplined application of a rigorous change management methodology.

4

Implementation Architecture

If you're going to do something, do it well.

—ANONYMOUS

Introduction

You can improve your creativity by learning about and using tools that help you see and understand the world from new perspectives.

Without an effective integration of BPI project planning techniques and change-management implementation planning techniques, you are left with multiple plans: an organizational design plan, a change-management plan, a communications plan, and a training plan. Attempting to manage multiple plans without clear milestones and integration points has frustrated many project managers and, as we pointed out in Chapter 1, cannot be an option to effective project execution. Such segmented plans result in what we term "bolt-on" change management. The "bolt-on" approach to dealing with the human aspects of change management generally occurs as an afterthought and only when the project runs into trouble. As the project manager confronts poor sponsorship, high levels of resistance, cultural conflict, and a lack of change-management expertise, there's a last-minute rush to attach a few change-management solutions in a vain attempt to recover the project's integrity. The result may be no change or change that is superficial, short-term, or distorted. The improvement project will likely end without meeting its stated objectives.

As you recall, we introduced in Chapter 2 the MOC Implementation Architecture, which is the fourth risk area in strategic change implementation. It is through the disciplined application of this architecture that you address the four tactical risk areas: sponsor commitment, change agent skills, cultural alignment, and target resistance. In this chapter we describe the overall structure of this implementation methodology and introduce specific change-management tools and techniques. This discussion will not be specific to BPI projects. Chapters 5 through 8 will provide a detailed look at how the architecture is best integrated with various BPI projects.

The MOC Sequence for Building Implementation Architecture

To adhere to the MOC structure, all project management initiatives must integrate the following sequence of change-management activities into the project plans in order to improve the overall probability of success. These activities are categorized into seven major phases:

Phase I. Clarify the Project: Identify the scope of the project and the level of commitment required for success.

Phase II. Announce the Project: Develop a tailored change-announcement plan.

Phase III. Conduct the Diagnosis: Following a well-structured announcement, analyze remaining resistance and the organization's capacity to implement the initiative.

Phase IV. Develop an Implementation Plan: Specify the precise actions needed for the change project to be successfully implemented on time and within budget.

Phase V. Execute the Plan: Apply the necessary concepts and/or techniques to fully achieve the human and technical objectives of the project on time and within budget.

Phase VI. Monitor Progress and Problems: Periodically prepare a formal report on the implementation status of the project.

Phase VII. Evaluate the Final Results: Prepare a final report on the extent to which the human aspects of the project actually achieved its stated objectives on time and within budget.

The challenge in applying this architecture is in ensuring that the tasks within all phases are effectively managed in concert with the other elements of the overall project plan. This enables the project team to implement the change with little or no rework.

The key to any successful project implementation is to respect the structure and discipline that the architecture provides while being flexible about applying it. More specifically, as a project manager, you will want to consider all of the phases of the architecture in each phase of your project, regardless of the project type (e.g., merger, process redesign, and systems implementation) or the number of phases in your organization's project or program methodology. The flexibility of the MOC implementation architecture comes into play by applying the appropriate elements of the architecture in one or more of the phases of your project plan. However, prior to the first phase of the architecture, preparatory activities are designed to lay the foundation for success. Figure 4-4 at the end of this chapter shows where the different MOC assessments, surveys, and tools can be applied during each of the seven phases of the MOC Implementation Architecture.

Preparation

In Chapter 2 we discussed the key roles in the change process—initiating and sustaining sponsors, change agents, targets, and advocates. In preparing to initiate a project, advocates and sustaining sponsors are focal.

It's assumed here that you have not yet achieved sponsorship for your proposed project. For example, you may not have sponsorship to begin a BPI project or, after starting the BPI project and identifying a business solution, you need the sponsorship to move forward to implement the solution. Our point here is that, without sponsorship, you are an advocate looking for an initiating sponsor. The following discussion illustrates the key tasks you should perform as an advocate and the tasks your initiating sponsor must perform once you've won his or her support.

Advocates

The job of the advocate is to persuade potential initiating and sustaining sponsors to support the project you hope to initiate or to take naive sponsorship to the level of strength needed for success. The first step is to outline the parameters of the change project using the *Change Project Description Form*. (This and all other MOC tools are also described on the CD-ROM.) This tool helps you fully detail the project, from a change-management perspective. Key outcomes of using this critical tool include:

- A brief description of the project
- Key components of the project
- The technical and human objectives of the project
- The identity of possible constraints to the success of the project
- The primary reason driving the decision to proceed with the project
- A listing of key sponsors associated with the project
- An explanation of why the project is important to the key sponsors
- An explanation of why the change is important to the organization
- A listing of the key targets of the project
- A listing of the ways to help the targets perceive the change as desirable and possible
- A description of the sponsors' expectations of resistance
- A listing of the change agents' responsibilities

The resulting description will be given to the prospective sponsor. As noted, this tool identifies the major role players.

To ensure that you miss no key players and better understand their roles and relationships, however, we also recommend using the *Role Map Application Tool*. This tool will help you develop a graphic representation of the key people, influential relationships, political realities, and organizational structures that are essential to the success of a specific component of a major change project. The instrument will help you discern the possible flow of the change; understand the issues, problems, and opportunities involved; and plot the terrain of the change environment. The following dimensions of each component of a project are identified:

- ► The primary targets of the project
- ► The key sponsors and advocates who will influence the targets
- ► The key initiating and sustaining sponsors who will legitimize the project
- ► The advocates of the project
- ► Key change agents for the initiating sponsors, sustaining sponsors, targets, and advocates
- ► Those people who play more than one primary role
- ► The key relationship structures (i.e., linear, triangular, and square)
- ► The location of weak and/or strong sponsorship
- ► Targets who are supportive or resistant to the changes involved in the project
- ► The level of preparation of key agents to handle sponsors, targets, and advocates
- ► The level of preparation among key advocates to influence their sponsors and targets

The output of this tool is the role map diagram, which will not only provide you with a better understanding of the key players in the projects, but also provide your potential sponsor with a visual sense of the scope of the project. Figure 4-1 is a typical example of a role map diagram.

FIGURE 4-1. Typical role map diagram

Role map diagram—The graphic representation of the key people, influential relationships, political realities, and organizational structures that are integral to the success of a major change.

The role map diagram should be a "living document" that is referred to and updated throughout the implementation process.

Initiating Sponsor

Again, as you recall from our discussion of the process of change in Chapter 2, there are several activities required of a competent sponsor. A potential sponsor will want to understand the planned desired future state (e.g., decreased cycle time or a higher level of quality), the identification of the pain associated with remaining with the current state, and a remedy (e.g., installing new software, other equipment, or downsizing). This information would have been gathered as you completed the *Change Project Description Form*. The tool, *Pain Management Strategies: Sponsor*, provides a step-by-step guide for developing an effective presentation to your potential sponsor. This tool helps you plan how to orchestrate information that increases the potential sponsor's dissatisfaction with the status quo. It enables you to convincingly present the price for the status quo as being higher than the price for transition. The tool is designed to convey "pain" information in such a way that it penetrates the sponsor's frame of reference and produces the level of urgency necessary to get him or her to commit to sponsor your project.

The outcome of using the tool is a well-planned "pain message" strategy covering such issues as:

▶ Possible resistance expected from a sponsor
▶ Assessment of the sponsor's commitment for this project
▶ An evaluation of the strength of the pain associated with the status quo and whether it's sufficient to generate the necessary sponsor commitment

Like the *Role Map Application Tool*, the *Pain Management Strategies: Sponsor* tool will be quite useful once the project is sponsored and you begin working with other potential sustaining sponsors who will be necessary to the project.

Should the proposed project be fairly complex, requiring the sponsorship of several individuals and groups, an advocacy team may be required. It will be critical that everyone on the team be familiar with the change-management methodology and end up giving a consistent advocacy message. Some training may be required.

The Project's MOC Implementation Team (CIT)

Project MOC Implementation Team (CIT)—The person or group responsible for developing and implementing the MOC plan for the project.

Once you have gained the support of an initiating sponsor, that person must begin the process of building an implementation team. The initiating sponsor must elect people from key groups—including sustaining sponsors, agents, advocates, and targets—to serve on the CIT. This team should be large enough to have ample representation from each stakeholder group. An ideal number of members on the core project team is six to eight. Larger groups are significantly harder to manage and potentially less effective. However, the formal core team composition can be supplemented by part-time subject-matter experts who join the team for a limited time when their content expertise is needed. Another key decision for the sponsor is whether or not to appoint a project team facilitator.

A project team facilitator could be the project manager or a designated change-management facilitator. This person's task is to conduct the initial project team meeting to explain the basic purpose of the team. At the meeting, he or she will ask team members to review the original *Change Project Description Form* and the *Role Map Application Tool* to familiarize themselves with the change project. Project team members may be asked to revise the description based on their related knowledge and will be given any input the initiating sponsor may now have.

It's critical that the members of the project team be familiar with the implementation architecture. At minimum, a half-day change-management briefing covering critical concepts is required. Specialized training may be necessary, particularly for key sponsors, change agents, and critical targets. These decisions will, of course, be made based on the results of various diagnostics that are completed later in the sequence. Once the team is in place, the seven-phase Implementation Architecture outlined earlier in this chapter may be applied to the project. The remainder of this chapter will be devoted to discussing each of these phases.

Phase I: Clarify the Project

The intent of Phase I is to clarify the scope of the project and the level of commitment required to succeed. The goal is to focus the parameters of the project to identify affected people, time and budget constraints, and the nature, scope, objectives, and implications of the entire change effort. It is critical that the initiating sponsor(s) clearly understand(s) the change so that the appropriate commitment can be built and adequate resources allocated.

The change facilitator and/or project manager conduct(s) this clarification process while working with the initiating sponsor(s) of the project. The process will define the project, identify key players, and review the organization's history of implementation problems. It will establish the priority of the project, assess initiating sponsor commitment to it, and determine if a select or comprehensive application of Implementation Architecture is warranted.

Once the project has been defined and clarified, the project team is formed. The project team is composed of key people from the organization. Personnel on the project team would ideally consist of one or more representatives from the following groups: initiating sponsors, sustaining sponsors, change agents, and key targets. Members of the project team are instructed in the use of the MOC methodology so that a common language and common frame of reference for appropriate change management are established.

Phase I Process

The CIT completes the following activities:

Outline the parameters of the change project using the *Change Project Description Form* and the *Role Map Application Tool.*

Get a clear view of where you need to go

▶ Determine if the project requires the deployment of the full seven-phase architecture, using *When to Apply Implementation Architecture*. This assessment tool is designed to determine if a specific project will generate major or minor disruption in the organization. In addition, it will aid in identifying tangible and intangible factors that contribute to the true cost should the project fail to meet its objectives on time and within budget. It will also identify the human factors that contribute to the risk of failure. If the project does not need the full sevenphase sequence (i.e., the cost and risk of failure of fully implementing the project are not high), the team may proceed with an unbundled, more bolt-on application of the architecture.

▶ Analyze the degree to which the change will disrupt the expectations of the people affected, using *Predicting the Impact of Change*. A change has high impact when it disrupts the expectations of the individuals involved. This interactive tool enables the team to assess the impact the project will have upon the targets of the change and to take appropriate steps to minimize and manage the effects of the disruption. This self-scoring tool provides an assessment of the degree to which certain aspects of the project are likely to cause high impact. Sample items include the following.

– The degree to which the change is easy to communicate and will be understood

– The degree to which people feel they have or can attain the knowledge and skill necessary to implement the change

– The degree to which the change requires people to learn new information or view existing information differently

An overall Impact Factor score is derived, estimating the risk of failure related to the impact of the change.

There are two primary types of MOC assessment tools: diagnostic and interactive. The diagnostic tools are designed to uncover barriers that could jeopardize project outcomes. These tools allow for the valid and reliable sampling of specific groups within an organization. Scoring and analysis is completed by ODR's Diagnostic Services. Interactive tools have been constructed to facilitate dialogue about potential barriers. They were not designed to sample reliably populations within an organization. These are self-scoring tools. For organizations that have not developed an assessment tool, organizations such as ODR and Ernst & Young LLP can provide help in administering, scoring, and analyzing MOC assessments.

▶ Analyze the current level of dysfunction within the affected area, using the *Overload Index*. This diagnostic tool assesses behavior related to "future shock"—the point at which no more change can be accommodated without dysfunctional behaviors. Individuals throughout the organization are asked to indicate how frequently they observe each type of behavior and the level of its impact on their work group. Individuals are also asked to record any additional symptoms of overload that may be unique to their situation. A report is generated summarizing results for the total group and for any subgroups identified by the organization. The information in this report allows the project team to systematically assess its current state of functioning related to change. It can be used to help key decision makers determine whether additional changes can be accommodated or whether they will push the organization over the future shock threshold.

▶ Analyze past implementation barriers that must be overcome, using the *Implementation Problems Assessment* or the *Change History Survey*. Past implementation experience sets the stage for expectations of current and future change. It is important to understand where problems may have occurred in the past so that they can be corrected and effective implementation plans laid for the future. An organization's track record of change implementation is one of the clearest indicators of the likelihood of future success. The interactive tool, *Implementation Problems Assessment,* identifies common implementation barriers. It allows an organization to benefit from mistakes of the past in addressing the implementation issues of future change projects.

A related tool is the *Change History Survey*. This diagnostic identifies issues in an organization's history that have been significant barriers to the successful implementation of previous change initiatives. The survey should be completed by a sample of individuals representing important constituencies within the organization. Conducting the survey early in the project allows important concerns to surface about inhibitors that have influenced past change efforts. This enables managers responsible for change projects to quickly assess implementation barriers and their implications. This information is presented in a report that summarizes the factors that distinguish successful organizations from those that fail when implementing change.

▶ Assess sponsor commitment to the project, using the interactive tools, *Sponsor Evaluation, Sponsor Checklist, Senior Team Value for Discipline,* and *Expectations for a Successful Change Project.* It is imperative that the team fully understand the strength of its sponsors' commitment, particularly as you prepare to launch the project. Let's look at each of these tools separately.

The *Sponsor Evaluation* identifies critical aspects of sponsor commitment. It pinpoints those areas that should be addressed so that sponsor commitment can be raised to increase the likelihood of your project's success. (It may also be completed by a target or change agent to evaluate his or her sponsor(s) or by the sponsor as a self-evaluation.) This self-scoring tool provides an assessment of a sponsor's level of commitment. Each item is assessed in terms of its contribution to the level of risk of implementation failure. Examples of some of the dimensions are as follows.

– How dissatisfied is the sponsor with the way things are?
– Does the sponsor understand the long-term impact the change will have on the organization?
– Is the sponsor willing to commit the resources needed for the change to succeed?
– Will the sponsor use rewards and pressure to gain support for the change?

An overall Sponsor Factor score is derived, estimating the risk of failure related to the specific sponsor.

The *Sponsor Checklist* identifies critical aspects of a sponsor's strategic preparation (overall readiness to sustain numerous, overlapping, and demanding changes) and crucial components of a sponsor's tactical preparation (overall readiness to initiate and implement a particular change effort). The tool helps focus on those areas that need to be addressed to strengthen sponsor commitment. A sampling of some of the strategic aspects includes the following:

– Support and encouragement of resilience
– Assessing the change-knowledge level of employees
– Consideration of organization's adaptation capacity before adding changes
– Monitoring of change-related dysfunction
– Requiring structured approaches to managing change

A sampling of the tactical aspects includes the following:
– Mechanism to monitor progress and problems

– Action to ensure synergistic teamwork
– Strong initiating and sustaining sponsorship

Two overall scores are derived: the Strategic Preparation score estimates implementation risk for future changes, based on the organization's readiness to sustain change in general, and the "Tactical Preparation" score estimates the risk from the level of preparation to undertake a specific change project. An overall interpretation, based on the combination of Consistency and Strength Factor scores, describes the likelihood of achieving both short-term and sustained success.

The *Senior Team Value for Discipline* assesses the degree to which the senior team is perceived to consistently incorporate disciplined thinking and action in their approach to major change. The information that is generated will help an executive team determine the specific action steps needed to become more effective sponsors. This self-scoring tool provides an assessment of the extent to which a senior team displays characteristics related to a value for discipline. These characteristics are as follows:

– Analysis before action
– Combining intuition with other data
– Process rather than event orientation
– Focus on what happens after initial excitement
– Will build on others' solutions
– Motivated by sustained change
– Open to influence from employees
– Motivated by familiar challenges
– Use of structure in implementation
– Application of consequences

An overall Value for Discipline Factor score is derived, estimating the risk of failure related to senior team discipline.

The *Expectations for a Successful Change Project* tool helps sponsors and change agents clarify their expectations regarding how a major project with important implications for the organization would ideally be implemented. This self-scoring tool provides an assessment of the extent to which expectations about important aspects of a change project are realistic. These aspects include the following:

– Cost of the implementation process
– Level of resistance generated
– Number of projects that can be implemented at once
– Comfort level during transition
– Top-down versus bottom-up flow of change
– Focus on success of the change versus liking the change
– Openness to conflict
– The use of pain as a driving force
– Importance of planning

An overall Expectations for a Successful Change Project Factor score is derived, estimating the risk of failure related to unrealistic expectations.

Critical Groundwork

You can improve your creativity by learning about and using tools that help you see and understand the world from new perspectives.

During this phase, critical groundwork for the success of a project is completed. The business reasons for undertaking the effort are clearly articulated and a real attempt is made to learn the organization's history of change implementation and not repeat any negative history. The effort's contributions to organizational goals and objectives are identified, as are its relationships with the organization's other work and projects. The support of critical managers is secured.

It is important to recognize the business reasons for changing an organization's practices. The stimulus for change could be unanticipated events or circumstances, an edict from someone higher up in the organization, or the information gained from benchmarking activities as part of a continuous improvement approach. Whatever the stimulus, it can have far-reaching influence on the visibility, conduct, and ultimate success of the project. Change for the sake of change rarely results in significant improvement. In general, when the business reasons for change are more evident, there is greater buy-in throughout the organization and there are greater chances for success.

Once the reasons for initiating the change have been clearly identified, you can work in your role as the project manager to help the initiating sponsor set the context for the change that will occur.

Set Context—Clarify how a BPI effort fits with the organization's business strategy.

What specific organizational goals and objectives will be realized or supported by this change? How will it affect other initiatives and ongoing work? What benefits will result, such as return on investment or improved capabilities and morale? What are expectations concerning return on change? Context and implications often become more evident as the effort proceeds, but it is important to be as clear as possible regarding these issues early in the effort. It's also critical to learn from how some of these issues were addressed during past project implementation activities.

Often, project managers and sponsors implement one change after another without ever realizing the full benefit of their efforts. Changes are introduced yet never fully implemented, and the barriers to successful implementation are never identified. Therefore, mistakes are repeated with new change projects. The costs of poor implementation are high: wasted time and money, low morale, and eroding confidence in management.

One of the best indicators of likely success in current or future change projects that a project manager can use is the organization's track record in implementing past changes. Project managers need an objective, systematic way of identifying issues from the past that can be implementation barriers in the present. This information provides early warning for potential problems and possible implementation failure, determines the organization's predisposition toward change, and analyzes any barriers that may arise during the implementation process. The *Change History Survey*, discussed earlier, is designed to do this.

This completes our discussion of the process and tools of Phase I. Our goal was to avoid unnecessary naiveté at the beginning of the project, clarify the scope of the change, identify potential change resistance, and ensure sponsor commitment. With this goal achieved, your team has laid a solid foundation for Phase II, building and delivering the announcement of the project to those who will be affected by it.

Phase II: Announce the Project

The intent of Phase II is to develop a tailored change announcement plan. The goal of this "communication plan" is the careful rollout of all change project information to the affected constituencies. Preplanning and sensitivity to the unique needs of various groups will minimize disruption and set the stage for acceptance of the need for the change. The project team completes the communication planning process.

Phase II Process

The CIT completes the following activities:

▶ If the key groups affected by the change project have not been identified, use the *Communicating Change: Project Analysis* to apply the *Role Map Application Tool*. Successful implementation of change requires the cascade of information to the targets. A thorough analysis of the project and key constituencies is the starting point of effective communication. The *Communicating Change: Project Analysis* tool asks pertinent questions about the key people and groups in a given change project. As part of the process, a role map diagram is developed (or reviewed and refined as the preliminary diagram should have been made during your "Preparation" activities, discussed earlier in this chapter) that delineates the different roles and key constituencies affected by the change.

▶ Determine the frame of reference of each identified group using the *Communicating Change: Constituency Analysis*. Following the project analysis, developing and delivering a successful change announcement requires a careful and thorough analysis of each constituency. This tool helps the team determine the frame of reference for each constituency identified during analysis. This information is then used to develop approaches to announcing the change for each key group. Completion of the tool provides the following:

- Identification of the change's level of disruption as major or minor
- Determination of the organization's change implementation history and its implications for the current project
- Assessment of the synergy among targets, agents, and sponsors
- Levels of current and required commitment toward the change
- Assessment of different frames of reference among the constituencies
- Identification of actions required following the announcement

▶ For each identified group, develop an announcement statement that conveys the organization's overall situation, the forces compelling the change, and where the change is taking the organization. Use the *Communicating Change: Statement Development*. Following a thorough analysis of the project and its critical constituencies, successful change announcements must be tailored to each constituency. This tool helps you create a statement to meet the particular needs of each key constituency affected by the project. The completed tool provides the following information:

- Identification of appropriate pain messages
- Objective measures of success
- An explanation of both the desirability and accessibility of the remedy
- Individual and organizational consequence management structures
- Identification of pessimism generators
- Identification of information channels
- Description of the level of sponsor commitment required
- Identification of implementation support structure

▶ Plan how best to announce the change project to each group, using the *Communicating Change: Announcement Plan*. This planning document helps determine how the change statement will be delivered to the key constituencies of a change project. It helps identify who should make the announcement, how the change announcement should be conveyed (via a speech, in a video, or through a memo), and to whom it should be addressed (individuals or groups). By answering questions such as these, the optimum change announcement plan can be developed for each constituency. The key outcomes of using this tool include:
- Identify the components, sequence, and timing of release of the announcements
- Develop appropriate formats, styles, and tone for each delivery
- Specify when, where, and by whom each delivery will be made
- Plan the actions required prior to making the announcements
- Cascade the plan throughout the organization
- Sequence the events around the announcements for maximum effect

   The sustaining sponsors become much more active at this time. They should complete the following activities:
- Establish methods to allow people affected by the change project to raise concerns and receive answers to questions about the change project
- Schedule and promote the announcement of the change project among identified groups
- Announce the change project according to the *Communicating Change: Announcement Plan*

Once the change project announcement plan is completed and executed, it is likely that concerns will arise around such issues as sponsor commitment and target resistance. The team must now direct its efforts into diagnosing the strength of sponsor commitment and target resistance as well as other areas of key risks, such as change agent skills and culture.

Phase III: Conduct the Diagnosis

The goal of Phase III is to analyze the organization's capacity to make a particular change, in order to determine if implementation barriers remain that could jeopardize the success of the change. This diagnosis should be made only after completing the formal announcement of the change project. A well-designed announcement will help ensure that all targets (and other role players) thoroughly understand the project and how it will impact them. This understanding allows you to assess reliably what forms their resistance might take, for instance, and how strong existing commitment may be. This diagnostic data, coupled with the rich dialogue that typically occurs during Phase II, provides the basis for developing a comprehensive implementation plan. Also, this diagnosis does not assess the organizational climate. Generalized assessments tend to be too broad to accurately pinpoint specific risk areas and levels of risks associated with the particular mix of role players and the technical requirements of each unique change effort.

The MOC diagnostic tools assess certain risk factors to determine the likelihood for success and the cost and risk of failure. Data from this diagnosis help determine if the change project warrants further diagnosis, additional planning, or reconsideration. To carry out the diagnosis, the project manager can use a survey such as the *Landscape Survey* for individuals or groups most affected by the change. This diagnostic tool provides an analysis of risk areas within the organization that may threaten your project. Information is collected using a survey instrument designed to address key elements in the successful implementation of a particular change. This information is presented in a report that summarizes the degree of risk for important constituencies affected by the change. The report can be stratified by department, level, or other variables. The report also includes prescriptions for addressing the identified risk area.

The *Landscape Survey* should be administered following the announcement of the change project, so that the respondents have sufficient knowledge of the change. Conducting the assessment before the implementation strategies are fully developed allows for the results to be used in developing the implementation plans. The data from the assessment also serve as a benchmark from which to track the progress of the change. Administering the survey several times over the course of the change project is a good mechanism for assessing the effectiveness of actions taken to address critical issues, charting the progress of the change, and finally, evaluating the effectiveness of implementation. Figure 4-2 displays the XYZ Corporation's average score on each risk factor, compared with the average scores of all other organizations that have completed the *Landscape Survey.*

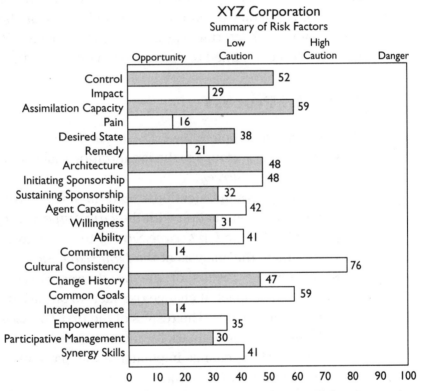

FIGURE **4-2. Example landscape survey results, combined samples**

Based on the diagnostic results, the project manager may administer and report on any of the self-scoring, interactive tools, such as the *Sponsor Evaluation, Sponsor Checklist, Synergy Survey,* or *Culture*

Assessment (the latter two will be described later in this chapter). For instance, if the results of the *Landscape Survey* indicate weak sponsor commitment, further analysis may be required using the *Sponsor Evaluation*. This secondary analysis may refine the project manager's understanding of the situation by clarifying the exact dimensions of the commitment problems. These tools also may be used in focus groups.

A special situation arises when the diagnosis indicates a significant discrepancy between the existing culture (or one or more subcultures) and the type of culture the organization would need for the change to succeed. When this is the case, it will be necessary to conduct culture audits in carefully selected areas of the organization. These audits will determine precisely which aspects of the current culture should be modified to ensure adequate support for the project.

Phase III Process

The CIT should complete the following activities:

▶ Identify key groups in the organization that should complete the *Landscape Survey*.

▶ Develop communications materials to distribute to target groups in conjunction with the *Landscape Survey*.

▶ Administer the *Landscape Survey* to select groups.

▶ Complete the analysis of the *Landscape Survey*.

▶ Review the results of the *Landscape Survey*. Evaluate the potential impact of change risk factors on various groups affected by the change. The results of the first *Landscape Survey* can be used as a benchmark for future surveys conducted during the course of the change implementation, particularly during Phases VI and VII of the sequence.

▶ Discuss the risk factors outlined for each group and build consensus among project team members on the data's implications for the change project.

Some risk factors or groups may require further analysis. If the results of the *Landscape Survey* pinpoint organizational subgroups with High Caution (successful implementation may be at risk) or Danger (successful implementation is definitely at risk) risk factors or if consensus cannot be reached on the implications of the data, one or more of the interactive tools may be needed. Decide which tools may be appropriate and plan how to administer them. The project team may choose to have specific people or groups complete the interactive tools or to use the tools as discussion drivers for focus groups.

▶ Develop an initial plan to proactively address the variables identified in the *Landscape Survey*, including potential barriers to the project's implementation, using the *Preliminary Implementation Plan (PIP)*.

▶ Once the goals, key individuals, and possible barriers to a project's implementation are identified, the next step is to build a constructive plan to proactively address all of these variables. This planning document helps change agents translate the information and analysis from the *Landscape Report* or use any of the individual assessment tools into tangible action steps. The tool identifies and prioritizes risk factors, concerns, and specific tasks. It also identifies who will be responsible for these tasks and deadline dates. The plan is used to clarify key issues and reconfirm sponsor commitment before using the more comprehensive, *Organizational Change Implementation Plan* in Phase IV. Once completed, this tool helps agents develop the following.

– A brief definition of the change project

– A tabular display of diagnostic data summarizing the risk factors identified by the *Landscape Survey*

– An analysis of relationships and/or patterns among various risk factors that may create an interaction effect and an even greater level of risk of failure

– A prioritized listing of specific areas of implementation concerns

– A sequenced action plan that lists the concerns, steps that can be taken to minimize them, people responsible for those actions, and due dates

▶ Review the goals and layout of the PIP with the project team and establish a work plan for finalizing the PIP. The project team should reach consensus on key barriers to the change project and develop action plans to reduce their effects. As mentioned earlier, various interactive tools can be used to further analyze risk factors identified by the *Landscape Survey*. For example,

– Analyze the degree to which the change will disrupt the expectations of the people affected, using *Predicting the Impact of Change*.

– Determine the organization's history of change project implementation and problems that might need to be overcome for this project, using the *Implementation Problems Assessment*.

– Assess the sustaining sponsor's level of commitment to the change, using the *Sponsor Evaluation* and the *Sponsor Checklist*. If sustaining sponsor commitment is insufficient:

– Educate sustaining sponsors with pain management and reframing techniques,

– Replace sustaining sponsors with people who possess legitimizing power, or

– Prepare for the project to fail.

▶ Evaluate the level of synergistic teamwork within, between, and among key groups using the *Synergy Survey*. This tool examines several issues related to synergy. It determines whether or not the key players in a project are able and willing to interact, integrate their ideas, show mutual appreciation and understanding, and implement plans to achieve common goals. The tool assesses the degree to which each of the four prerequisites and four skills related to synergistic interaction is present with reference to a particular project. A sample of some of the issues addressed includes the following:

– Common goals: Is there a clear, shared goal?

– Interdependence: Do people recognize that they must combine their skills and abilities with those of others in order to achieve the goal?

– Appreciative understanding: Are people able to discover value in ideas that differ from their own?

An overall Synergy Factor score is derived, estimating the risk of failure related to interpersonal synergy. If the level of synergy is insufficient for successful change implementation, conduct a synergy training program.

▶ Assess the level of resistance among key target groups, using the *Change Resistance Scale*. This interactive assessment tool is designed to be completed by targets. This self-scoring tool assesses the extent to which resistance is an issue in a specific change. Sample items that targets are asked to address include the following:

– Do you believe that this change is really needed?
– How involved have you been in the planning for this change?
– How clear has communication been about this change?
– Do you believe that adequate rewards are being provided to accomplish this change?
– How compatible do you believe this change is with existing organizational values?
– Do you believe that your boss or other politically important individuals and groups are genuinely supportive of this change?

An overall Resistance Factor score is derived, estimating the risk of failure related to target resistance. If resistance is being expressed openly, it can be addressed by sponsors and agents through problem solving. But if it is covert, targets should be taught to resist openly.

▶ Assess the consistency between the organization's current culture and the desired culture, using the *Culture Assessment*. As we noted in Chapter 2, culture (the patterns of beliefs, behaviors, and assumptions of an organization) can be an extremely powerful force either to facilitate or to obstruct change. In fact, whenever there's a conflict between culture and change, culture always wins. This assessment tool evaluates both the strength of your existing culture and the consistency of that culture with the proposed change. It can be used to modify and position a change project to make it more readily accepted by the organization. A change that is inconsistent with the existing culture or a subculture critical to the success of your project is more likely to fail. This is especially true if the culture is strong. This self-scoring tool assesses the degree to which the change and the existing culture are compatible and the strength of the existing culture. Consistency between the change and the culture is assessed on the following dimensions:

– Management processes
– Motivation
– Decision making
– Performance appraisal
– Communication
– Leadership
– Teamwork
– Business
– Structure
– Change implementation

Strength of the existing culture is assessed on the following dimensions:

– History
– Common beliefs, behaviors, and assumptions
– Shared belief, behavior, and assumption patterns
– Consistency of behaviors and beliefs
– Consistency of assumptions with belief and behavior patterns
– Clear and consistent signals about beliefs, behaviors, and assumptions
– Localization of operations
– Strength and duration of leadership
– Stability of membership
– Consciously communicated and rewarded beliefs, behaviors, and assumptions

Two overall scores are derived. The "Consistency Factor" score estimates the risk of failure related to cultural inconsistency.

The "Strength Factor" estimates the difficulty of altering the current culture. An overall interpretation, based on the combination of Consistency and Strength Factor scores, describes the likelihood of success.

▶ If the *Landscape Survey* and the *Culture Assessment* reveal a high degree of inconsistency between the current and desired cultures, further action may be needed. One option is to modify the change project to more closely fit with the current culture. An alternative is to change the organization's culture systematically, over time. If the latter course of action is required, a *Culture Audit* is needed. As we've indicated before, if you find that the culture is likely to act as a barrier to the success of your change project, you should delay the project until the necessary changes in the culture are made. The *Culture Audit* is a resource-consuming process.

▶ Select and evaluate the skills of change agents using the *Change Agent Selection Form* and the *Change Agent Evaluation*. The *Change Agent Selection Form* is an interactive assessment tool that identifies characteristics that successful change agents must possess. The form is designed to facilitate discussions between agents and sponsors about expectations for agent performance. This self-scoring tool is used to assist sponsors and potential agents in the rationale used to select and develop agents. The dimensions it explores include the following:

- Is the candidate perceived as highly credible?
- Has the candidate earned sponsor trust and respect?
- Does the candidate demonstrate a high tolerance for ambiguity?
- Does the candidate thrive on challenge while avoiding stress levels associated with burnout?
- Is the candidate aware of the formal and informal power structure and know how to use it?

An overall Change Agent Potential score is derived, estimating the risk of failure related to the specific agent.

The *Change Agent Evaluation* identifies the skills and attributes needed by designated change agents and pinpoints those skills that are weak. It can be used as a self-evaluation tool or by those who train and/or supervise change agents. Examples of these attributes include the following:

– Good understanding of change management concepts and principles
– High levels of political support and credibility
– Effective management of ambiguity and uncertainty
– Working within the sponsor's expectations

An overall Change Agent Evaluation Factor score is derived, estimating the risk of failure related to the competence of the agent. If the *Change Agent Evaluation* indicates that agents are not sufficiently skilled, they must be trained as quickly as possible.

► Convene the project team to review the results of the interactive tools that were used to add to the organization's understanding of the nature and scope of the change project.

► The interactive tools should be reviewed item by item, page by page. If multiple tools were completed by individual project team members or groups of team members, all of these responses should be shared.

► The project team change facilitator should use the discussion to build consensus regarding the data's implication for the change project.

► One team member should record the results of the discussion and complete a final copy of each tool that reflects the consensus that was achieved.

► Depending on the number of tools completed and the length of discussion on each, more than one meeting may be required to review the interactive tools.

► Once the CIT has formulated its own interpretation of the nature and scope of the change project, determine if other groups should be sampled to verify or challenge the team's perceptions. The completed *Role Map Application Tool* would be helpful for this task.

▶ Revise the PIP to reflect any new data gathered with the interactive tools.

▶ Depending on the results of the *Culture Assessment*, the sponsors may need to modify the change project or sanction a *Culture Audit* to determine how the current culture and/or subcultures might be changed to arrive at the desired culture.

▶ Set up ongoing methods to ensure that rumors regarding the change project are overtly voiced and then addressed by the project's sponsors.

▶ Communicate the status of the change project and the results of the *Landscape Survey* to the affected groups. Use various communication methods—including presentations, question-and-answer sessions, videos, memos, and newsletters—to ensure that all groups are fully updated.

By this point the team should have the data necessary to complete the PIP. The next step will be to develop a comprehensive plan (*Organizational Change Implementation Plan* or OCIP), based on your sponsor's feedback on the PIP. This is the focus of Phase IV.

Phase IV: Develop an Implementation Plan

The goal of this phase is to specify the actions necessary to successfully implement the project on time and within budget. The implementation plan's purpose is to clarify strategies, tasks, responsibilities, and time frames for lowering the implementation barriers identified in Phase III. A written plan also ensures proper sponsorship for such actions.

The project manager or change facilitator should educate the project team in the use of a disciplined approach to change implementation and then help the team create a preliminary implementation plan that integrates the technical aspects of the project and the change-management elements. This plan is then reviewed with the appropriate sponsors for approval and/or modification. The initiating sponsor and the project manager will determine if additional data are necessary to fully represent initiating and sustaining sponsor commitment, target resistance, cultural alignment, and/or change agent skills (i.e., the four tactical risk areas). Based on the collection of all data required, the CIT completes a final version of the OCIP for review by the steering committee. The completed OCIP includes detailed descriptions of the major aspects of a comprehensive implementation plan, including the following:

- Implications of status quo
- Implications of desired future state
- Description of the change
- Outcome measures
- Burning platform criteria
- Comprehensive or select application of implementation architecture
- Disruption to the organization
- Barriers to implementation
- Primary sponsors, change agents, targets, and advocates
- Tailoring of announcement for each constituency
- Approach to pain management strategies
- Actions to disconfirm status quo
- Alignment of rhetoric and consequence management structure
- Management of transition state
- Level of commitment needed from which people
- Alignment of project and culture
- Strategies to improve synergy
- Training for key people
- Tactical action steps
- Major activities
- Sequence of events

The completed implementation plan should be evaluated using the *Implementation Plan Evaluation*. This self-scoring tool assesses the primary human aspects of a plan that may be potential hot spots in need of attention prior to moving ahead with a change. Each item is assessed in terms of its contribution to the level of risk of implementation failure. Sample dimensions are as follows:

▶ The project's impact on available adaptation resources

▶ How individual and group resilience will be developed and maintained

▶ The avoidance of "black holes"

▶ How high levels of resolve will be generated among the key constituencies to sustain the implementation process

An overall "Implementation Plan" factor is derived, estimating the risk of failure related to the specific implementation plan.

We also recommend the use of project management tools such as Microsoft Project (see Figure 4-3) to integrate BPI and MOC phases with a disciplined approach to project management.

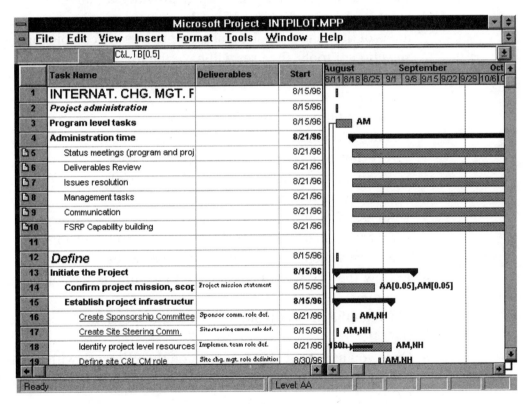

FIGURE **4-3. Sample project plan**

Phase IV Process

The project manager must ensure that the following occurs:

▶ Submit the completed PIP to the appropriate sponsors for their review. Use strategies outlined in the *Implementation Plan Advocacy Kit* to gain sponsor support for the PIP. This kit includes a packet of MOC tools and concept summaries to help change advocates understand how to make the advocacy role effective when implementing major change. It provides guidance to people in the advocacy role. It gives advocates information critical to understanding major change and how the advocacy role can promote success. It provides a planning instrument and interactive tools to focus management on critical areas of the change implementation process. By completing this selection of tools, the user will have the following:
  – A five-part outline for advocating a *Preliminary Implementation Plan*
  – Interpretations of the advocate's role
  – A description of how pain drives change
  – A review of key pain management concepts
  – A pain management plan for the sponsor(s)
  – A review of how people react to change
  – An assessment of the sponsor(s)
  – An assessment of the targets' resistance to the change
  – An assessment of the key change participants' synergy
▶ Review the PIP with the sponsors to ensure its feasibility and accuracy.
▶ Convene the project team to review the sponsors' feedback on the PIP.
▶ Once you have provided feedback on the PIP, work with the initiating sponsor to sanction the project team to complete the OCIP.
▶ Work with the initiating sponsor and the project team to revise the OCIP to ensure that its information, including its assignment sheets and time-frame activity charts, is feasible and accurate.

Once your sponsor has approved the plan, you may begin implementation.

Phase V: Execute the Plan

The goal of Phase V is to fully achieve the human and technical objectives of the change project on time and within budget. The execution of the implementation plan is intended to achieve the project goals by reducing resistance and increasing commitment to the project.

Work in this phase will focus on applying the change-management concepts, techniques, and philosophy to build sponsor commitment, build target support, develop pain management strategies, increase synergy, decrease resistance, apply reframing skills, build the appropriate corporate culture, and use the special change agent skills taught in a change-management class.

Based on the various formal and informal assessments of key role players made during Phases I, II, and III, or if new people had been assigned to the project, training needs often will have been identified and met for some individuals and groups. However, if sponsors, agents, targets, or advocates do not understand how to perform their roles at this point (and these needs may have gone undiscovered until the formal diagnosis during Phase III), the appropriate change-management training will help them learn the skills they need. This training should be included as part of the implementation process. Once these skills are taught, there must be sufficient follow-up assistance available to help people as they apply the implementation architecture for the first time.

Phase V Process

The project manager should ensure that the following occurs:

▶ Conduct assessments, including *Landscape Surveys* and *Overload Indexes*, at regular intervals after implementation starts. Provide sponsors and change agents with data to compare against benchmark results collected in Phase III, the diagnosis phase.

▶ Actively monitor project implementation.

▶ Review implementation-monitoring plans with the appropriate sponsors. Make revisions as needed.

▶ Ensure that sponsors, agents, targets, and advocates have the required skills and knowledge to perform their roles in the implementation process. Conduct MOC training programs as needed. These programs might include any of the following:
  – *Building Resilient Organizations for Turbulent Times*
  – *Building Implementation Architecture*
  – *Managing Organizational Change Tactics of Implementation*
  – *Developing Personal Resilience*
  – *Resilience Orientation*
  – *Increasing Change Knowledge*
  – *Resilience Coaching*
  – *Sponsor/Agent Contracting Workshop*
  – *Team Resilience Process*
  – *Sponsor Development Series*
  – *Target Training*

▶ Work with the sustaining sponsors to communicate the status of the change project to the affected groups. Use various communication methods—including presentations, question-and-answer sessions, videos, memos, and newsletters—to ensure that all groups are fully updated.

Once the implementation process begins, it's critical that the project manager and his or her sponsor monitor what's happening. It's usually necessary to make appropriate revisions to the plan throughout the process.

Phase VI: Monitor Progress and Problems

The goal of Phase VI is to periodically generate a formal report on the status of the project. The intent of this report is to present the sponsors with systematically and objectively collected data in order to advise them of progress and problems.

Most large-scale organizational changes are so complex that it's impossible to determine at a glance if true progress is being made. Project managers set clear goals, an implementation plan is created, and resources are allocated to bring the plan to life. The intent of the change is announced and meetings are held, facilities are changed, incentives are provided, and hardware and software are acquired. But is there substantive progress being made toward achieving the project's goals on time, within budget, and at the required performance level? Often, managers complain that they do not know about problems with a change project until there's a crisis.

A series of specially designed evaluations, based on success factors determined at the beginning of the project, given periodically to key people, reveals a great deal about the progress of a change project. Tracking a change project in this way allows sponsors to identify problems early and allocate resources to address pockets of resistance or other implementation inhibitors. In this way, crises can be avoided and changes can be implemented more efficiently and effectively.

During the planning phase (Phase IV), the project manager should have selected interim dates for collecting tracking data. Key representative sponsors, agents, and targets are identified and asked to participate in this data collection.

Phase VI Process

The project manager should ensure that the following occurs:

▶ Implement procedures designed to monitor the implementation. Use an especially tailored version of the *Landscape Survey* and the *Overload Index*. During this phase, data should be collected on a regular basis and compared with data collected before the project implementation.

▶ Routinely convene the project team to review data gathered during this phase. Build consensus on causes of factors that might impede implementation.

▶ Revise the implementation plan to address barriers that are viewed as a problem in the implementation.

▶ Present monitoring data to the appropriate sponsors. Sponsors should address the barriers with the appropriate sustaining sponsors and targets. Review revisions to the implementation plan intended to address these barriers.

▶ Revise the implementation plan as needed.

The goal of Phase VI is to keep project implementation on track by consistently and periodically monitoring your results against your plan. These findings, of course, should be regularly shared with your sponsors to keep them advised of progress, to seek their advice where needed, and to continue to build and maintain their support for the project. This iterative process should continue until the implementation is complete.

This leaves one last but critical activity, evaluating the results of your projects in a formal and systematic way.

Phase VII: Evaluate the Final Results

The primary goal of Phase VII is to generate a final report on the extent to which the change project has achieved its stated objectives within the allotted time and budget constraints. The intent is to present the sponsors with systematically and objectively collected data to help them determine if the tangible and intangible objectives of the project have been achieved. The evaluation report will also provide insight into key lessons to be learned and potential problem areas that may arise regarding future change projects.

Delivering the final report

Phase VII Process

The project manager should do the following in this phase:

- ▶ Determine if the implementation of the change project has actually achieved the objectives within stated parameters as identified by the critical success factors of the project that were delineated in earlier phases. A final *Landscape Survey* is completed for this purpose.
- ▶ Review the final report with the initiating sponsor. Determine key learnings based on what worked well and what did not work well throughout the project.
- ▶ Prepare a follow-up communication to the targets on the success of the implementation and the importance of their roles.

Summary

The effective integration of BPI project management and a disciplined approach to change management will dramatically improve the odds of successful project implementation. Even though we have presented the implementation architecture in phases, the project manager also should look at all of the phases at each step in his or her project to identify other points for integrating change management with the technical aspects of the project. We will provide guidance on how to integrate change management with the phases of process improvement in Chapters 5, 6, 7, and 8.

There is no reason why any project manager should treat change management as magic. More important, the successful project manager must have change management as a core competency of effective project management.

Finally, Figure 4-4 lists the MOC assessments, planning tools, and training that are used in applying the seven-phase MOC Implementation Architecture.

The names of the MOC assessments, planning tools, and training listed in Figure 4-4 are exact titles of ODR products. These titles will be used throughout the book. In addition to the overviews found in this chapter, a description of each assessment, survey, and tool can be found on the CD-ROM that accompanies this book. These descriptions will allow you to begin developing your own questionnaires in order to meet your project requirements. On the other hand, if you would like to purchase copies of ODR's products, please contact Ms. Connie Floyd, ODR, Inc., 2900 Chamblee-Tucker Road, Bl15, Atlanta, GA 30341, phone: (770) 936-2470 Ext. 126, e-mail: cfloyd@odr.odrnet.com.

Concepts are useless until someone finds a way to put them to use.

MOC Assessments, Planning Tools, and Training	Pre-Work†	Phases						
		I	II	III	IV	V	VI	VII
Change Agent Evaluation (A)	✓			✓				
Change Agent Selection Form (A)	✓			✓				
Change History Survey (A)*		✓						
Change Project Description Form (P)	✓	✓	✓	✓	✓	✓	✓	✓
Change Resistance Scale (A)				✓				
Communicating Change: Project Analysis (P)			✓					
Communicating Change: Constituency Analysis (P)			✓					
Communicating Change: Statement Development (P)			✓					
Communicating Change: Announcement Plan (P)			✓					
Culture Assessment (A)				✓				
Culture Audit (A)				✓				
Expectations for a Successful Change Project (A)		✓						
Implementation Plan Advocacy Kit (P)					✓			
Implementation Plan Evaluation (A)					✓			
Implementation Problems Assessment (A)				✓				
Landscape Survey (A)*		✓		✓		✓	✓	✓
MOC Training for Sponsors, Agents, Targets, and Advocates (T)	✓	✓			✓			
Organizational Change Implementation Plan (P)					✓	✓	✓	✓
Overload Index (A)*		✓			✓			
Pain Management Strategies: Sponsor (P)	✓							
Postmortem Process **								✓
Predicting the Impact of Change (A)		✓		✓				
Preliminary Implementation Plan (P)					✓			

FIGURE 4-4. MOC assessments, planning tools, and training (continued on the next page)

Role Map Application Tool **(P)**	✓	✓	✓	✓	✓	✓	✓	✓
Senior Team Value for Discipline **(A)**		✓						
Sponsor Checklist **(A)**		✓		✓				
Sponsor Evaluation **(A)**		✓		✓				
Synergy Survey **(A)**		✓		✓				
When to Apply Implementation Architecture **(A)**		✓						
†Pre-Work Used preliminary to starting Phase I. *This assessment tool is scored by ODR's Diagnostic Services. **This project-effectiveness evaluation tool is not MOC specific.								

FIGURE **4-4.** (Continued)

5

How MOC Fits into Project Management Methodology

For a project to be successfully managed, the change it creates must be managed.

Introduction

Up to this point, we have been discussing MOC concepts and approaches. In this chapter, we will show you how these concepts support and integrate into the project management concepts. When you stop to consider how MOC is most often used, you will soon realize that it is applied to major changes in the organization's operations, products, and services. Usually, these major projects need to be managed in order to ensure that they produce the desired results and are completed on time and within budget.

Meeting or exceeding stakeholders' needs and expectations invariably involves balancing competing demands among:

▶ Scope, time, cost, and quality
▶ Stakeholders with different needs and expectations
▶ Identified requirements (needs) and unidentified requirements (expectations)

Managing Organizational Change®—The disciplined application of a comprehensive set of structured procedures for the decision-making, planning, execution, and evaluation phases of the change process. It does not focus on what is to be changed.

Project—A temporary endeavor undertaken to create a unique product or service.

It is obvious from these two definitions that project management and MOC go together like apple pie and ice cream. For the sake of this book, let's consider project management as being the pie that serves as the foundation and MOC as the ice cream that brings out the flavor of the total combination. To help you understand this relationship, we will provide a short overview of the project management methodology as defined by the Project Management Institute's book titled *A Guide to the Project Management Body of Knowledge* and the ISO/SC-1006 document titled *Guidelines to Quality in Project Management*.

Performance improvement results mainly from a number of large and small projects undertaken by the organization. These projects involve all levels within the organization and can take less than a hundred hours or as much as millions of hours to complete. They are a critical part of the way an organization implements its business strategies.

It is extremely important that these multitudes of projects be managed effectively to meet the stakeholders' needs and expectations. This undertaking is made more complex because conflicting demands are often placed upon those who manage these projects, such as:

- Scope
- Time
- Cost
- Quality

Stakeholders have different identified requirements (needs) and unidentified requirements (expectations). As a result, different stakeholders often place conflicting requirements on a single project. For example, management may want a project to reduce labor cost by 80% while organized labor wants the same project to create more jobs.

The Project Management Institute in Upper Darby, Pennsylvania, is the leader in defining the body of knowledge for project management. Its Project Management Body of Knowledge (PMBK) approach to project management has been widely accepted throughout the world. In addition, the International Standards Organization's technical committee 176 has released an international standard, *ISO/DIS 10006—Guidelines to Quality in Project Management*. These two methodologies complement each other and go hand in hand.

Program—A group of related projects managed in a coordinated way. Programs usually include an element of ongoing activities.

Large projects are often managed by professional project managers who have no other assignments. However, in most organizations, individuals who serve as project managers spend only a small percentage of their time managing a project. A project could be as small as one person implementing a change that was suggested by a quality circle.

In any case, the individual project manager is responsible for defining a process by which a project is initiated, controlled, and brought to a successful conclusion. Success is defined in the following terms:

- ▶ Project completed on time
- ▶ Project completed within budget
- ▶ Outputs meet specification
- ▶ Customers are satisfied
- ▶ Team members gain satisfaction as a result of the project

A good project manager would probably follow General George S. Patton's advice: "Don't tell soldiers how to do something. Tell them what to do and you will be amazed at their ingenuity."

Although it's very difficult to get everyone to agree to what is meant by a project life cycle, the definition in U.S. DOD's document 5000.2 (Revision 2-26-92, titled "Representative Life Cycle for Defense Acquisition") provides a reasonably good starting point. It is divided into five phases (see Figure 5-1):

- ▶ Phase 0—Concept Exploration and Definition
- ▶ Phase I—Demonstration and Validation
- ▶ Phase II—Engineering and Manufacturing Development
- ▶ Phase III—Production and Deployment
- ▶ Phase IV—Operations and Support

A life cycle that we like better for an organization that is providing a product and a service is the following (see Figure 5-2):

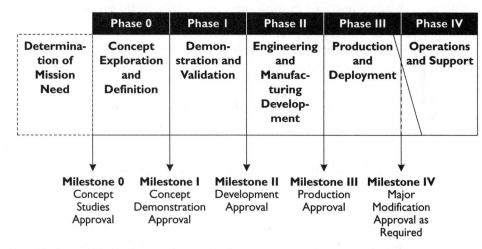

FIGURE 5-1. Representative life cycle for defense acquisition, per U.S. DOD 5000.2

- ▶ Phase I—Concept Definition
- ▶ Phase II—Design and Development
- ▶ Phase III—Creating the Product or Service
- ▶ Phase IV—Installation
- ▶ Phase V—Operation and Maintenance
- ▶ Phase VI—Disposal

Traditionally, projects have followed a pattern of phases from concept to termination. Each phase has particular characteristics that distinguish it from the other phases. Each phase forms part of a logical sequence in which the fundamental and technical specification of the end product or service is progressively defined.

PHASE					
I	**II**	**III**	**IV**	**V**	**VI**
Concept and Definition	Design and Development	Creating the Product or Service	Installation	Operation and Maintenance	Disposal

• New product opportunities • Analysis of system concept and options • Product selection • Technology selection • Make/buy decisions • Identify cost drivers • Construction assessment • Manufacturability assessments • Warranty incentives	• Design trade-offs • Source selection • Configurations and change controls • Test strategies ŸRepair/throwaway decisions • Performance tailoring • Support strategies • New product introduction	• System integration and verification • Cost avoidance/cost reduction benefits • Operating and maintenance cost monitoring • Product modifications and service enhancements • Maintenance support resource allocation and optimization	• Retirement cost impact • Replacement/ renewal schemes • Disposal and salvage value

FIGURE 5-2. Typical product life cycle

The successful project manager understands that there are four key factors to consider when developing the project plan. All four factors overlap to a degree, but they should be considered first independently and then all together (see Figure 5-3).

The 10 Elements of Project Management

To put it simply, project management is an approach to planning and managing projects so that the desired results are obtained in the future.

> *The trouble with the future is that it usually arrives before we are ready for it.*
> —ARNOLD H., *THE EMPLOYEE HANDBOOK FOR ORGANIZATIONAL CHANGE*

In order to manage a project effectively, the individuals assigned will be required to address the 10 elements outlined in Figure 5-4. The

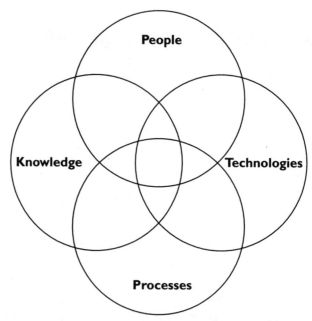

FIGURE 5-3. The four key project management factors

 Project Management Institute included only the first nine elements listed in Figure 5-4. The PMI did not include MOC® as a separate element, but placed part of it under the element entitled "Project Risk Management." Of course, the depth and detail to which each element needs to be evaluated and managed will vary greatly depending upon the scope and complexity of the project. We will present a project-management strategy for a complex project that can be cut back to a single-person project by just considering the controls needed to meet the project's objectives.

A Guide to the Project Management Body of Knowledge, published by the Project Management Institute, summarizes the nine project management knowledge areas as follows.

Project Integration Management

A subset of project management that includes the processes required to ensure that the various elements of the project are properly coordinated. It consists of:

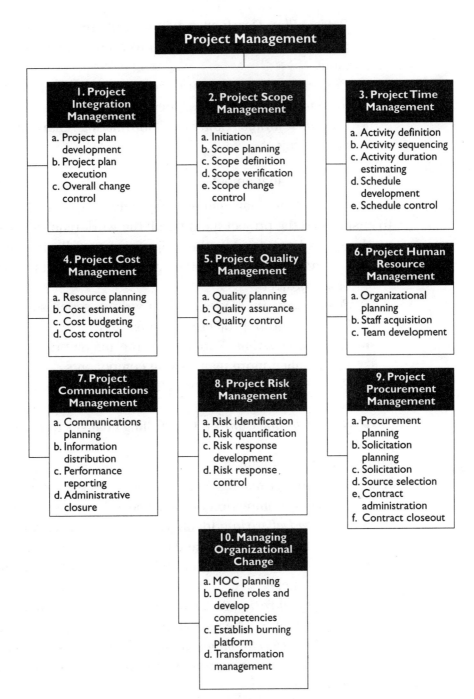

Project Management

1. Project Integration Management
a. Project plan development
b. Project plan execution
c. Overall change control

2. Project Scope Management
a. Initiation
b. Scope planning
c. Scope definition
d. Scope verification
e. Scope change control

3. Project Time Management
a. Activity definition
b. Activity sequencing
c. Activity duration estimating
d. Schedule development
e. Schedule control

4. Project Cost Management
a. Resource planning
b. Cost estimating
c. Cost budgeting
d. Cost control

5. Project Quality Management
a. Quality planning
b. Quality assurance
c. Quality control

6. Project Human Resource Management
a. Organizational planning
b. Staff acquisition
c. Team development

7. Project Communications Management
a. Communications planning
b. Information distribution
c. Performance reporting
d. Administrative closure

8. Project Risk Management
a. Risk identification
b. Risk quantification
c. Risk response development
d. Risk response control

9. Project Procurement Management
a. Procurement planning
b. Solicitation planning
c. Solicitation
d. Source selection
e. Contract administration
f. Contract closeout

10. Managing Organizational Change
a. MOC planning
b. Define roles and develop competencies
c. Establish burning platform
d. Transformation management

FIGURE 5-4. The 10 elements of project management

- *Project Plan Development:* Taking the results of other planning processes and putting them into a consistent, coherent document.
- *Project Plan Execution:* Carrying out the project plan by performing the activities included therein.
- *Overall Change Control:* Coordinating changes across the entire project.

Project Scope Management

A subset of project management that includes the processes required to ensure that the project includes all the work required, and only the work required, to complete the project successfully. It consists of:

- *Initiation:* Committing the organization to begin the next phase of the project.
- *Scope Planning:* Developing a written scope statement as the basis for future project decisions.
- *Scope Definition:* Subdividing the major project deliverables into smaller, more manageable components.
- *Scope Verification:* Formalizing acceptance of the project scope.
- *Scope Change Control:* Controlling changes to project scope.

Project Time Management

A subset of project management that includes the processes required to ensure timely completion of the project. It consists of:

- *Activity Definition:* Identifying the specific activities that must be performed to produce the various project deliverables.
- *Activity Sequencing:* Identifying and documenting interactivity dependencies.
- *Activity Duration Estimating:* Estimating the number of work periods that will be needed to complete individual activities.
- *Schedule Development:* Analyzing activity sequences, activity durations, and resource requirements to create the project schedule.
- *Schedule Control:* Controlling changes to the project schedule.

Project Cost Management

A subset of project management that includes the processes required to ensure that the project is completed within the approved budget. It consists of:

▶ *Resource Planning:* Determining what resources (people, equipment, materials) and what quantities of each should be used to perform project activities.

▶ *Cost Estimating:* Developing an approximation (estimate) of the costs of the resources needed to complete project activities.

▶ *Cost Budgeting:* Allocating the overall cost estimate to individual work items.

▶ *Cost Control:* Controlling changes to the project budget.

Project Quality Management

A subset of project management that includes the processes required to ensure that the project will satisfy the needs for which it was undertaken. It consists of:

▶ *Quality Planning:* Identifying which quality standards are relevant to the project and determining how to satisfy them.

▶ *Quality Assurance:* Evaluating overall project performance on a regular basis to provide confidence that the project will satisfy the relevant quality standards.

▶ *Quality Control:* Monitoring specific project results to determine if they comply with relevant quality standards and identifying ways to eliminate causes of unsatisfactory performance.

Project Human Resource Management

A subset of project management that includes the processes required to make the most effective use of the people involved within the project team. It consists of:

- *Organizational Planning:* Identifying, documenting, and assigning project roles, responsibilities, and reporting relationships.
- *Staff Acquisition:* Getting the human resources needed assigned to and working on the project.
- *Team Development:* Developing individual and group skills to enhance project performance.

Project Communications Management

A subset of project management that includes the processes required to ensure timely and appropriate generation, collection, dissemination, storage, and ultimate disposition of project information. It consists of:

- *Communications Planning:* Determining the information and communications needs of the stakeholders: who needs what information, when they will need it, and how it will be given to them.
- *Information Distribution:* Making needed information available to project stakeholders in a timely manner.
- *Performance Reporting:* Collecting and disseminating performance information. This includes status reporting, progress measurement, and forecasting.
- *Administrative Closure:* Generating, gathering, and disseminating information to formalize phase or project completion.

Project Risk Management

A subset of project management that includes the processes concerned with identifying, analyzing, and responding to project risk. It consists of:

- *Risk Identification:* Determining which risks are likely to affect the project and documenting the characteristics of each.
- *Risk Quantification:* Evaluating risks and risk interactions to assess the range of possible project outcomes.

- ► *Risk Response Development:* Defining enhancement steps for opportunities and responses to threats.
- ► *Risk Response Control:* Responding to changes in risk over the course of the project.

Project Procurement Management

A subset of project management that includes the processes required to acquire goods and services from outside the performing organization. It consists of:

- ► *Procurement Planning:* Determining what to procure and when.
- ► *Solicitation Planning:* Documenting product requirements and identifying potential sources.
- ► *Solicitation:* Obtaining quotations, bids, offers, or proposals as appropriate.
- ► *Source Selection:* Choosing from among potential sellers.
- ► *Contract Administration:* Managing the relationship with the seller.
- ► *Contract Closeout:* Completion and settlement of the contract, including resolution of any open items.

Managing Organizational Change® (MOC®)

This part of project management is not part of the PMBK concept covered in *A Guide to the Project Management Body of Knowledge.* MOC is directed at the people side of the project. It helps prepare the people affected by the project to accept and, when required, to become committed to the change and often even look forward to it. The MOC part of project management consists of:

- ► *MOC Planning:* Defining the level of resistance to change and preparing a plan to offset the resistance.
- ► *Define Roles and Develop Competencies:* Identify who will serve as sponsors, change agents, change targets, and change advocates. Then, train each individual on how to perform the specific role.

- ▶ *Establish Burning Platform:* Define a situation in which the major cost of the status quo becomes prohibitively expensive. In such circumstances, major change is not just a good idea—it is a business imperative. (This will be discussed later in this chapter.)
- ▶ *Transformation Management:* Implement the MOC plan. Test for black holes and lack of acceptance. Train affected personnel in new skills required by the change.

Unfortunately, many organizations go for buy-in on new processes or systems after they introduced it, and the results can be catastrophic.
            —ROBERT KRITGEL

How MOC® Fits into Project Management Methodology

It is imperative that the MOC activities be integrated and completely aligned with the project management activities. This is accomplished by making the MOC plan part of the project management plan. Then, involve as many of the project management team members as possible in implementing the MOC plan.

MOC as Part of Project Management

Project managers must be as skilled and familiar with Managing Organizational Change® concepts as they are with financial management. In fact, the skills that the project managers have related to Managing Organizational Change often have a much greater impact upon the outcome of the project than financial controls. The degree of resistance to change impacts cost, schedule, resource requirements, and the performance of the end output from the project. No longer can project managers limit their project design to just the resources consumed by the project. An effective project management plan must prepare the targets (the people who need to change) so that the results of the project will be effectively assimilated into the organization.

Too often, project managers look at the four key project management factors—process, knowledge, technology, and people—and limit their people's thinking to the make-up of the project team. As a result, the project team is made up of technology experts who have little or no knowledge or concern about the people who are impacted by the project and have to live with the project results day after day.

The project manager must be skilled at:

▶ Being a change agent
▶ Being a change advocate
▶ Being a change facilitator
▶ Being a change target

Change Facilitator—The individual who leads and directs the change-management activities for a project. He or she provides the just-in-time MOC training and change-management guidance to the PIT, sponsors, and others requiring that level of training. The change facilitator can be viewed as a "black belt" change agent. Often internal or external consultants serve as the change facilitators.

At some point during most projects, the manager will be required to assume each of these roles. You will note that we have added a new change role to the ones previously discussed. The change facilitator is the change management expert for the project. This individual must have the training and experience to understand MOC® concepts and apply them to the specific project. He or she will serve as the MOC authority and trainer for the project. The change facilitator assesses the organization's resistance to the project and prepares the MOC plan and its integration into the overall project plan. Once the plan is prepared, the change facilitator will be held responsible for the implementation of the plan.

The change facilitator should be one of the first members of the project team to be identified, as he or she will play an important role in helping the project manager select project team members who can embrace key change concepts. The people who make up a project team are a key MOC consideration. In small projects, the change facilitator assignment can be handled by the project manager if he or she has the proper level of training. But for major projects, an individual should be assigned who has MOC as a sole responsibility.

Not everyone can be the change facilitator. Too often, organizations feel that any person who has attended an MOC class or read a book on MOC is capable of performing the role of the change facilitator. Of course, this is not true.

If you categorize people as being one of the four types discussed in Chapter 2—Thinkers, Feelers, Intuitors, and Sensors—a change facilitator would need to be effective in all four areas but extremely good in the sensor role (networker).

This is a sample of the text for the definition, or these are more synonyms and usages that are commonly found in the English language.

Only people who feel very comfortable functioning in sensor roles and who are already experienced networkers should be considered to serve as the change facilitator. The change facilitator needs to have and maintain a network of contacts who serve as sensors to define the level of organizational resistance. The facilitator needs to be able to identify potential "black holes" before they become bottlenecks in the project. He or she must be skilled in using problem-solving techniques and team skills. In addition, the change facilitator should be experienced in adult education concepts. The change facilitator should also understand the organization's big picture and have knowledge of any other projects that are going on or will be started that relate to the same group of people who will be affected by this project. But most of all, the change facilitator must have excellent people skills and be very knowledgeable about how people react to different conditions.

The change facilitators and the change agents have a lot of common skills. Usually only one change facilitator will be assigned to a project. This facilitator will train the inexperienced change agents who are assigned to the project. Often, highly skilled technical people need to serve part-time as change agents as well as implementing their specific technical change into the new process. Because the change facilitator must have a very in-depth understanding of the change process and have extensive past experience in effectively using the change methodologies, outside consultants are often used for this job.

In large organizations that are undergoing a lot of change, individuals who have effectively functioned as change agents on a number of projects are often designated as change facilitators. In cases where the change agents assigned to the project already have the skills to do their assigned tasks and can provide the required MOC® training to the project team, advocates, targets, and sponsors, a change facilitator need not be assigned to the project team.

MOC Planning as Part of the Project Plan

The change facilitator will prepare a specific part of the project plan that will be referred to as the Managing Organizational Change® plan. In addition, the change facilitator will input MOC requirements into the following parts of the project plan:

- Project integration management
- Project time management
- Project cost management
- Project quality management
- Project human resource management
- Project communication management
- Project risk management

The change management plan will include the following:

- Timing and scope of all MOC assessments that will be conducted
- Degree to which the organization and the targeted individuals must accept the project's output
- MOC training plans
- Target plus/minus analysis and communication approach
- Project impact strategy
- MOC roles and responsibilities of all project team members and impacted organizations
- Timeline chart of MOC activities (Figure 5-5 is a typical timeline chart for an ISO 9000 quality management system project.)
- Definitions of integration dependencies

Managing Organizational Change Activities Keyed to EMS Phases

Change Management Activities	Phase I Assess	Phase II Plan	Phase III Redesign	Phase IV Implement	Phase V Audit	Phase VI Improve
Identify, document, and communicate cost of the status quo (business imperative)	■	■	■	■		
Create and communicate the future-state vision (people, process, and technology)	■					
Clarify the change and obtain initiating sponsor understanding and commitment	■					
Create needed infrastructure and implementation architecture	■	■				
Conduct a high-level change risk assessment (the eight risk factors)		■				
Create a high-level QMS-wide organizational change plan		■				
Create role maps to identify all personnel having key change roles		■				
Conduct tier-level change risk assessments (the eight risk factors)		■				
Conduct change-readiness assessments		■				
Assess organizational alignment (structure, compensation, rewards, etc.)		■				
Assess enablers and barriers		■				
Develop tier-level transition management plans		■				
Develop a communication plan		■				
Cascade sponsorship (communications, training, performance management)			■	■		
Implement the communication plan			■	■	■	■
Provide change management training for sponsors, change agents, and others			■	■		
Form change agent, sponsor, and advocate teams			■	■		
Provide training for targets (those affected by the change)				■	■	■
Implement organizational alignment enablers				■		
Analyze effectiveness of communications and training strategies				■	■	
Monitor commitment levels of sponsors, change agents, advocates, and targets				■	■	
Monitor and measure implementation effectiveness and schedule adherence					■	
Modify transition management plans as needed to ensure effectiveness					■	
Track and report planned versus actual activities and results					■	
Identify opportunities for continuous improvement of the change process						■

It is evident from this chart that most change management activities are iterative and not confined to one QMS phase.

FIGURE 5-5. Timeline for an ISO 9000 quality management system project

Figure 5-6 (pages 152-153) is a partial list of MOC assessments, planning tools, and training that could be used in each of the six project management phases. These are the same assessments, planning tools, and training already presented in Chapter 4.

In reality, MOC becomes part of the way projects are managed and a management factor as important as cost, quality, and schedule because those three factors are all affected if the change process is poorly managed.

Figure 5-7 (page 154) shows how the seven MOC phases relate to the six project phases defined in Figure 5-2.

Organizational Change Implementation Plan

The challenge that faces the change facilitator and the rest of the project team is to implement all of the individual sections that make up the project plan and still meet the cost, schedule, and performance requirements. For the change facilitator, it involves activities such as the following:

► Conducting assessments
► Attending project reviews
► Developing target plus/minus analysis
► Communicating project objectives and visions
► Communicating with the targets
► Defining required commitment levels
► Managing resistance to the project
► Ensuring that the targets have an excellent vision of how the project will impact them
► Building commitment to the project
► Ensuring that the targets' concerns are considered
► Ensuring that suggestions made by the targets are acted upon and that the people who made the suggestions get feedback and credit.

The MOC activities are among the first activities that should get under way in a project. Just ask yourself, "In my organization, how long does it take for the rumor mill to spread a story like 'Management

	MOC Assessments, Planning Tools, and Training	Project Management Phases					
		I	II	III	IV	V	VI
1.	Adaptation Capacity Audit	✓		✓			
2.	Change Agent Evaluation	✓		✓			
3.	Change Agent Selection Form	✓		✓			
4.	Change History Survey	✓	✓				
5.	Change Knowledge Assessment		✓		✓		
6.	Change Project Description Form	✓	✓	✓	✓	✓	✓
7.	Change Resistance Scale		✓	✓			
8.	Coaching Styles Inventory and Guide			✓	✓		
9.	Communicating Change: Announcement Plan	✓	✓	✓	✓		
10.	Communicating Change: Constituency Analysis	✓	✓	✓	✓		
11.	Communicating Change: Project Analysis		✓	✓	✓		
12.	Communicating Change: Statement Development		✓	✓	✓		
13.	Communicating Style Survey and Guide	✓	✓	✓			
14.	Culture Assessment		✓	✓	✓		
15.	Culture Audit		✓	✓	✓		
16.	Expectations for a Successful Change Project	✓	✓				
17.	Focus Group Tools*			✓	✓		
18.	Force Field Analysis*			✓	✓		
19.	Implementation Plan Advocacy Kit			✓	✓		
20.	Implementation Plan Evaluation			✓	✓		
21.	Implementation Problems Assessment	✓	✓				
22.	Individual Error Rate Measurements*				✓	✓	✓
23.	Influence Style Survey and Interpretation Manual		✓	✓	✓		
24.	Landscape Surveys			✓	✓	✓	
25.	MOC Training for Sponsors, Agents, Targets, and Advocates	✓	✓	✓	✓		

FIGURE 5-6. MOC assessments, planning tools, and training and their use in the six project management phases (continued on next page)

	MOC Assessments, Planning Tools, and Training	Project Management Phases					
		I	II	III	IV	V	VI
26.	Organizational Change Implementation Plan (OCIP)			✓	✓		
27.	Overload Index	✓			✓	✓	
28.	Pain Management Strategies: Sponsor	✓	✓	✓			
29.	Pain Management Strategies: Target			✓	✓		
30.	Personal Power Survey	✓		✓			
31.	Personal Resilience Questionnaire and Profile		✓		✓		
32.	Postmortem*					✓	
33.	Predicting the Impact of Change	✓	✓	✓			
34.	Preliminary Implementation Plan		✓	✓	✓		
35.	Process Modeling*		✓	✓			
36.	Process Walk-Through Checklist*		✓	✓			
37.	Rewards and Recognition Tools*		✓	✓			
38.	Role Map Application Tool	✓	✓	✓			
39.	Senior Team Value for Discipline	✓					
40.	Simulation Modeling*			✓	✓		
41.	Sponsor Checklist	✓	✓	✓	✓		
42.	Sponsor Evaluation	✓	✓	✓	✓	✓	
43.	Synergy Survey		✓	✓			
44.	When to Apply the MOC Methodology	✓	✓	✓			

* Use of this tool is not limited to the MOC methodology

FIGURE 5-6. (Continued)

is reengineering our jobs and 80% of us will be laid off'?" We don't know about your specific organization, but at most of the organizations we work with, it does not take weeks, or even days, and often not even hours. The rumor mill spreads out these juicy bits of false information in minutes. Even before a decision can be reached whether or not to reengineer a process, the rumor mill will have many people

Seven MOC Phases	Project Management Phases					
	I Concept and Definition	**II** Design and Development	**III** Creating the Product or Service	**IV** Installation	**V** Operation and Maintenance	**VI** Disposal
Phase I–Clarify	▓▓					
Phase II–Announce	▓▓	▓▓				
Phase III–Diagnose		▓▓				
Phase IV–Plan	▓▓	▓▓	▓▓	▓▓	▓▓	▓▓
Phase V–Implement						
Phase VI–Monitor				▓▓	▓▓	
Phase VII–Final Evaluation					▓▓	

FIGURE 5-7. Integration of the seven MOC phases and the six project phases

upset. These rumors generate a momentum that, if not checked, will be detrimental to the success of the project. As a result, the MOC® activities must start long before the project team takes the time to document a project plan. Often, these activities need to continue long after the project has been implemented.

We will not discuss each line on the MOC plan because we have discussed most of them in detail in the first part of this book and we will be presenting a detailed plan for a process redesign project in Chapter 6. But we would like to discuss two critical categories:

- ▶ Training
- ▶ Target Plus/Minus Analysis

Training

In today's hectic environment, everyone needs to understand his or her personal emotions about change and have skills to help relieve the tension related to change. For this reason, we believe that everyone from the boardroom to the boiler room needs to have training to handle the hectic change pace that he or she faces. This type of training should not be included in the project plan because it should be applied across the board for all projects and programs. If the organization has not provided personal change management training to every member, it will be necessary to provide it to all of the people who will be affected by the project.

In addition, anyone designated on the Role Map diagram as a change agent, sponsor, or advocate should receive training for his or her assigned role. Everyone needs to understand why the individual assessments are conducted and how the data will be used. All of the members of the project team should be trained to understand all of the concepts related to Managing Organizational Change® and should be skilled in applying these concepts. In our experience, the people who implement a project usually have good technical background but are poorly prepared to deal with the people side of the equation. The project manager and the change facilitator need to be very proficient in applying the organizational change management concepts.

Target Plus/Minus Analysis

As we have discussed, change is a process. For individuals to start to move through this process, they must feel that they will benefit from the change. One of the major challenges that a project team faces is to surface the benefits of making the change.

This, in reality, is a pain management process. It involves surfacing the pain related to the current process, what we call "establishing the burning platform." This term for getting people who will be affected by change to leave the current state and accept the change was originated by Daryl Conner, based upon the following story:

The Burning-Platform Story
At nine-thirty on a July evening in 1988, a disastrous explosion and fire occurred on an oil-drilling platform in the North Sea off the coast of Scotland. One hundred and sixty-six crew members and two rescuers lost their lives in the worst catastrophe in the twenty-five-year history of exporting North Sea oil. One of the sixty-three crew members who survived was a superintendent on

Mochan. His interview helped me find a way to describe the resolve that change winners manifest.

From the hospital bed, he told of being awakened by the explosion and alarms. He said that he ran from his quarters to the platform edge and jumped and jumped fifteen stories from the platform to the water. Because of the water's temperature, he knew that he could live a maximum of only twenty minutes if he were not rescued. Also, oil had surfaced and ignited. Yet Andy jumped 150 feet in the middle of the night into an ocean of burning oil and debris.

When asked why he took that potentially fatal leap, he did not hesitate. He said, "It was either jump or fry." He chose possible death over certain death ....

He jumped because he had no choice—the price of staying on the platform, of maintaining the status quo, was too high. This is the same type of situation in which many business, social, and political leaders find themselves every day. We sometimes have to make some changes, no matter how uncertain and frightening they are. We, like Andy Mochan, would face a price too high for not doing so.

An organizational burning platform exists when maintaining the status quo becomes prohibitively expensive. Major change is always costly, but when the present course of action is even more expensive, a burning-platform situation erupts.

The key characteristic that distinguishes a decision made in a burning-platform situation from all other decisions is not the degree of reason or emotion involved, but the level of resolve. When an organization is on a burning platform, the decision to make a major change is not just a good idea—it is a business imperative.

From *Managing at the Speed of Change*

People are willing to pay the price for solving a problem or capturing an opportunity. Both problems and opportunities can be subdivided into *current* and *anticipated* (see Figure 5-8).

How Motivation Drives Change

People are willing to pay the price for solving a problem or capturing an opportunity.

	Problem	Opportunity
Current	**Situation:** "We're in trouble now." **Motivation:** The immediate loss of our market dominance, job security, organizational survival, etc.	**Situation:** "If we act immediately, we can take advantage of this situation." **Motivation:** The loss of a potential advantage that is within our grasp.
Anticipated	**Situation:** "We're going to be in trouble." **Motivation:** The impending loss of our market dominance, job security, organizational survival, etc.	**Situation:** "In the future, we could be in a position to profit from what is going to happen." **Motivation:** The loss of a potential advantage that is possible to achieve in the future.

FIGURE **5-8. Pain related to the current process**

It is pretty obvious to people that the stress of a rapidly changing organization can be difficult and unpleasant. What's not so clear to us sometimes is how much trouble we're in for if the organization fails to change.

    —Price Pritchett, The Employee Handbook for Organizational Change

Employees normally understand the problems in the current process as they directly relate to each of them, but not as they relate to the total organization. Most employees do not have the information available to understand the pain related to lost opportunity and anticipated pain. Management and the project team need to define and communicate this pain to all the targets. This is called "establishing the burning platform." Then, the project team needs to provide a clear vision of the future-state process so that the employees can assess the pain that's related to the future state. (In the MOC® methodology, the proposed future-state solution is often called the remedy.) In addition, management must provide the employees with an understanding of what pain they will experience during the transitional period. (e.g., working overtime to make up for lost productivity as a result of the training program or having to learn a new system.) If the current-state pain is not greater than the pain anticipated in the best-value future-state solution plus the pain anticipated for the transition period, the only way that management will be able to get the employees to accept the change is by dragging them along, kicking and fighting (see Figure 5-9).

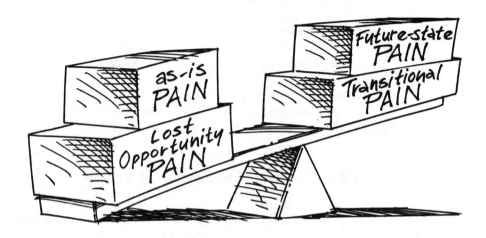

FIGURE 5-9. Target plus/minus analysis

You will note in Figure 5-9 that there are two ingredients of pain related to the current process (the A end of the plank), the as-is pain and the lost-opportunity pain. The employees probably have an excellent understanding of the as-is pain. But they have no way of assessing the magnitude of the lost-opportunity pain, the pain that will result if the process is not changed. Therefore, management must help the employees understand and quantify lost-opportunity pain. At the B end of this plank is the pain related to the future-state solution. No process is perfect, of course; all processes have some disadvantages. Management and employees must realize that even the best-value future-state solution will still have some pain associated with it. The B end of the plank is also weighted down by the pain that occurs during the transitional state. When starting out on the change process, management and employees anticipate what the pain will be during the transitional state and the future state—the anticipated pain.

Change only occurs when individuals make a choice to change.
We have to establish with people that there is less pain in moving.
    —WILLIAM BRIDGES, *MANAGING TRANSITIONS*

Transformation Management

Very simply put, you can think of transformation management as the conversion of resistance to the project to commitment to the project. We need to change the general attitude from "It can't be done" to "We will get it done." That's what is meant by changing resistance into commitment. To make this transformation, we need to do the following:

► Define the pain related to the current state.
► Define an achievable remedy.
► Prepare a future-state vision statement.
► Define a what's-in-it-for-me scenario (for the targets, the organization, and the team).
► Understand the reasons for resistance.
► Respect those who resist.
► Be truthful with the targets.
► Listen intently to the targets.
► Develop win-win scenarios.
► Align the change with the organizational culture.
► Don't move so fast that we overstress the system.
► Set up reward systems that encourage people to change.
► Maintain open communications.
► Stop talking and start listening.
► Look at the situation from the perspective of the people who are resisting.
► Recognize that resistance is normal.
► Understand the emotional cycles related to change and specific bail-out points related to how the individual perceives the change.
► Help targets through the bail-out points.
► Provide everyone with required change training.

- ▶ Build models so the targets can observe the change and gain hands-on experience with the change before it is implemented.
- ▶ Involve as many of the targets as possible in the change decisions.

Too many people who are implementing a project take resistance to the project personally. In truth, resistance is good and normal. Resistance to change is just human. From the beginning, we are trained to question everything that can affect us. Our mothers warn us not to touch the stove because we may get burned and to put on our coats in the winter because it's cold outside. We are taught to question everything, every change, to be sure that it's good for us before we accept it. I would like to buy a new car every year, but I resist that transformation after doing a cost benefit analysis. Every change meets resistance. Individuals ask, "What's in it for me?" Each person performs a cost benefit analysis of the change and either accepts or rejects the change. The degree of resistance to the change varies according to the individual's experience, age, and culture. In general, the more bad experiences an individual has had with change or the older the person is, the more he or she resists change. The way people express their resistance to change could be classified into two categories:

- ▶ Covert resistance is a marked, concealed reaction to the change.
- ▶ Overt resistance is the expression of open and honest opposition to the change.

In Chapter 1 we discussed some of the reasons employees and management resist change.

Although the individual resistance classification approach is not part of the MOC® methodology, H. James Harrington has found that individuals' resistance to change can be classified into six categories.

- ▶ *Arbitrary resistance.* This is characterized by individuals who are just against everything. It does not make any difference if it is good or bad—they are against it.
- ▶ *Justified resistance.* These are individuals who have realized that the change is going to hurt them and, as a result, are going

to do everything possible to prevent it. For example, a change that will cause the organization to release employees.

▶ *Informed resistance.* In this case, the individuals understand that the change that is going to impact them and have an idea that will lessen that impact on them or will make the change more effective. These individuals are not against the change, but have a strong feeling that the proposed change should be restructured to improve the benefits to the organization's stakeholders.

▶ *Mistaken resistance.* These are individuals who are reacting to gossip or false information and, as a result, have turned against the change, but they can change their opinion when provided with the correct information.

▶ *Uninformed resistance.* These are individuals who have not been provided enough information about the change. We all resist changes that we don't understand.

▶ *Fearful resistance.* These are individuals who can imagine all sorts of bad things happening to them if there is any change in their comfortable environment. These individuals oppose any progress.

For each of these six categories, answer the following questions and write your answer on a piece of paper:

1. What do they say about the change?
2. What do they do related to the change?
3. What is their attitude after the change is implemented?

Everyone has two choices in life. You can choose to make the best of any situation, or you can choose to let it get you down and act as a victim. The best thing to do is to choose it as a learning experience and better yourself.

—Patty Haworth, Celestial Seasonings, Inc., *Quality*, August 1998

It's extremely important that the project team recognize the type of resistance that it faces and then provide communication to the targets to offset the various types of resistance. Usually sound information, good vision statements, and future-state models can convert everyone whose resistance does not fall into the classifications of *arbitrary* or *justified* from resistance to commitment.

Generic Change Management Approach Applied to a Complex Project

The following is a list of tasks that would typically be undertaken when change management is applied to a complex project.

Project Start-Up and Preparation
- ▶ Initiate Project
- ▶ Define Project Charter
- ▶ Clarify Scope of Organizational Change
- ▶ Develop Project Plan
- ▶ Review and Approve Project Charter and Project Plan
- ▶ Kick Off the Project

Current People Infrastructure Description
- ▶ Describe the Current Organizational Environment
- ▶ Define Current Change Management Process
- ▶ Review and Approve Current People-Infrastructure Stage

Enterprise People-Infrastructure Definition
- ▶ Define People-Enablement Framework
- ▶ Review and Approve Enterprise People-Infrastructure Stage

Pilot Planning
- ▶ Assess Change Management Enablers and Barriers
- ▶ Define Pilot-Phase Strategies
- ▶ Develop Pilot-Phase Transition Management Plan
- ▶ Develop Initial Pilot-Phase Schedule
- ▶ Develop Initial Project Charters—Pilot
- ▶ Review and Approve Pilot-Planning Stage

Transition Management

- ▶ Refine Transition Enablers and Barriers Assessment
- ▶ Refine Transition Management Infrastructure
- ▶ Develop Transition Management Plan
- ▶ Review and Approve Transition Management Stage

Future State Design

- ▶ Perform People-Enabler Detailed Analysis
- ▶ Define People-Enabler Design
- ▶ Review and Approve Future-State Design Stage

People-Enabler Development

- ▶ Develop People Enablers

Training Development

- ▶ Develop Training Program
- ▶ Prepare for Training
- ▶ Review and Approve Training Development Stage

Business Case Refinement

- ▶ Conduct Cost/Benefit Analysis
- ▶ Analyze Risk and Return
- ▶ Review and Approve Pilot Business Case Refinement Stage

Implementation Planning

- ▶ Develop Implementation Plan
- ▶ Develop Initial Project Charters—Implementation
- ▶ Review and Approve Implementation Planning Stage

Communications Management

- ▶ Implement Communication Plan
- ▶ Develop Communications Status Report
- ▶ Conduct Change Communication Intervention
- ▶ Refine Implementation Management Infrastructure
- ▶ Review and Approve Communications Management Stage

Staff Training

- ▶ Conduct Training
- ▶ Review and Approve Staff-Training Stage

Change Implementation Monitoring
- ▶ Track and Monitor Enablers and Barriers Management Plan
- ▶ Review and Approve Change Implementation Monitoring Stage

Evolution Planning
- ▶ Verify Business Value
- ▶ Identify Evolution Options
- ▶ Develop Evolution Vision
- ▶ Develop Evolution Plan
- ▶ Review and Approve Evolution Planning Stage

Project Review and Assessment
- ▶ Review Project Performance
- ▶ Close Down Project

Project Management Weapons

Projects can be managed skillfully or haphazardly. To be a skillful project manager, the individual must be able to use at least 69 different weapons (tools) effectively. Twelve of these are MOC weapons. With so many weapons, it's easy to see that managing a project is not for the weak of heart or the inexperienced.

The Seven MOC® Support Patterns

The following is a list of support patterns that we have found useful in applying MOC to projects and associated factors. These are the key elements of the *Landscape Survey*.

Support Pattern 1: The Nature of Change
Why major change is difficult to assimilate:
- ▶ **Control:** The extent to which respondents feel they are unable to control what happens to them (direct control) or anticipate the sequence of events (indirect control).

▶ **Micro-Level Impact:** The extent to which individuals do not perceive the change as affecting their day-to-day activities.

▶ **Assimilation Capacity:** The extent to which individuals do not have adequate personal resources to deal with the demands presented by change.

Support Pattern 2: The Process of Change

The key elements and the flow of events involved in human transition:

▶ **Pain:** The extent to which individuals fail to see the status quo as leading to either problems or missed opportunities.

▶ **Desired State:** The extent to which the targets are unable to envision the way things are supposed to be once the change is fully implemented.

▶ **Remedy:** The extent to which individuals fail to acknowledge the value of the specific change being implemented.

▶ **Architecture:** The extent to which respondents fail to recognize a workable plan to move from the status quo to the desired state.

Support Pattern 3: The Roles of Change

The roles that are central to change in organizational settings:

▶ **Initiating Sponsorship:** Inadequate support from those persons who initially sanction the change.

▶ **Sustaining Sponsorship:** Inadequate support from those persons who sanction the change at local levels within the organization.

▶ **Agent Capability:** Inadequate level of skill possessed by those persons who are responsible for facilitating the implementation of the change.

Support Pattern 4: Resistance to Change

How and why resistance forms:

▶ **Willingness:** The extent to which the change is incongruent with respondents' goals and values.

▶ **Ability:** The extent to which respondents do not perceive that they do not have the skills and abilities needed to accomplish the change.

Support Pattern 5: Commitment to Change

The sequence of events involved in people becoming committed to a change:

▶ Commitment: The extent to which the respondents' level of commitment to the change does not match the level needed for the change to succeed.

Support Pattern 6: Culture and Change

Why organizational culture is so important to the success of a change:

▶ **Cultural Consistency:** The degree to which the beliefs, behaviors, and assumptions required by the change are inconsistent with those currently in existence.

▶ **Change History:** The extent to which respondents currently hold negative expectations, based on their experience with previous changes, about the organization's capacity for implementing change.

Support Pattern 7: Synergy and Change

Why powerful teamwork is at the heart of achieving change objectives:

▶ **Common Goals:** The extent to which targets do not see themselves as working toward a clear, shared goal in the change.

▶ **Interdependence:** The extent to which targets do not recognize the necessity of working collaboratively with coworkers to accomplish the change.

▶ **Empowerment:** Perceptions by the targets that their contributions regarding the change are not valued or influential.

▶ **Participatory Management:** The extent to which managers fail to seek the highest appropriate levels of input from targets regarding the change.

▶ **Synergy Skills:** The extent to which respondents do not use the skills necessary for synergistic interaction in the change process.

Summary

A thought to the wise: "If you can't change the situation, you can change the way you handle it."

MOC is a critical project management skill that must be part of all major project management initiatives. Not having MOC plans integrated into the project plan greatly increases the risk of not completing the project on schedule and within budget or providing an output that the customer does not value. MOC is the 10th ingredient in the project management toolbox. In the next chapter, we will look at the MOC methodology in greater depth as it is applied to a typical redesign project.

It is inadequate to manage just project cost, schedule, and quality. Without managing the project's social impact, most projects will fail to reach their full potential.

References

Bridges, William, *Managing Transitions: Making the Most of Change* (Reading MA: Addison-Wesley, 1991).

Conner, Daryl R., *Managing at the Speed of Change: How Resilient Managers Succeed and Prosper Where Others Fail* (New York: Villard Books, 1993).

International Standards Organization, *Guidelines to Quality in Project Management*, Q10006-1997 (Geneva: International Organization for Standardization, 1997).

Pritchett, Price, and Ron Pound, *The Employee Handbook for Organizational Change* (Dallas TX: Pritchett & Associates, 1995).

Project Management Institute, Standards Committee, *A Guide to the Project Management Body of Knowledge* (Upper Darby PA: Project Management Institute, 1996).

6

Applying MOC to a Process Redesign Project—Phases I and II

Reengineering projects fail because they ignore the human part of the equation:
Reengineering = Process + Technology + People + Knowledge.

Introduction

For major projects to be effective in any organization, four ingredients need to be considered:

- ▶ Process
- ▶ Technology
- ▶ People
- ▶ Knowledge

Failure to understand and manage any one of these four factors can destroy what otherwise would have been a very effective improvement project. This is particularly true with the five breakthrough business process improvement (BPI) technologies:

- ▶ Process reengineering
- ▶ Process redesign
- ▶ Process benchmarking
- ▶ Fast Action Solution Technique (FAST)
- ▶ High Impact Team (HIT)

These five business process improvement technologies can swiftly bring about changes that decrease cost, cycle time, and error rates from 30% to 90% while improving output quality (see Figure 6-1). The business process improvement projects make up some of the most important projects organizations have been undertaking.

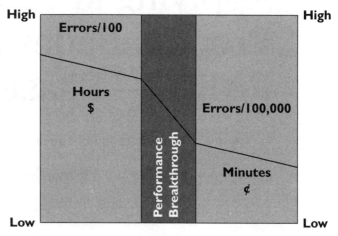

FIGURE 6-1. Performance breakthrough

These types of drastic improvements can be accomplished only when an organization drastically changes the way the employees interface with the process. We have read every major book on process reengineering, process redesign, and process benchmarking, but only in one of these major books was the people side of the equation discussed, and then only very briefly. Is it any wonder that reengineering got such a bad reputation, when its success depends upon challenging the basic paradigms that the present process was built upon without taking into consideration the impact that changing these paradigms would have on the individuals involved in the process?

Jim Harrington wrote the first book on process redesign/reengineering, *Business Process Improvement*, published by McGraw-Hill in November 1991. This book was based upon eight years of successful and not-so-successful process redesign/reengineering projects. In October 1989, Ernst & Young purchased the company that H.J. Harrington was then president of and overlaid the Managing Organizational

Change® (MOC®) process from ODR®, Inc. on the business process improvement concept his team was using.

Suddenly, a light bulb went on. His book and his consulting concepts did an excellent job of defining the process and the enabling technologies, but it did not address the people side of the equation adequately. Using his original approach, he could provide the clients with a near-perfect process that met their needs, but not the assurance that the people who implemented the process would be ready to embrace or even accept the drastic changes. Putting it very simply, his original formula was:

Best Practices + Best Technology = High Performance

The new formula is:

Best Process + Best Technologies + Energized, Knowledgeable People = Highest Performance

This realization added vast new dimensions to process reengineering, process redesign, and benchmarking. Suddenly, success rates jumped twofold and the actual performance of the completed projects improved by an additional 20% to 30%. Over 95% of the business process improvement projects are success stories, and failures are usually the result of upper management changing priorities.

To succeed with a business process improvement (BPI) project, you need the following:

- A reason for the organization to improve
- A process that will have a significant impact upon the organization if it were improved a minimum of 30%
- Trained BPI technologists
- Dedicated resources
- Good simulation modeling tools
- Effective management of change methodologies
- A good understanding of the process enablers
- Upper management interest and support
- An effective implementation team
- A lot of momentum

Even more important, you need to have people ready and willing to accept and even embrace the new process.

The lack of any one of these ingredients will cause the project to fail, or at least not produce the results that it should have produced.

In a benchmarking study of 57 organizations from six continents conducted by ProSci of Loveland, Colorado, directed at identifying best practices in business process reengineering and process design, the firm reported: "When asked what they would do differently next time, many companies cited change management as one of the top two areas for improvement." The other area for improvement was the use of dedicated resources for the projects. Top management sponsorship and change management were cited most frequently as the most important steps in the reengineering or process redesign activities. Based upon this study, the greatest reengineering or redesign obstacles that the 57 organizations faced were:

▶ inadequate management support
▶ change resistance
▶ team members had too little time to devote to the project
▶ poor or inadequate training

It's not our intent to train the reader on how to do process redesign but rather to use the process redesign technology as a mannequin on which we will hang the change management concept so that the undesirable bulges are covered up and the interesting curves accentuated. In this chapter, we will discuss the first two phases of a process redesign project. Phases I and II are designed to characterize the process that is under study and to implement some quick fixes. In Chapter 7 we will discuss Phases III and IV of a process redesign process. Phase III is used to develop the future-state process design and during Phase IV the future-state process design is implemented.

Overview

The purpose of Chapters 6 and 7 is to take the change management concepts discussed in this book and apply them to a process redesign project. This will allow the reader to see how the change management concepts can be effectively applied to a particular methodology. Understanding the change management concepts is an important first step, but the real payoff occurs when you are able to apply these concepts to your job. This often is the most difficult part in the transformation that converts theories into practice. Taking a classroom concept and applying it to the maintenance shop or the development laboratory is the real challenge.

We will start by defining some common terms that need to be understood:

Process Redesign—A methodology used to streamline a current process with the objective of reducing cost and cycle time by 30% to 60% while improving output quality from 20% to 200%.

Process Reengineering—A methodology used to radically change the way a process is presently designed by developing an independent vision of how it should perform and using a group of enablers to prepare a new process design that is not hampered by the present process paradigms.

Enabler—A technical or organizational facility/resource that makes it possible to perform a task, activity, or process. Examples of *technical* enablers are personal computers, copying equipment, decentralized data processing, voice-response acceptance, etc. Examples of *organizational* enablers are self-managed work teams, virtual departments, network organizations, and education systems.

Future-State Solutions (FSS)—A combination of corrective actions and changes that can be applied to an item (process) being studied to increase its performance and its value to the stakeholders.

Best-Value Future-State Solution (BFSS)—A solution that results in the most beneficial new item as viewed by the item's stakeholders. It is the best combination of implementation cost, implementation cycle time, risk, and performance results (examples: return on investment, customer satisfaction, market share, risk, value added per employee, time to implement, cost to implement, etc.).

Process Improvement Team (PIT)—A group of individuals, usually from different functions, assigned to improve a specific process or subprocess. They design the best-value future-state solution using methodologies such as process redesign, process reengineering, and process benchmarking.

BPI Approaches

Three of the BPI approaches (process benchmarking, process redesign, and process reengineering) are covered in the book *Business Process Improvement*. Fast Action Solution Technique (FAST) and High Impact Team (HIT) are more recent concepts designed to identify and rapidly harvest the low-hanging fruit that has grown within our business processes.

Process Benchmarking

Process benchmarking is an old methodology that was given new life when Xerox gave it primary credit for its turnaround and its winning of the Malcolm Baldrige Award. This approach is very misunderstood today. Most people think they are benchmarking when they compare their process performance measurements with another organization's measurements. This is only an early step in the benchmarking process. This type of activity should correctly be called *comparative analysis*.

Benchmarking—A systematic way to identify, understand, and creatively evolve superior products, services, designs, equipment, processes, and practices to improve the organization's real performance by studying how other organizations are performing the same or similar operations.

Comparative Analysis—The act of comparing a set of measurements with a set of similar measurements for a similar item.

Typically, the benchmarking process will reduce cost, cycle time, and error rates between 20% and 50%. A typical benchmarking project takes three to five months to design a best-value future-state solution (BFSS). Based on our experience, this is the correct approach to use on 5% to 20% of an organization's major processes.

· Roller Skate Redesigned ·

Process Redesign (Focused Improvement)

You can improve your creativity by learning about and using tools that help you see and understand the world from new perspectives.

The process redesign approach focuses the efforts of the process improvement team (PIT) on refining the present process. Process redesign is normally applied to processes that are working fairly well today. Typically, process redesign projects will reduce cost, cycle time, and error rates between 30% and 60%. With process redesign, it takes between 80 and 100 days to define the BFSS. This is the correct approach to use with approximately 70% to 90% of major business processes. This approach is used if improving the process's performance by 30% to 60% would give the organization a competitive advantage.

Process Reengineering (New Process Design or Process Innovation)

If you have always done it that way, it is probably wrong.
—CHARLES KETTERING

Process reengineering is the most radical of the five BPI approaches. It is sometimes called *process innovation* because its success relies heavily on the PIT's innovation and creative abilities. Process reengineering is also called *big picture analysis* or *new process design*. We like the term "new process design" most because it uses the same approach that would have been used if the organization were designing the process for the first time.

Process reengineering, when applied correctly, reduces cost and cycle time between 60% and 90% and error rates between 40% and 70%. It is a very useful tool when the current-state process is so out of date that it is not worth salvaging or even influencing the BFSS. Process reengineering is the correct answer for 5% to 20% of the major processes within an organization.

Roller Skate Re-engineered.

FAST (Fast Action Solution Technique)

Fast Action Solution Technique is based on an improvement tool first used by International Business Machines Corporation in the mid-1980s. General Electric refined this approach in the 1990s and called it "Workout." Ford Motor Company further developed it under the title "RAPID." Today, Ernst & Young extensively uses this approach (which it calls "Express") with many clients around the world. It is also often used by other organizations throughout the Americas.

Fast Action Solution Technique (FAST)—A breakthrough approach that focuses a group's attention on a single process for a one- or two-day meeting to define how the group can improve the process over the next 90 days. Before the end of the meeting, management approves or rejects the proposed improvements.

FAST can be applied to any process level, from a major process down to the activity level. The FAST approach to BPI centers around a single one- or two-day meeting that identifies root causes of problems and/or no-value-added activities designed into a present process. Typical improvement results from the FAST approach are reduced cost, cycle time, and error rates between 5% and 15% in a three-month period. The potential improvements are identified and approved for implementation in one or two days; hence the term FAST was given to this approach.

Impact of Different BPI Approaches

Figure 6-2 compares how typical process benchmarking, process redesign, and process reengineering methodologies improve cycle time for a process. It clearly shows the different levels of improvement that three of the BPI approaches, combined with continuous improvement, have on a typical process over a 36-month period.

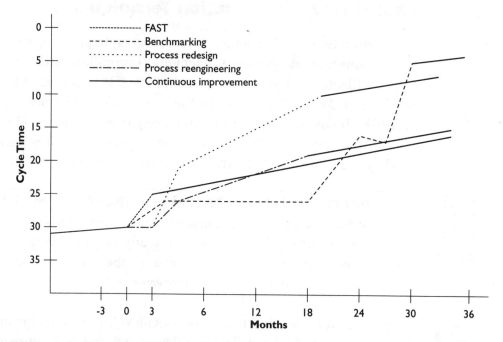

FIGURE 6-2. Comparison of four breakthrough approaches on the cycle time of a typical process

BPI and Change Management

Although change management concepts should be used in all five of the business process improvement methodologies each time they are applied, we will use process redesign as our example in this chapter.

The Five Phases of Process Redesign

The complexity of our business environment and the many organizations involved in the critical business processes make it necessary to develop a very formal approach to process redesign. This methodology is conveniently divided into five subprocesses (phases) that consist of a total of 36 activities (see Figure 6-3).

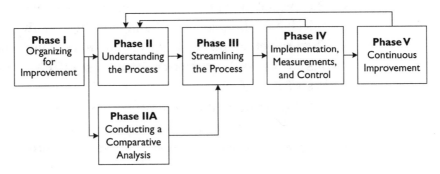

FIGURE 6-3. The five phases of process redesign

	Weeks													
	2	4	6	8	10	12	14							
Process Redesign Phase														
I. Organize	▓	▓												
II. Understand			▓	▓										
III. Streamline					▓	▓	▓							
IV. Implement								▓	▓	▓	▓			
MOC Phases														
I. Clarify	▓													
II. Announce	▓													
III. Diagnose			▓	▓		▓	▓							
IV. Plan		▓				▓								
V. Implement			▓	▓	▓	▓	▓	▓	▓					
VI. Monitor					▓	▓	▓	▓	▓	▓	▓	▓	▓	
VII. Final Evaluation														▓

FIGURE 6-4. The process redesign phases compared with the MOC phases

Phase I: Organizing for Improvement

An executive improvement team (EIT) is formed. Process owners and process improvement teams (PITs) are assigned, process boundaries are defined, total process measurements are developed, and initial business process improvement project plans are developed and approved. The outputs from Phase I are follows:

- ▶ The executive improvement team (EIT) is educated in the process redesign methodology (including the MOC methodology).
- ▶ The project scope is clearly articulated through the use of various tools and processes, such as ODR's *Change Project Description Form*.
- ▶ Employee communication processes are started.
- ▶ Critical processes are defined.
- ▶ Process improvement teams (PITs) and process owners are assigned.
- ▶ Process boundaries are established.
- ▶ Process measurements of effectiveness, efficiency, and adaptability are developed and goals are set.
- ▶ PITs are trained in team operating methods and the process redesign methodology.
- ▶ Project change management plans are developed and included in the project plan.
- ▶ Project plans are prepared and approved.

Phase II: Understanding the Process

The PIT flowcharts the process, develops the simulation model, conducts a process walk-through to understand the process, defines problems, and measures cycle time and cost. Additional studies are conducted to fill in any void in the database. The processes and procedures are aligned and quick-fix improvements are implemented.

Phase IIA: Conducting a Comparative Analysis

Often in parallel with Activities 1 through 6 of Phase II, a comparative analysis study is conducted to allow the matrix of the process under study to be compared with other similar processes.

Phase III: Streamlining the Process

The PIT now focuses its efforts on streamlining the process. The PIT will systematically work its way through the 12 streamlining steps in Activity 1 to develop a group of future-state solutions. During Activities 4, 5, and 6 the PIT will define a best-value future-state solution and get it approved by management. The outputs from Phase III are:

- The PIT is trained in the 12 streamlining steps and seven basic problem-solving tools.
- Process problems are addressed.
- Process improvement projections and implementation-cost and cycle-time estimates are completed for each option.
- Options are analyzed and a preferred process (best-value future-state solution) is defined.
- A *Preliminary Implementation Plan* for the best-value future-state solution is prepared and approved.
- Project plans are updated.
- The PIT is rewarded based on the projected process improvement.

Phase IV: Implementation, Measurements, and Control

Increased emphasis is placed on the management of change during Phase IV. The best-value future-state solution is phased in with the appropriate number of trial runs that verify the magnitude and impact of each change. The simulation model is updated to reflect these changes. The outputs from Phase IV are:

- An implementation team is formed and trained in project management, process improvement, and change management.
- Final improvement plan for the best-value future-state solution is developed and approved.
- Department improvement teams (DITs) are formed and trained to help with the implementation.

- ▶ The best-value future-state solution is implemented in keeping with the implementation plan and the result of each change is measured.
- ▶ Internal process performance measurements and feedback systems are defined and put in place.
- ▶ Management control systems are implemented.
- ▶ The MOC plan is implemented and updated.
- ▶ The implementation team is rewarded based upon how effectively the new process was implemented.

Phase V: Continuous Improvement

Process improvement plans are reviewed by the EIT and approved. The process evolves through a series of six qualification levels. Each time a change to the process is implemented, the simulation model is updated. The outputs from Phase V are:

- ▶ The department improvement teams take over the responsibility of continuous improvement for their part of the process.
- ▶ Process changes are implemented.
- ▶ Process improvement results are measured.
- ▶ Process simulation model is updated.

Managing Organizational Change Applied to Process Redesign

As with any project, the MOC activities should be embedded into the process redesign project plan and be an important part of the project activities. The following is a list of MOC assessments, surveys, and tools that can be used during the first four phases of a business process improvement project (see Figure 6-5).

To understand how change management is applied to process redesign, we will present what happens in each of the first four phases of the process redesign methodology, one at a time. At the end of each phase, we will explain how change management is applied during that phase. For details related to each of the activities in each of

MOC Assessments, Surveys, and Training Tools	Process Redesign Phases			
	I	II	III	IV
1. Adaptation Capacity Audit	✓		✓	
2. Change Agent Evaluation	✓		✓	
3. Change Agent Selection Form	✓			
4. Change History Survey	✓			
5. Change Knowledge Assessment	✓		✓	
6. Change Project Description Form	✓	✓	✓	✓
7. Change Resistance Scale			✓	
8. Coaching Styles Inventory and Guide			✓	✓
9. Communicating Change: Announcement Plan	✓	✓	✓	
10. Communicating Change: Constituency Analysis	✓	✓	✓	
11. Communicating Change: Project Analysis		✓	✓	
12. Communicating Change: Statement Development		✓	✓	
13. Communicating Style and Survey Guide	✓	✓	✓	
14. Culture Assessment		✓	✓	
15. Culture Audit		✓	✓	
16. Expectations for a Successful Change Project	✓	✓		
17. Focus Group Tools*		✓	✓	✓
18. Force Field Analysis*		✓	✓	✓
19. Implementation Plan Advocacy Kit			✓	✓
20. Implementation Plan Evaluation		✓		✓
21. Implementation Problems Assessments	✓			
22. Individual Error Rate Measurements*			✓	✓
23. Influence Style Survey and Interpretation Manual		✓	✓	✓
24. Landscape Surveys		✓	✓	✓

FIGURE 6-5. MOC assessments, surveys, and training tools used in the first four phases of process redesign (continued on next page)

	MOC Assessments, Surveys, and Training Tools	Process Redesign Phases			
		I	II	III	IV
25.	MOC Training for Sporsors, Agents, Targets, and Advocates	✓	✓	✓	✓
26.	Organizational Change Implementation Plan (OCIP)			✓	✓
27.	Overload Index	✓	✓		✓
28.	Pain Management Strategies: Sponsor	✓	✓	✓	✓
29.	Pain Management Strategies: Target		✓	✓	✓
30.	Personal Power Survey	✓		✓	
31.	Personal Resilience Questionnaire and Profile			✓	✓
32.	Postmortem*				✓
33.	Predicting the Impact of Change			✓	
34.	Preliminary Implementation Plan			✓	✓
35.	Process Modeling*	✓	✓	✓	
36.	Process Walk-Through Checklist*		✓		
37.	Rewards and Recognition Tools*			✓	✓
38.	Role Map Application Tool	✓	✓	✓	✓
39.	Senior Team Value for Discipline	✓			
40.	Simulation Modeling*		✓	✓	✓
41.	Sponsor Checklist	✓	✓	✓	✓
42.	Sponsor Evaluation	✓	✓	✓	✓
43.	Synergy Survey	✓	✓	✓	✓
44.	When to Apply the MOC Methodology	✓		✓	

* Use of this tool is not limited to the MOC methodology

FIGURE **6-5. (Continued)**

the four phases, read *Business Process Improvement* by H. James Harrington (McGraw-Hill, 1991).

Phase I—Organizing for Improvement

Phase I—Organizing for Improvement is subdivided into eight activities (see Figure 6-6).

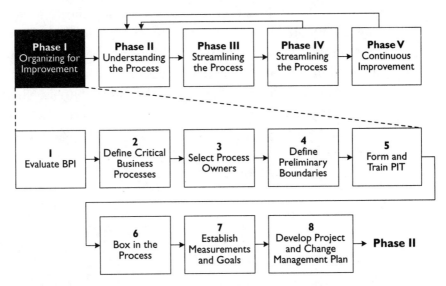

·FIGURE 6-6. **The eight activities that make up Phase I**

Effectiveness—The extent to which the output of a process or subprocess meets the needs and expectations of the customers. A close synonym of effectiveness is *quality*. Effectiveness is having the right output at the right place at the right time at the right price. Effectiveness impacts the process's direct and indirect customers.

Efficiency—A measure of the resources (human, money, cycle time, etc.) that a process consumes in order to produce its output. A close synonym of efficiency is *productivity*.

Adaptability—The flexibility of the process that handles future, changing customer expectations and today's individual special customer requirements. It is managing the process to meet today's special needs and future requirements.

Applying MOC to Phase I

Now let's go back and look at the eight activities that took place during Phase I and determine how management of change should be used during this part of the process redesign cycle. Contrary to what most people believe, Phase I is one of the most important parts of the Managing Organizational Change® process. Typically, Activities 1, 2, 3, and 4 will take place over a two-month period. Activities 5, 6, 7, and 8 will occur during a three-day period, approximately. Figure 6-7 is a timeline chart for Phase I. "Time zero" on the chart is when the process owner starts to work in the project. (Activities 1 through 3 are establishing the BPI projects throughout the organization.) The individual process redesign project starts with Activity 4, when the process owner starts work on the project.

Activity	Weeks									
	-6	-5	-4	-3	-2	-1	1	2	3	4
1. Evaluate the applicability of BPI	▓	▓	▓	▓						
2. Define critical business processes					▓	▓				
3. Select process owners						▓				
4. Define preliminary boundaries							▓			
5. Form and train PIT							▓	▓		
6. Box in the process										▓
7. Establish measurements and goals								▓		▓
8. Develop a project plan										▓

FIGURE **6-7. Phase I typical process redesign timeline chart**

Introduction to Applying MOC to Phase I

Employees complain of being burned out, used up, overloaded. Too many of us are just plain tired, overdosed on change, sick of ambiguity and uncertainty.
    —PRICE PRITCHETT, *A SURVIVAL GUIDE TO THE STRESS OF ORGANIZATIONAL CHANGE*

We now turn to exploring the application of the Managing Organizational Change® principles, tools, and techniques, not just at the organization-wide level, but rather to specific major process redesign initiatives. We will be reviewing redesign phases and activities and identifying opportunities for integrating MOC plans and activities into the appropriate stages in the redesign work plan.

That integration is key to project success, which we define as meeting both human and technical objectives, on time, and within budget. The change aspects of any project should be fully integrated into each phase and activity within the project, not addressed separately or as an afterthought. Every step of the way, we should be asking ourselves which activities should be included to enhance the probability that changes will be fully and effectively implemented.

Chapters 1, 2, 3, and 4 stressed the importance of creating nimble organizations capable of effectively managing within an increasingly turbulent environment. The focus was on the capability and resilience of the entire organization. To review key points at the organizational level before exploring project-specific change strategies:

We saw the value of assessing the strategic factors related to an organization's overall capacity to assimilate new change initiatives (the Human Due Diligence™ Audit). (Note: Human Due Diligence is a registered ODR trademark.) This audit, typically tailored for each organization, would include the assessment of previous change implementation projects (we have found that an organization's past successes and/or problems in change implementation typically predict what might happen during future implementation projects) and an inventory of other ongoing projects that are currently drawing on overall capacity.

All of these factors, then, contribute to an objective understanding of an organization's resilience—its ability to absorb the disruption of major change without debilitating dysfunction. Indeed, the greater an organization's overall capacity for initiating changes, the more likely its specific process improvement initiative will achieve success *with minimum disruption and, therefore, minimal draw on your organization's capacity for implementing other important initiatives.*

Nothing endures except change.
—HERACLITUS, CA 500 B.C.

Nimbleness—The ability for an organization to consistently succeed in unpredictable, contested environments by implementing important changes more efficiently and effectively than its competitors, thereby maintaining its desired return on change (ROC_{hg}).

On the tactical project level (i.e., process redesign), an additional set of MOC® tools and techniques is required to make sure that the overall project is implemented as effectively and efficiently as possible. With these tools, the project manager and all others involved will make dramatic gains in terms of conserving human resources by channeling employees' energies toward productive commitment and away from nonproductive resistance.

Price Pritchett and Ron Pound wrote in *The Employee Handbook for Organizational Change*: "Zero defects is an alien concept in managing transition and change. If the organization waited until the changes could be made perfectly, they would never be made at all."

MOC Applied to Phase I, Activity 1: Evaluate the Applicability of BPI

MOC should be applied at the very outset of the project, even during the evaluation of applicability of BPI. It's important that the people conducting that evaluation be sensitive to change issues and to the potential for organizational and individual disruption that the project represents. It is a leading practice for organizations to identify a cadre of progressive thinkers who have the ability and desire to lead change projects and who understand the emotions that change generates in the organization and its people. These are the people whom Rosabeth Moss Kanter calls the "Change Masters."

All project managers must be change masters in addition to having an excellent understanding of the organization's processes. The individuals assigned to determine if BPI methodologies are applicable should already be competent change masters or, at the very least, be the type of people who embrace change and who can be readily trained to master MOC principles and methods.

Behaviorally based interviews of those who will be conducting the evaluation can be a significant help in selecting people with a positive orientation to change and with the skills for implementing it. A number of assessment tools are available to aid in the selection process, including *Personal Resilience Questionnaire, Personal Power Survey, Influence Style Survey, Coaching Styles Inventory, Communicating Style Survey, Change Knowledge Assessment, Sponsor Evaluation, Change Agent Evaluation, Change Agent Selection Form, Synergy Survey,* and *Change Resistance Scale.*

If the decision is to implement the BPI methodologies, then it's very important to provide management with enough information about the BPI methodologies so that the managers understand it well enough to know what is going on and to be able to answer questions that employees may ask. Be sure that the management team understands that the processes to which BPI will be applied will not be identified until Activity 2. Communications at this point in the BPI cycle are focused on helping the organization understand the BPI concepts. No one knows who will be impacted by the BPI methodologies at this early stage.

MOC Applied to Phase I, Activity 2: Define Critical Business Processes and Select Processes for Improvement

Just-in-time training for executives, sponsors, and evaluators should be provided to ensure that they have the information they need about the nature of change. It should include an understanding of basic change principles and concepts. It is important at this early stage that executives understand resistance, that it's a normal and natural human reaction to the prospect of change and disruption of their expectations and way of life. All too often, executives see resistance as a sign either that there is something wrong with the planned change or that employees are simply obstructing progress. Neither is necessarily true.

If the organization decides to apply the BPI methodologies, it's important to start communications about the projects at this time. Communicating about a major change project is not as simple as one might think. Key aspects include thoroughly understanding the project, understanding the various constituencies to be affected and how they will be affected, and finally drafting well-crafted statements targeted for each constituency. Also, keep in mind that the use of these and other MOC® planning tools may be iterative as the project moves forward, expands, and becomes more focused on specific solutions or changes. Communication is not a "one-shot" endeavor; the content and constituencies are likely to change throughout the life cycle of the project. Everyone in the organization will need to know what the projects are, why the organization is doing it, and when it will happen. The real question they want answered is how it will affect them. In most cases, no one will have an answer to that question this early in the process. It's extremely important to answer that question as soon as the information is available, as accurately as possible. When the organization decided to use BPI, it dropped the first shoe. Everyone has heard the horror stories about how process improvement has reduced headcount by as much as 90%. People will begin looking around and worrying that they will not be among the 10% who are left. Many good people will start looking for jobs elsewhere—people that the organization cannot afford to lose.

Factors that the executive committee should consider in selecting processes to be redesigned include, in addition to the business considerations previously mentioned, change-relevant factors such as:

▶ the extent of anticipated disruption to those who operate the process, using the tool, *Predicting the Impact of Change*

▶ the change capacity of the people involved in the processes, using the *Adaptation Capacity Audit*

▶ past history of successful implementation of change in that process, using an *Implementation Problems Assessment*

▶ leadership within the potential projects and the process that will be redesigned

▶ the subculture of each process itself (differences can frequently be found among production, engineering, finance, and/or R&D with respect to change attitudes), using a *Culture Assessment* and comparing results for each group

▶ other changes that are already going on in the organization or that are planned to start in the next 12 months

It should be kept in mind, however, that it is possible to "over assess" a particular constituency, so care should be taken in determining when and to what depth the assessments should be conducted. At this early stage, informal use of assessment tools, perhaps in a focus group setting, will provide the data needed, while reserving the potential for more rigorous assessments of specific target constituencies when specific processes have been identified or solutions approved for implementation.

When the matrix is designed that will be used to select BPI projects, your organization's existing change capacity and the likely demand of your project on that capacity are just as important selection factors as "Impact on the Customer" or "Potential for Improvement."

Before the end of this phase, the executive team must answer the question, "What are we going to do with the surplus people after the processes have been reengineered or redesigned?" This is a difficult

question to answer when you consider that, for processes targeted for cost reduction, an average of 40% of the people will be surplus. For example, if 12 processes are selected for BPI and seven of those have cycle time reduction targets, 10 have quality improvement targets, and eight have cost-reduction targets (a process can have more than one type of improvement target) and if the schedule calls for four cost-reduction projects the first year, two the second year, and two the third year, the executive team can estimate the number of surplus people by assuming that the head count required to perform the activities will be reduced by 40%.

The first thing the executive team should do is stop hiring to fill openings in the affected processes and use subcontract or temporary workers to fill essential vacancies. Through effective planning, many of the surplus personnel who accrue in the second and third years will be from the ranks of temporary workers, who knew that their jobs were temporary. We have found that personal resilience training can make a critical difference to the permanent employees, whether they are relocating from one department to another or from one city to another. The training is also helpful to those who are being laid off. The training not only provides the platform for constructively discussing the issues before them, but also helps them identify their strengths, renew themselves, and begin planning their futures.

For those people who will become surplus during the first year, there are many options that should be considered before layoffs. The executive team should approach the surplus issue very creatively, consider all potential options, and release a "no layoff" policy whenever possible. Available alternatives are discussed by H. James Harrington in *The Down Side to Quality Improvement* and in Chapter 1 of *Total Improvement Management: The Next Generation in Performance Improvement.*

The executives will start to implement the cascading sponsorship activities for the managers involved in the processes to which the process redesign methodology will be applied. At the end of Activity 2, these managers are all targets who need to become sustaining sponsors before the process redesign project reaches Phase II.

It's crucial for the executive team to communicate with all employees working on processes to which BPI will be applied. Although it may be difficult or uncomfortable, honest and candid communications about the number of people affected and about the plans for dealing with the surplus are essential. Your people will respect you for it.

MOC Applied to Phase I, Activity 3: Select the Process Owners and Executive Sponsors

Identify key people in the organization to spearhead the change. Choose them on their personal characteristics, not their place on the hierarchy. You want people who will be very strong supporters of the project and who have open minds. Look at new hires the same way. They must be flexible and open to new things. Hire risk takers, then make it safe for them to experiment and possibly fail.

—MICHAEL TOFOLO, *MANAGEMENT REVIEW*, MARCH 1998

During this activity, the critical project management roles of process owners and executive sponsors are filled. The key roles in the change process, including sponsors, were defined earlier. The importance of their role cannot be overstated and they must be selected with the same diligence as the project itself. Of all the potential risks associated with the effective management of change, ineffective sponsorship is the most critical. Other risks, while potentially serious, can be mitigated through the efforts of knowledgeable sponsors. But without effective sponsors, project success is significantly less likely. Typically, the executive sponsor of a process redesign project is the initiating sponsor and the process owner is one of the sustaining sponsors, as defined earlier, and frequently also serves as the project manager. Experience has identified a number of key principles to keep in mind with respect to sponsorship:

▶ **Sponsorship is critical to successful change.** Significant change within a target population will not occur unless the appropriate sponsors show sufficient commitment.

▶ **Weak sponsors must be educated or replaced, or failure is inevitable.** When sponsors who do not fully understand the change implications are unwilling or unable to take the actions necessary to secure the critical resources or are unwilling or unable to fulfill their role requirements, they must be educated or replaced. Otherwise, the change effort will fail to meet its stated objective(s).

▶ **Sponsorship cannot be delegated to agents.** Sponsorship can be delegated only to those who have legitimization power; therefore, it cannot be delegated to agents. Change agents can be charged with implementation responsibilities but should never be asked to legitimize change.

▶ **Initiating and sustaining sponsors must never attempt to fulfill each other's functions.** *Initiating* sponsors have the organizational power to start the change process and they can legitimize the process for all affected targets. *Sustaining* sponsors maintain the change process because they have the logistical, economic, and political proximity to the targets; they are closer to the action.

▶ **Cascading sponsorship must be established and maintained.** There must exist a cascading, direct line of active sponsorship from the *initiating* sponsors to the *sustaining* sponsors or the change effort will fail to achieve its objective(s).

Although the process owner will frequently be selected on the basis of process knowledge, his or her role as a critical sustaining sponsor suggests that sponsorship skills are equally important to the ultimate success of the project.

The process owner serves as the project manager for individual process redesign projects. He or she must understand all of the project management activities defined in Chapter 4 and particularly the MOC® strategy and approaches. Very important factors in selecting process owners are their ability to manage how they react personally to changes that affect them and their impact on others during the change cycle. Those process owners who are not "change masters" when selected must gain those skills very quickly. The process owner role goes well beyond that of other sustaining sponsors, as owners need to provide help and guidance to all the other sustaining sponsors and change agents throughout all phases of the project.

MOC Applied to Phase I, Activity 4: Define Preliminary Process Boundaries

Even before identifying the specific processes that will be the subject of improvement projects, high-level communications about the overall need for improvement—the "business case"—and the "burning platform" should begin the awareness process.

It's never too early to begin thinking about the communications that will be necessary at the very beginning of the project, as you anticipate and answer the questions that will be at the top of employees' minds as soon as word of the project gets out. If word has not already spread, it certainly will when the selection of improvement team members commences. Establishing process boundaries will define the scope of the improvement effort and allow preliminary identification of those employees who are likely to be affected. Now is the time to plan a communications strategy and design the initial communications to address the potential concerns of this group.

Build on the communications plan developed in Activity 1, but with more focus, now that we know which organizations and people will be affected and the processes where the redesign will occur. The first plan was very general, but now we can be more specific. We still don't know the nature of the change, so that aspect of the communications plan will be added later in the process.

At this stage, you will not have complete answers to all these questions, but it will serve you well to be aware of the issues that will have to be addressed. Answer the questions that you can now and make a list of those that will have to be answered later in the process.

A Communications Approach Provides Employees with Answers to the Questions at the Top of Their Minds

Do I have a job?

Does the new direction of the organization include me?

How will my job and role be affected?

How will it be different from what I do now?

How will success be measured?

Will my pay be linked to performance?

Will I have a new boss?

What will he or she be like and what will be expected?

Are there behaviors that I will need to change?

How will I personally benefit from this change?

What will I get and what will be taken away from me?

Where is the organization going?

Why do we need to change to get there?

How will we get there?

What's our strategy and how can I help make it happen?

What is the difference between how we work now and how we will work in the future?

How will the organization benefit from the changes?

Who specifically will benefit?

MOC Applied to Phase I, Activity 5: Form and Train the Process Improvement Team

When the process owner creates a block diagram of the process, the managers of all involved groups or departments identified automatically become change targets. Defining preliminary process boundaries also enables the preparation of the initial Role Map diagram for the project, the first cut at identifying all those who will affect or be affected by the changes to come. Identify not only all the target populations and individuals, but also all sponsors, change agents, and advocates. The Role Map diagram shows the dynamics of relationships among them as well.

As you recall, an important principle related to the roles of change is that everyone should first be treated as a target. For instance, even though a particular person is technically a sponsor, he or she must first be seen as a target. That person's resistance must be identified and managed and his or her commitment must be built to the level appropriate to that of an effective sponsor. This is also true of potential change agents. Sponsors must become effective sustaining sponsors; their transformation into that role is the responsibility of the process owner and the initiating sponsor. The first interview with those managers is key to beginning the transformation process. The process owner must take advantage of this early opportunity to get the managers connected and involved in the redesign process, to understand their concerns and personal issues, and to gain their support. This is the opportunity to help those managers understand why it is crucial that they provide needed resources.

During this single meeting, a skillful process owner will make significant progress toward transforming each manager from a target to a sustaining sponsor. This requires that the process owner do a lot of homework before knocking on the manager's door and be well prepared to anticipate and answer any questions the manager may have. It is very helpful to prepare a list of potential questions or concerns that may be raised and to have candid, factual, and honest answers ready. Typical questions managers raise at this stage include:

- ► Where do I get the people to do the work of those people who are spending time on the process improvement team?
- ► Who will pay for this effort?
- ► When will it begin and end?
- ► What if I don't like the proposed changes?
- ► What's in it for me?

After the interview, the process owner should prepare minutes of the meeting, to document the manager's concerns, suggestions, and commitments, to capture the information, and to demonstrate that the process owner was listening. Pay particular attention to the questions and concerns that were not on the original list, so they can be added in preparation for interviews with other managers. MOC training for the process improvement team (PIT) is critical to the success of the project.

During the formation of the PIT, attention should be given to including employees, staff personnel, and managers who can add value as effective advocates of the change that will ensue. You should look for a fundamentally positive orientation toward change and a high degree of credibility with peers. We have previously noted that one aspect of individual resilience is a fundamental orientation that sees change as an opportunity rather than a threat.

Change produces a crisis when it significantly disrupts our expectations. The Chinese express the concept of crisis with two characters. The top character represents *potential danger*; the lower one conveys *hidden opportunity*. Type-D or danger-oriented people see change as a threat, frequently responding with defensive reaction mechanisms such as denial, distortion, or delusion. Opportunity-oriented or type-O people, while recognizing the dangers and experiencing the same feelings of disorientation, see change as a potential advantage to be exploited, rather than a problem to be avoided. The extent to which PIT members and key leaders have the type-O orientation will impact the ease with which they will be able to function as effective advocates with their peers. The process owner should evaluate each PIT candidate and reject all type-D candidates.

At the first PIT meeting, a project charter and team operating articles should be prepared. Typical rules that would be included in the team operating articles are:

- ▶ All meetings will start within five minutes of the scheduled time.
- ▶ No meeting will run past the scheduled quitting time.
- ▶ An agenda will be prepared for each meeting.
- ▶ No one will interrupt another person when he or she is speaking.
- ▶ All tests should be completed on or ahead of schedule.
- ▶ No one will belittle another team member.
- ▶ No phone interruptions during meetings.
- ▶ There will be a 10-minute break every two hours.

> ▶ No break will start more than five minutes later than the sched-uled time.
> ▶ No cellular phones or pagers will be allowed in the meetings.
> ▶ No one will discuss a subject that is not on the agenda unless the PIT first agrees to adjust the agenda.

The operating articles often call for a major change in the way the organization functions, but become a key part of ensuring that the pro-ject is completed on time within budget and meets the performance objectives. It is extremely important that all members agree with the PIT's operating articles. After the members have agreed to the articles, the PIT members' performance should be measured to ensure that each PIT member complies with the articles. This is the job of the process owners, although any of the PIT members can point out a noncompli-ance that the process owners may have overlooked. Each noncompli-ance will be called an *error*. At regular scheduled intervals, the process owner will publish an error report for each PIT member, which is then distributed to the PIT and the executive committee (see Figure 6-8).

Change Roles for PIT Members

In Chapter 2 we defined the various roles necessary for the successful implementation of change. At different times and in the face of differ-ent challenges, PIT team members may carry out the roles of sustain-ing sponsors, agents, targets, and advocates. Many change projects will require that members wear more than one hat. It is not unusual for people to say, "I am an agent for my boss, but a sponsor to my people."

The process owner, management, and supervisory personnel on the PIT must understand their role as sustaining sponsors and be pre-pared to take a very active role in sustaining communications and ensuring necessary resources. They have the proximity to the targets to legitimize the change for them and to reinforce the behavior need-ed to sustain it.

The PIT will develop the future-state solution. This is not a change agent role. Some of the individuals on the PIT may also serve as change agents, responsible for developing and implementing the activ-ities that support the MOC part of the project. The change agent is not

Bob Maas's Project 1596–Error Rate Report

Type of Errors	Data				
	6/1	6/8	6/15	6/22	6/29
Late for meeting	3	1	4	2	0
Left meeting early	4	3	2	0	0
Interrupted others	3	5	10	6	3
Did not meet commitments	0	8	9	6	3
Phone call interruption	3	2	4	1	2
Pager interruption	8	8	4	2	0
Deviated from agenda	10	15	10	3	5
Weekly total	31	42	43	20	13
Project total	31	73	116	136	149

FIGURE **6-8. Typical individual error rate report**

responsible for designing or implementing the technical part of the project. This often calls for the same person to wear two or more hats. At one point, he or she will be wearing a technical hat and then quickly change it for a change agent's hat. Until the specifics of the change are defined, you will not know for sure who all the change agents will be, but it's quite likely that some of the PIT members will fill that role. Agent success depends on the ability to diagnose potential problems, develop a plan to deal with them, and execute the change effectively.

At some time in the project, most PIT members will also be targets—the individuals who must change. Remember that the term *target* is used because these people are the focus of the change effort and play a crucial role in the short- and long-term success of the project. To increase the likelihood of success, they must be educated to understand the changes they are expected to implement and they must be involved appropriately in that process.

Advocates are the individuals who want to achieve the change, but who lack the power to sanction it. In process redesign projects, some of the most powerful and effective advocates are the peers of those targets who are not on the PIT. When peers whom targets know and respect—their coworkers—clearly support the change, the potential for acceptance, and even commitment, increases significantly.

Select PIT members carefully, giving consideration not only to their process expertise, but also to their potential for effectively carrying out their change roles. Are they type-O people? Will they be open to the change themselves? Are they willing to challenge the status quo, existing assumptions, and conventional wisdom? Can they play the devil's advocate? Can they also be "angel's advocates," helping to develop and improve upon other's ideas? If otherwise logical team members do not bring these additional skills to the team, consider including others who will add these essential ingredients.

To aid in selecting PIT members, have each candidate's manager fill out a *Personal Resilience Questionnaire* that defines the manager's view of the candidate. Each candidate should also fill out a *Personal Resilience Questionnaire.* In addition, the process owner should fill out the same form after interviewing the candidate. Based upon these three inputs, the process owner should have a good idea of the candidate's change readiness. If for some reason type-D people have to be assigned to the PIT, the process owner needs to increase the time estimates required to complete the process redesign project and be more conservative in setting improvement goals. The presence of one or two type-D people on the PIT will double the time required to complete Phases I through III and reduce the gain that will result from the project by 15% to 25%.

Based on the process owner's assessment of the potential for disruption that the project represents, the magnitude of the changes it is likely to bring, and the level of MOC experience of the process managers and the other PIT members, it may be necessary to add a change facilitator to the PIT.

Change Facilitator—The individual who leads and directs the change management activities for a project. The change facilitator has mastered MOC methodologies and tools. He or she provides the just-in-time MOC training and change management guidance to the PIT, sponsors, and others requiring that level of training. The change facilitator can be viewed as a "black belt" change agent. Often internal or external consultants serve as the change facilitators.

Redesign projects frequently require at least a part-time change facilitator and reengineering projects almost always require them. This person will provide change training for the PIT team members and targets, provide MOC guidance, coordinate change initiatives, and evaluate effectiveness. Significant previous change experience is a must for this role. The change facilitators are often called *change consultants*.

Training for PIT Members to Fulfill Their Roles Effectively

We have already discussed various evaluation tools, such as the *Sponsor Evaluation* and *the Change Knowledge Assessment*. We have also mentioned the importance of providing training and/or coaching to help the team members strengthen any areas of weakness these tools may have revealed. The PIT should work with someone who is skilled in the MOC methodology to be sure that members are trained and have the skills to execute the MOC concepts. If this is the first time that PIT members have undertaken a process redesign project, a change facilitator is often used to supply this service. Knowledge of change management principles will help the PIT members understand the implementation risks associated with their projects and create appropriate change management strategies and plans. High-level change management education should have been provided prior to the establishment of any specific change project. Now that specific projects have been identified, it's the time to provide more specific education and training.

For example, PIT members will need to appreciate the impact of a very compressed timeline on the change process. One aspect of resilience is the ability to assimilate a high rate of change. The process redesign methodology is fast-paced, going from project identification to implementation in a matter of weeks, not months or years. This pace puts a premium not only on the resilience that the organization has nurtured, but also on project-specific change management plans. The impact of future shock that creates high levels of dysfunctional behavior must be avoided at all costs.

PIT members also need to understand the instruments and tools available to them, both to understand project-specific risks and to develop mitigation strategies and plans. Knowing which tools to use at which stage and how to use them will make their job much easier.

Typical tools that all PIT members must be skilled in using include:

- ▶ *Change History Survey*
- ▶ *Implementation Problems Assessment*
- ▶ *Predicting the Impact of Change*
- ▶ *Sponsor Evaluation*
- ▶ *Change Agent Evaluation*
- ▶ *Role Map Application Tool*
- ▶ Techniques for Managing Resistance

MOC Applied to Phase I, Activity 6: Box in the Process

You can improve your creativity by learning about and using tools that help you see and understand the world from new perspectives.

When the preliminary process boundaries were defined in Activity 4, we suggested developing a preliminary Role Map diagram to help identify all the people who will be affected. Role Map diagrams should be thought of as living documents, continually being refined as new information becomes available. Once the process is boxed in, we will have a more clear understanding of just what the process includes and does not include. This is the time, then, to make the first modifications to the Role Map diagrams. Be sure to include in the map anyone whose behavior will need to change or who will be impacted by the change. Since boxing in the process helps to identify all the inputs and outputs to the process, don't forget to include corporate staff people, suppliers, customers, subcontractors, and the like. Also, now is the time to begin specifically identifying sustaining sponsors and advocates, since their commitment and support are crucial to successful implementation.

Communications Revisited

One of the first and most critical tasks of the PIT is to design and implement a comprehensive, project-specific communication plan. The key elements of such a plan were defined in Chapter 4.

Earlier communications were necessarily general and addressed the organization's need to improve, a vision of the future, and what improvement will mean to the organization and its people. Now that specific projects have been identified, there is an opportunity and a need to build on those earlier communications. Tell people as soon as possible the scope of the project and why it was selected. Many questions will arise. What are the improvement objectives? Are we trying to reduce cycle time? If so, by how much? Are we trying to reduce costs? Reduce the number of people? If so, how will that affect me? Will I lose my job? Will I be transferred? Will I have to do a different job? Do I have the skills that will be needed? Will I have a new boss?

The plan should address, at minimum, the "What's in it for ....?" questions:

- ▶ What's in it for me?
- ▶ What's in it for the organization?
- ▶ What's in it for us?
- ▶ What's in it for them?

Some of these questions will be impossible to answer at this early stage, when the specific changes have not yet been identified. But it's important to appreciate the concerns that people will have, address those that can be answered immediately, and let people know when and how they will be informed about these things. Also, identify the process owners and PIT members, so they will know whom to contact for further information. There is nothing that will feed people's resistance more than feeling that not only are they powerless to influence their future, but they don't know what is going to happen—fear of the unknown.

Keep in mind that there are three populations with which you need to maintain communications: the people to be affected immediately, the people to be affected only later, and the people not likely to be affected at all. Now is a good time to put at ease those who are not likely to be affected and to give the others a sense of when and how they will be affected by the changes.

Another major objective of early communications is to keep good people, to prevent them from leaving as soon as they get wind of change. Very close and regular communications with these people can go a long way toward retaining their much-needed skills. Talk with them early and often about the opportunities the change will create for them and about any specific retention plans that have been put in place.

Lance Dublin, chairman and CEO of The Dublin Group of San Francisco, stated in *Quality*, August 1998 ("Smooth Sailing in a Sea of Change"), "Companies confuse propaganda with communication. They think if they just talk at people enough, people will embrace the change. That's a big mistake, because you need two-way communication so people can find a way to get committed to the change."

MOC Applied to Phase I, Activity 7: Establish Measurements and Goals

The biggest change needed during this activity is in the minds of the PIT members themselves, who typically have thought of measurement only from their own limited perspective, their own part of the process. They focus on micro measurements because that has been their frame of reference. It's the job of the process owner to lead PIT members to a new and broader focus—macro measurements of the total process.

Measurements start with effectiveness, efficiency, and adaptability. For our purposes, effectiveness includes not only the effectiveness of the process being improved, but also effectiveness in implementing the change. Was it completed on time and within budget? Does it meet defined performance objectives? What were the levels of conformance? How are we going to measure the behavior necessary to achieve project objectives?

The introduction of measurements is frequently a significant change issue in itself. Resistance to measurement is common and comes from many sources. Concerns frequently expressed include the following: Why start measuring now? Wasn't my work good enough?

Fast enough? How is the data going to be used? Is the measurement system fair? Why waste time measuring when I could be doing the work? Will measurement highlight my weaknesses? Why measure the process now when we're going to change it anyway?

Your communications plan and change management plan should therefore anticipate these reactions and treat measurement itself as a potential change issue to be specifically addressed.

Setting radical breakthrough goals (reductions of 30% to 60%) for the key measurements often causes another cultural shock. Most people are used to improvement goals of 3% to 5% per year. At times they may strive to meet a 10% improvement goal in one year. Now, all of a sudden, the PIT is expected to define how the process can be improved 30% to 60% in the next 12 weeks. (Example: Reduce the cost of performing the process from $60,000 to $30,000 per week.) Often many of the people in the PIT will be thinking, "If the process can be improved that much, doesn't that mean that we've been doing a poor job all along?" Often we hear comments like "You cannot make that kind of improvement in the process the way we run our business." Our answer to this is "Yes, you are right. You cannot have breakthrough the way you are operating today. We will need to change our approach to the way we do business radically to get radical improvements."

Setting ambitious breakthrough improvement goals for the key measurements requires a great deal of work on the part of the process owner to get all of the PIT members to sign up for these aggressive goals. A key part of the MOC process is convincing the PIT members that radical improvement in the process is not only feasible but attainable.

MOC Applied to Phase I, Activity 8: Develop Project and Change Management Plans

MOC plans (MOCP) are evolving documents. A high-level plan should be included in the first iteration of the project plan, then reiterated in more detail during later phases, as more information is obtained. Remember that the entire timeline is compressed, so you can't wait until Phase III to begin developing your MOCP. It's important to think ahead and conduct change activities on a just-in-time basis. The MOCP at this point is primarily directed at the MOC activities in Phases I, II, and III.

The MOC plan must take into account the way that targets perceive the change. Do they perceive it as a positive or a negative?

Typical changes that many employees might perceive as positive include:

► Ones that add more people to the process
► Ones that reduce overtime, but not headcount
► Ones that will increase the amount of money people receive
► Ones that provide a bigger and better work environment

Typical changes that employees might perceive as negative include:

► Ones that increase their workload
► Ones that cut costs
► Ones that reduce headcount
► Ones that change the organization structure
► Ones that require less skill to do the job
► Ones that require more skill to do the job
► Ones that provide better measurement of the work the individual is performing

However, you cannot make assumptions about how an individual target will perceive a particular change. What one person perceives as a positive, another may perceive as a negative. For example, people sometimes see a reduction in force as positive because they are already looking for an opportunity to change jobs or because they know they will be retained and the reduction will give them new opportunities within the organization when others are laid off. But few will be candid enough to admit their self-interest, particularly when it appears to be at the expense of another.

Typical cycles of response to both positively and negatively perceived change were discussed in Chapter 2. Since different people view projects differently, effective MOC plans will design diverse approaches to respond to resistance, whether it results from emotional response or from actual negative impact on the individual. Remember: a positive emotional response to change does not mean that there is an absence of disruption. Even those big changes we see as good (getting a new baby, a new job with greater responsibilities, etc.) take energy and time, so we all resist on some level, if only by becoming physically tired. There will still be resistance. Remember that even changes that the individual views as positive have a bail-out point in the cycle.

A change management plan developed at this stage should:

▶ Address how to avoid the dysfunctional characteristics of future shock

▶ Call for "soberly selling" the change to prepare people for informed pessimism

▶ Address all the key elements of change as a process (pain, remedy, and vision)

▶ Outline how to develop and maintain synergistic relationships

The project plan should also include a vision statement that paints a picture of how the future-state process will function. It should not include the process improvement goals. In some cases, this vision statement is not prepared until the flow chart for the process is prepared in Phase II, Activity 1, because the PIT may not understand the present process well enough to define the process vision statement at this point in the process redesign cycle. You can evaluate each plan using the MOC *Implementation Plan Evaluation*.

Remember that the MOC plan is an integral part of the project plan, not a stand-alone plan. It must change as the project plan changes. Figure 6-9 is a sample MOC timeline chart that is included in the project plan.

Appendix B contains a typical MOC timeline project plan of the four phases of a process redesign project.

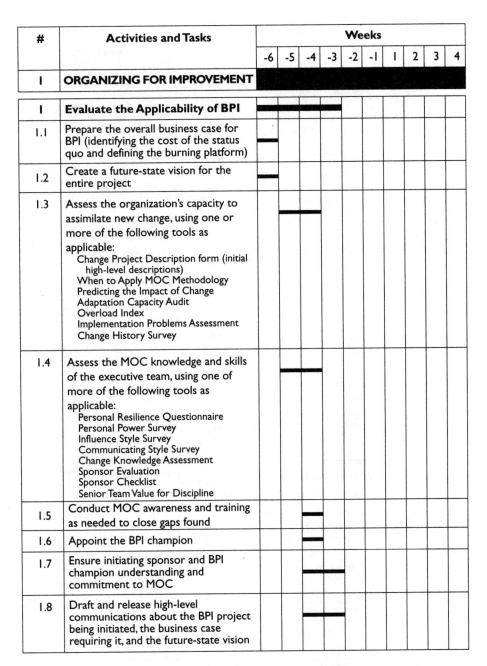

#	Activities and Tasks	Weeks									
		-6	-5	-4	-3	-2	-1	1	2	3	4
I	**ORGANIZING FOR IMPROVEMENT**										
1	**Evaluate the Applicability of BPI**										
1.1	Prepare the overall business case for BPI (identifying the cost of the status quo and defining the burning platform)										
1.2	Create a future-state vision for the entire project										
1.3	Assess the organization's capacity to assimilate new change, using one or more of the following tools as applicable: Change Project Description form (initial high-level descriptions) When to Apply MOC Methodology Predicting the Impact of Change Adaptation Capacity Audit Overload Index Implementation Problems Assessment Change History Survey										
1.4	Assess the MOC knowledge and skills of the executive team, using one of more of the following tools as applicable: Personal Resilience Questionnaire Personal Power Survey Influence Style Survey Communicating Style Survey Change Knowledge Assessment Sponsor Evaluation Sponsor Checklist Senior Team Value for Discipline										
1.5	Conduct MOC awareness and training as needed to close gaps found										
1.6	Appoint the BPI champion										
1.7	Ensure initiating sponsor and BPI champion understanding and commitment to MOC										
1.8	Draft and release high-level communications about the BPI project being initiated, the business case requiring it, and the future-state vision										

FIGURE 6-9. Typical MOC timeline chart for Phase I of a process redesign project (continued on pages 210-212)

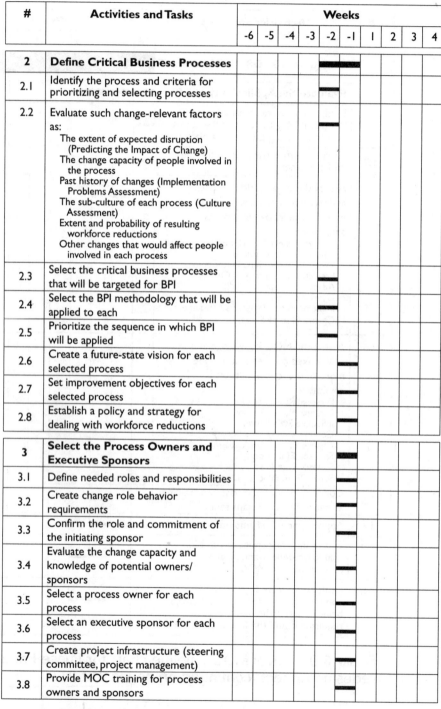

#	Activities and Tasks	Weeks									
		-6	-5	-4	-3	-2	-1	1	2	3	4
2	**Define Critical Business Processes**					▬▬					
2.1	Identify the process and criteria for prioritizing and selecting processes					▬					
2.2	Evaluate such change-relevant factors as: The extent of expected disruption (Predicting the Impact of Change) The change capacity of people involved in the process Past history of changes (Implementation Problems Assessment) The sub-culture of each process (Culture Assessment) Extent and probability of resulting workforce reductions Other changes that would affect people involved in each process					▬					
2.3	Select the critical business processes that will be targeted for BPI					▬					
2.4	Select the BPI methodology that will be applied to each					▬					
2.5	Prioritize the sequence in which BPI will be applied					▬					
2.6	Create a future-state vision for each selected process						▬				
2.7	Set improvement objectives for each selected process						▬				
2.8	Establish a policy and strategy for dealing with workforce reductions						▬				
3	**Select the Process Owners and Executive Sponsors**						▬▬				
3.1	Define needed roles and responsibilities						▬				
3.2	Create change role behavior requirements						▬				
3.3	Confirm the role and commitment of the initiating sponsor						▬				
3.4	Evaluate the change capacity and knowledge of potential owners/sponsors						▬				
3.5	Select a process owner for each process						▬				
3.6	Select an executive sponsor for each process						▬				
3.7	Create project infrastructure (steering committee, project management)						▬				
3.8	Provide MOC training for process owners and sponsors						▬				

FIGURE 6-9. (continued)

#	Activities and Tasks	Weeks									
		-6	-5	-4	-3	-2	-1	1	2	3	4
4	**Define Preliminary Boundaries**							■			
4.1	Define the preliminary scope of each process/project							■			
4.2	Create a preliminary Role Map diagram							■			
4.3	Create preliminary communications about the project							■			
5	**Form and Train the Process Improvement Team**							■	■		
5.1	Define required team member competencies, skills, resilience, etc.							■			
5.2	Process owner block diagram each process to the department level							■			
5.3	Meet with each affected department manager							■			
5.4	Select a PIT team member from each affected department							■			
5.5	Select additional PIT team members as needed (experts, customers, etc.)								■		
5.6	Select a change facilitator if warranted by the magnitude of the change								■		
5.7	Create a PIT charter								■		
5.8	Identify PIT member's existing skills and competencies, etc. using Sponsor Evaluation Change Knowledge Assessment								■		
5.9	Create a training plan to close the gap								■		
5.10	Conduct training and assess results							■	■		
6	**Box In the Process**										■
6.1	Clarify process/project scope–what is included and excluded?										■
6.2	Update the Role Map diagram based on updated scope information										■
6.3	Update the communications plan based on updated scope information										■
6.4	Implement the communications plan										■

FIGURE 6-9. (continued)

#	Activities and Tasks	Weeks									
		-6	-5	-4	-3	-2	-1	1	2	3	4
7	**Establish Measurements and Goals**										▬
7.1	Determine the metrics to be applied to the process/project										▬
7.2	Establish goals for each metric										▬
7.3	Create a project-specific change management data base										▬
8	**Develop Project and Change Management Plans**										▬
8.1	Create or update the project mission statement										▬
8.2	Give clear statement of the business case (the burning platform)										▬
8.3	Develop a set of PIT operating guidelines										▬
8.4	Create individual member assignments										▬
8.5	Incorporate the process measurements established in Activity 7										▬
8.6	Incorporate the improvement goals for each process metric										▬
8.7	Identify key barriers										▬
8.8	Incorporate the current version of the Role Map diagram										▬
8.9	Evaluate the extent, causes and sources of potential resistance										▬
8.10	Create preliminary plan for Phases II and III										▬
8.11	Set timetables for completion of Phases II and III										▬
8.12	Identify resource requirements										▬
8.13	Assess the plan using the MOC Implementation Plan Evaluation										▬
8.14	Communicate the plan to affected employees										▬

FIGURE 6-9. (continued)

Phase II—Understanding the Process

Unfortunately, most business processes are not documented and, when they are, often the procedures are not followed. During Phase II, the process improvement team (PIT) will draw a current-state picture of the present process, analyze compliance with the present procedures, collect cost, cycle-time, and error data, and align the day-to-day activities with the procedures (see Figure 6-10). There are 14 major activities in this phase.

The purpose of Phase II is for the PIT to gain detailed knowledge of the processes and the matrices for cost, cycle time, processing time, error rates, etc. related to the process being studied and to validate the improvement objectives that were defined in Phase I. The flowchart and simulation model of the present process will be used as the primary working tools in defining the improvement activities.

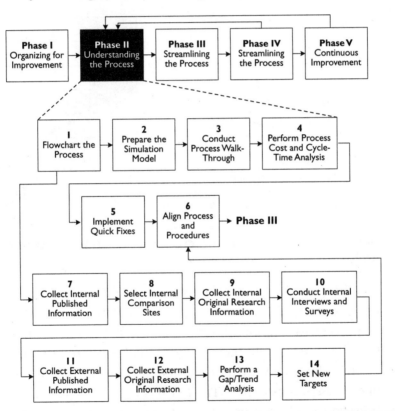

FIGURE 6-10. The 14 activities that make up Phases II and IIA

Applying MOC to Phase II

A groove can turn into a rut and a rut can become a grave.
    —ROBERT KRIEGER

It's time to stop working harder and start doing something different.

Now, let's go back and look at the six activities that took place during Phase II and determine how the management of change should be used during this part of the process redesign cycle. It is important to note that this phase will typically be completed in two to three weeks (Figure 6-11).

	5	6	7	8
1. Flowchart the process	■			
2. Prepare the simulation model	■	■		
3. Conduct the walk-through		■		
4. Perform process cost and cycle-time analysis		■	■	
5. Implement quick fixes			■	
6. Align process and procedures			■	■

FIGURE 6-11. **Typical timeline chart for Phase II of a process redesign project**

Although Phase II, Understanding the Current Process, lasts for a very short time, it's a crucial part of the MOC process. The PIT contacts employees throughout the process under study to discuss how they do their jobs and obtain their suggestions for improving the process.

Just think about where the redesign project is in the management of change process cycle. The PIT has not defined the future-state solution, so the change process has not entered into the transformation stage. From the employees' and management's point of view, nothing has changed except that there is a big cloud hanging over them and they are not sure what's going to happen to them.

An employee not sure what's going to happen next

The PIT and top management can talk in generalities, but the realities of the future-state solution cannot be defined until the end of Phase III. It's a time of uncertainty and doubt. Resistance to the change is strong, because no one knows enough about the upcoming change to decide if it will have a good or bad effect on him or her. Most people tend to resist changes that they do not understand. If managers handle the situation correctly, they can build confidence and trust. If they do not handle it correctly, a fifth column will form among the employees that will minimize the impact of the change upon the organization's performance. The major MOC focus during Phases II and III is on transforming resistance into support, at a minimum, or commitment when that is necessary to accomplish the project objectives. The first step begins with helping everyone to develop an open mind about upcoming changes.

Do you feel like you're in second gear and you're required to be going 100 miles per hour?
     —H. JAMES HARRINGTON

Applying MOC to the PIT

Don't forget to manage the change as it relates to the PIT. When the PIT members first come together, each member has his or her view and prejudice. Most of them join the PIT to protect the way the process now performs in their department or to get more resources. The general attitude that they have is "If my customers were realistic with their requirements, my suppliers lived up to their commitments, and we had 20% more resources, everything would work perfectly." Few if any of them understand the total process, nor do they even care. The biggest transformation that must take place during Phase II has to be in the PIT members themselves.

As the PIT starts flowcharting the process, usually this protective attitude becomes very apparent. When the engineering representative is defining the engineering part of the process, the manufacturing representative slips out to make a phone call and the industrial engineering representative scratches out a list of things that must be done before going home. When the manufacturing representative defines the manufacturing part of the process, the product engineering representative slips back to the office for a quick meeting and the sales representative reviews his or her e-mail. Everyone tends to overestimate the time required to do his or her job. The big MOC challenge is to transform this group of individuals with diverse interests who are focusing just on their subprocesses into a team of people who understand the total process and are each willing to compromise personal power for the good of the total process.

To bring about this transformation of each BPI member from cocoon to brilliant green and yellow butterfly is the most important job for the process owner in Phase II. To accomplish this, we suggest that the team meet eight hours or more a day during Phase II and that someone else be assigned to do the PIT members' assignments during this time period. In selecting the location for the PIT meetings, the advantage of being close to the process versus the advantages of fewer interruptions should be considered. In either case, the team members should strictly adhere to the PIT charter of conduct that was prepared in Phase I in terms of when members show up for meetings and what kind of interruptions are acceptable. In no case should cellular phones and pagers be allowed in the PIT meetings. During Phase II, the PIT assignment should be the only thing that the team members have on their minds. The organization should treat the team members as though they were on a fishing trip on a remote stream in Alaska.

When the PIT is flowcharting the process, have the person who knows that part of the process best describe the process. Have another team member flowchart the process. Select another person who has very little knowledge of the part of the process that's being discussed to flowchart the process.

This is a very effective way of stimulating questions and obtaining clarifications. Select another team member to record the critical estimated parameters related to each box on the flow chart. About every 30 minutes, have a fifth member of the PIT review the changes that have been made to the process flowchart. The object is to get as many people as possible actively involved in defining what goes on within the process. Every member of the PIT should be capable of discussing the details of the entire process by the time the process is totally flowcharted.

As the PIT prepares to conduct the process walk-through, it needs to be trained in the following areas:

▶ Effective listening skills
▶ Interviewing skills
▶ Nondirective communication
▶ Nonverbal communication
▶ Activity-based costing
▶ Establishing the burning platform

One skill that's very important for all of the PIT members but usually underdeveloped is interviewing. This is particularly true of technically oriented people.

As the process walk-through teams are formed, be sure that no more than one member of each team is an expert in the area being studied. Even then, the expert should serve as the recorder and the other members of the process walk-through team should be the interviewers. This ensures that the other members of the team understand the activity in detail and the person who knows the most about that part of the total process can point out after the meeting any critical points that were overlooked.

After completing the process walk-through for an individual department, the walk-through team should sit down with the influencing targets (targets who are the unofficial leaders in the department), review its findings, and ask them to add any comments and/or clarifications that they might have related to the data collected. Then, the team should sit down with the department manager and review all of its findings to ensure that nothing was misunderstood.

By the time the simulation model is updated to reflect the information collected during the process walk-through, all of the members of the PIT should have an excellent understanding of the total process.

Now, management must answer the question, "What's in it for the PIT members?" Surely, each member of the PIT is an important member of the organization and they were selected based upon their personal knowledge of the process, so they don't have to worry about losing their jobs. In addition, the organization has spent a great deal of time and effort widening their view of the organization. As a result, these are individuals who open up new career opportunities after the future-state solution is implemented. Many of the PIT members enjoy the process redesign activities so much that they want to do it again and make excellent facilitators for other PITs. Other PIT members become good second-level managers because of their increased knowledge of the business operations. Some of the PIT members are happy to be part of a team that improved the process's performance and want to go back to work in the improved process. At this point, management can show what's in it for the PIT members only by expressing sincere appreciation for their efforts and assuring them that they will be an important part of the new process and the organization. To do this, each PIT member's manager should sit down with his or her employee at the end of Phase II and find out what the employee would like to do when the redesign project is completed.

The Three S's—Sustaining Sponsor Support

Lou Gerstner, CEO of IBM, stated in *Management Review*, September 1997, "Change isn't something you do by memos. You have got to involve people's bodies and souls if you want your change effort to work."

Sustaining sponsor support during this phase is absolutely critical to the success of the project. A single casual, negative remark from a sustaining sponsor can do irreparable damage to the project. Each sustaining sponsor has his or her own agenda and degree of commitment to the project. The emotions can range all the way from complete belief that the redesign project is necessary for the organization to survive to fear that the redesign project will eliminate his or her job and put him or her in the unemployment line. Typical emotions are:

1. I am not for it. It's bad for me, but I'm going to do it because the boss told me I must. However, I'll look for a way to show him or her that it was a bad decision.
2. I am not for it, but I'll do it because the boss wants it done.
3. This too will pass. I can wait it out.
4. I'll support it, because if I don't it will be bad for me.
5. This cannot do any harm and it may do some good.
6. Supporting it will make me look good.
7. This has worked in other places; it should work here.
8. This will be good for the organization.
9. This will be good for the organization and me.
10. This is great. We should have done it sooner.

We have seen sustaining sponsors at all 10 levels who have agreed to assume the role and have been trained to do it. It's easy to see that the sustaining sponsor's attitude will have a significant impact on the targets who report to him or her. It's not enough to act the part of a sustaining sponsor. He or she must live it. They must walk the talk: employees listen to the tongue in your mouth, but they really believe when the tongue in your shoe communicates the same message. The PIT should look at the Role Map diagram and evaluate each sustaining sponsor's level of commitment to the project. The *Sponsor Evaluation* is used to assess his or her strength as a sponsor. It's simply a matter of observing if each sponsor is reflecting the kind of behavior and attitude desired in each stage of the commitment model (previously discussed) and then working with him or her to progress to a higher stage, if needed (see Figure 6-12).

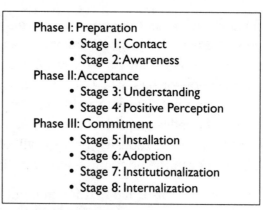

FIGURE **6-12. Commitment model**

Figure 6-13 depicts the pluses and minuses for each stage in the commitment model.

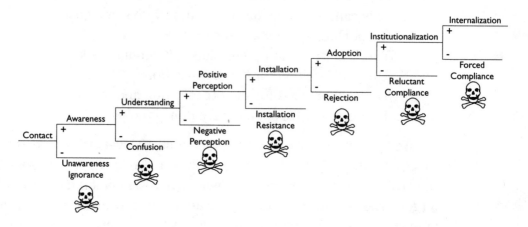

FIGURE **6-13. Stages in the commitment model: pluses and minuses**

The PIT members should then evaluate each sustaining sponsor in terms of his or her responsibilities related to the process under study and the impact that the targets who report to him or her have on the process. Based upon this analysis, the PIT should define the degree of commitment that is required from the individual to perform as a sustaining sponsor. In some cases, it's enough to be committed to the point that the sustaining sponsor would do the job because he or she is told to do the job by a higher-level manager (installation). Other sustaining sponsors on the same project must believe that the project is essential to the organization and themselves if the sustaining sponsors and the organization are going to move forward (internalization).

A third factor is then considered. This factor is the phase and activity in the process redesign project in which the individual sustaining sponsor must reach the required commitment level. In most cases, the sponsor must reach this level of commitment in Phase II before the process walk-through. But in some of the supporting areas (such as information systems, industrial engineering, and maintenance), the sponsor need not reach the required commitment level until just before his or her group gets involved in the redesign process. Sometimes this is as late as Phase IV. The commitment information is then combined (see Figure 6-14).

Name	Commitment		When Required?		Status
	Now	**Required**	**Phase**	**Step**	**Plus or Minus**
Bob T.	Installation	Internalization	I	4	-
Jen K.	Awareness	Adoption	II	2	-
Ruth M.	Institutionalization	Installation	IV	I	+
Jane H.	Understanding	Adoption	II	2	-
Marguerite H.	Positive Perception	Internalization	III	2	-
Bob M.	Awareness	Adoption	II	10	-
Tom A.	Adoption	Adoption	II	2	0
Tia K.	Contact	Internalization	II	2	-

FIGURE 6-14. Sustaining sponsor commitment analysis

For all of the sustaining sponsors who are not at the required level, a plan needs to be developed to help change their attitudes toward the project. In addition, the PIT should plan on helping them interface with the targets. High priority should be placed on the sustaining sponsors who directly interface with the employees in departments that will be part of the walk-through process. Be sure that a strong advocate is assigned to work with every sustaining sponsor whose commitment level is low.

New Process Vision

At the end of Phase I, the PIT has defined the objectives for the process redesign project but does not have enough information and knowledge to prepare a new process vision statement. At the end of Phase II, Activity 1, the PIT should prepare a preliminary vision statement. By the end of Phase II, all of the PIT members should understand the as-is process and its problems so that they will be able to prepare the final comprehensive vision statement that defines the new process design specification. The content of the vision statement plays an important part of the target's decision process. If the perceived pain related to the future vision statement isn't much less than the pain related to the as-is process, the employees will resist the change, greatly increasing the risk of failure. In truth, the vision statement is prepared more to provide the targets with an understanding of the new process than to provide guidance to the PIT. Most of the time, the PIT prepares the vision statement to communicate its objectives to management. This is a misuse of the vision statement, as the objectives that were prepared in Phase I fulfilled this need. As the PIT members prepare the mission statement, they should ask themselves, "When the targets read this, will they perceive the new process as much better for them than the present process?" If the answer is no, then the PIT may want to reconsider its process redesign strategy, because if the mission statement is not changed there will be a great deal of resistance to implementing the redesigned process.

Signs of a powerful vision:

- ▶ People are talking about it informally.
- ▶ The vision is reflected in new behaviors.
- ▶ Decisions are made and then they happen.
- ▶ People feel empowered to make decisions.
- ▶ Some employee enthusiasm exists.
- ▶ Clients are aware that something is different and better.

The bottom line is that change is only climatic when you don't know where you're going.
—CELESTIAL SEASONINGS, INC.

As-Is Process Pain

By the end of the process walk-through, the PIT has collected the data required to truly define the pain related to the as-is process as perceived by employees. The PIT needs to package this information so that it can be presented to the targets and management. The as-is pain as viewed by the employees is only a part of the pain related to the as-is process. The other part of the as-is pain is the lost opportunity pain that will result if the as-is process is not changed. The PIT must define the negative future impacts that will occur if the process is not changed (e.g., lost sales, excess inventory, inability to meet production requirements). Often, the lost opportunity pain far exceeds the present pain as viewed by the employees and management. The PIT will then combine the as-is pain and the lost opportunity pain to develop a picture of the total pain related to the current process.

Use the Right Words

The way the PIT, sustaining sponsors, and change agents talk about the redesign project has a big impact upon the targets. Realize that the typical employee believes that the only objective of a reengineering and redesign project is to eliminate his or her job. Employees may not say so, but that's what they're thinking. Is it any wonder that they are upset and have a tendency to blow the smallest comment out of proportion?

Most redesign projects have as one objective to reduce cost. To your employees, this means working harder and fewer employees doing the work. When the PIT or the sustaining sponsors share the objective of the redesign process with the employees as reducing product cost, reducing cycle time, and improving quality, it immediately reinforces the employees' fears. We like changing the objective of *reducing product cost* to *improving value added per employee*. It means the same thing, but focuses on the employees as adding value to the process; everyone wants to do work that is valued. Talk about eliminating bureaucracy. Why? Because everyone hates bureaucracy. Talk about making the process work better for the employees and making better use of their efforts. Don't talk about eliminating non-value-added activities. Talk about increasing the percentage of effort devoted to real-value-added activities. The way the future change is positioned verbally is very important to gaining acceptance by targets.

Targets

All people will resist change, but it's important to note that the degree of resistance will vary from person to person. This different reaction to the same change is because each individual evaluates the change based upon his or her past experiences, wants, beliefs, prejudices, hopes, fears, needs, and the information that is available.

Ernst & Young typically sees five types of reaction to change:

1. **Believers**—People who think, "If it's good for the whole organization, I'll go along with it because the organization has taken care of me and it will continue to do so." These are the people that salespeople love. If they find the place, they can buy almost anything. On a scale of 1 to 10, believers have a resistance rating of 1.
2. **Joiners**—People who want to know how the change will impact them and will go along with the change unless it has a significant negative impact on them or when it's in their best interest to go along with the change. They have a resistance rating of 3.

3. **Uncommitted**—People who sit on the fence and can be easily swayed in either direction based on the opinions of the key people they work with. At one point, they can be in favor of the change and then, a short time later, opposed to it. These people are not ready to take a position. They will sometimes look like joiners and sometimes like skeptics. They don't agree, but they don't disagree. When talking about the change, they often express the opposite point of view. They like to be in the position that allows them, after the change is implemented, to say, "See, I told you so." They are easily swayed by the joiners or the skeptics. They usually take a final position based upon the majority position or the position taken by someone that they respect. They have a resistance rating of 5.

4. **Skeptics**—People who feel they don't understand the change well enough to be sure that it's good for them. They usually believe that management is holding back data on the next impact of the change or they don't believe the change will produce the stated results. They like things as they are. They will try to convince the uncommitted and the joiners to agree with them. They have a resistance rating of 8.

   To modify a statement by John Kenneth Galbraith, "Faced with the choice between changing one's mind and proving that there is no need to do so, the skeptic gets busy on the proof."

   Ronnie Shakes captured the thinking of the skeptic with the following line: "I was going to buy a copy of *The Power of Positive Thinking*, but then I thought, 'What the hell good would that do?'"

5. **Naysayers**—People who fight change. It makes no difference if it's good or bad. Ogden Nash expressed the beliefs of a naysayer when he said, "Progress (change) might have been all right once, but it has gone on too long." Naysayers have a resistance rating of 10.

The objective is to get all the targets to be believers, but a project can succeed with a small percentage of the people in the other four categories. To succeed, you will need at least 80% of the targets in categories 1, 2, and 3. You cannot be successful if a naysayer holds any key position. It's primarily the sustaining sponsor's responsibility to break down the resistance of the targets who report to him or her and to make believers out of them. The pain management tool is most frequently used for this task. The sustaining sponsor is not required to accomplish this transformation alone. The PIT members also help in this transformation.

Jonathan Kozol provides a key thought for targets who are faced with a change that they don't like: "Pick battles big enough to matter and small enough to win."

Influencing Targets

In every organization there are formal leaders and informal leaders. In most departments there's someone who serves as the informal leader. Other employees look to this person and value his or her opinions. Management does not legitimize the position of informal leader. This is an individual whom the other employees greatly trust and respect because of his or her deeds. For example, if Joe says it's good, the rest of the employees go along with it because Joe knows, and if Mary thinks it's bad, everyone will jump in to discuss how bad it is. We call these informal leaders *influencing targets*. It should be the objective of all the PIT members to move these influencing targets to be advocates as well as targets.

Influencing Targets—A nonmanagement member of a group who sways other members of the group as a result of the trust and respect that they have for that person.

The PIT must identify the influencing targets in each department that is involved in the process and develop a plan to win their support of the redesign project before the process walk-through begins in that department (Phase II, Activity 3). Things that will typically help involve the influencing targets are:

▶ Ask them to review and comment on the flow diagram as it is being developed in Phase II, Activity 1.

▶ Have them assigned to coordinate the walk-through activities in their department.

▶ Schedule them to participate in the design experiments conducted in Phase II, Activity 4.

▶ Have them comment on the walk-through questionnaire.

▶ Use them as key communication contact points.

▶ Ask them to provide input on problems related to the present process and how to correct those problems.

▶ When faced with a situation you can't change, it's time to change the way you handle it.

Change Agents

The job description of change agents has them deal only with the implementation of MOC concepts, which are by nature very people-oriented. The task of change agents is very difficult because often the same person plays both a technical implementation role and a change agent's role. In that case, the person playing both roles has to be effective at handling three factors:

▶ Technology
▶ Processes
▶ People

One of the major reasons for process redesign failures is process designers and implementers who are unable to handle the people side of the equation. In some redesign projects, an individual will be assigned to serve as a change agent only. In most cases, the process designer will need to wear a technical hat at one point in time and a change agent hat at another time. In reality, most of the process designers need to have an excellent understanding of the MOC tools.

At the start of Phase II, all change agents identified on the Role Map diagram should complete a change agent attitude survey to help identify areas where the change agents need to improve. When the surveys have

Wearing more than one hat

been analyzed, the results should be presented to the change agents as a group and to each change agent individually as the survey relates to him or her. Plans need to be developed to correct any inadequacy.

MOC and the Process Walk-Through

The process walk-through provides a unique opportunity to gain in-depth understanding of the process and the people who make it function. It also provides an excellent opportunity to involve the targets in the process redesign. The PIT needs to consider the process walk-through as a two-way learning experience. The PIT members learn about the process and the targets gain understanding about why the process is being redesigned and what the redesign process is all about.

To help the targets gain understanding and to get their involvement, the PIT should start the process walk-through in a department by holding a department meeting. During this meeting, the team should review the process flowchart, placing particular emphasis on parts of the process that flow through that department. The department member should be asked to comment on the flowchart based upon his or her understanding of how the activities are really done. At this meeting, the PIT should explain what will take place during the process walk-through and how the data that are collected will be used. We have often made a game out of it by having all of the department members estimate the average cycle time through their department. Then, after the data are collected, a prize is given to the individual who gave the most accurate estimate. Also, during this meeting the PIT should pass out copies of the process walk-through checksheet so that the employees can comment on it and prepare for their upcoming process walk-through interviews.

During the individual interviews, the process walk-through team should encourage each employee to define the problems related to the process as he or she sees them and to recommend ways to improve his or her job. In addition, the PIT should also ask how to eliminate the problems that he or she defines. The PIT should be very obvious when it records the individual problems and recommendations so that the employee knows that the team is listening to his or her ideas.

The process walk-through is an important part of the pain management activities, since it probes the targets for problems that they're having with the current process. The process walk-through team will work with the targets to help them to surface the pain related to the current state.

In addition, the process walk-through team needs to explain to the targets the anticipated pain that will result if the process remains the same. (Example: "If we don't reduce the cycle time by at least 40%, our market share will be cut in half because our competition's cycle time is already 30% less than our cycle time. If we don't change, we estimate that our orders will drop by 50% and we will have to lay off 30 people due to lack of work and funds.")

The process walk-through team should also point out opportunities that will occur as a result of improving the process. (Example: "If we could decrease our cycle time by 60%, we would double our market share, which would give us all an additional one-month bonus at the end of the year.")

The process walk-through team should also provide the individual targets with the vision of how the process will operate after the future-state solution is implemented. This allows the targets to weigh the difference between the as-is process pain and the future-state process pain. This puts the targets in a much better position to decide whether or not to support the project. These one-on-one discussions can go a long way toward breaking down the walls of resistance that the targets have put around themselves. It's very important that the visions and pain picture painted by the process walk-through team be in complete harmony with the messages that the sustaining sponsors have communicated to the targets.

Also during the process walk-through, the walk-through teams need to define the subculture or what we would like to call the "personality" of each department. The organization has a culture based upon its goals, beliefs, and behavioral patterns. But within that culture, each department takes on a personality that reflects the manager's general perspective and his or her view of how the culture of the organization applies to his or her area.

In Tom's department, for example, schedules are sacred. He has never missed the committed delivery date. He's very willing to sacrifice quality and cost to meet schedules. In Mary's department, all decisions are made by teams. She requires that everyone agree with a decision; a majority vote is not enough. In Dave's department, every new activity needs to have a value proposition prepared for it before Dave will even consider it. If it doesn't improve his department's value-added per employee, he will not get his department involved.

The culture of the organization is one thing; the behavior in individual departments is driven by the personality of the formal leader of the department. As the walk-through team interviews people from each department and reviews the process activities for which the department is responsible, it needs to define the personality of the department (behaviors, beliefs, roles). The process can be designed to conform to the organizational culture and yet be totally unacceptable in a specific department because it does not fit with the personality of that department.

After collecting all the data from the process walk-through and putting them into the simulation model, the team should hold a second department meeting, to review the findings and suggestions made by members of the department. At this meeting, the team should highlight quick fixes (Phase II, Activity 5) that result from suggestions by department members.

Personnel Planning and the MOC

Typically, a process redesign project will result in a 30% to 60% reduction in the number of employees required for the process. This means that a plan is needed that defines what will be done with the surplus employees. The easy, inhumane answer is to just lay them off, but that's probably the last resort for social and business reasons.

Socially, the organization has an obligation to the employees who have helped the organization develop and progress. From a business standpoint, the organization has invested thousands of dollars in training and indoctrinating each of the employees. Dow Chemical, for example, estimates that it costs between $30,000 and $100,000 to lay off and replace a technical or managerial employee (*Total Improvement Management*, H. James Harrington and James S. Harrington). In addition, how can you expect employees to give freely of their ideas if employee ideas result in layoffs? The executive committee should go on record with a statement similar to the following one:

No one will be laid off as a result of the process redesign projects. Employees whose jobs are eliminated will be assigned to equivalent or higher-level jobs.

The authors know of a company that had a surplus of 63 employees and, instead of laying off anyone, had a contest to select 63 employees to go to the local university to study engineering subjects. The company paid their full salary, tuition, and book costs and required the students to maintain a B grade average. At the end of one year, all the students had been put back to work in value-added jobs. In addition, 58 out of the 63 continued night school and earned engineering degrees.

Right Associates conducted a survey of 909 organizations that downsized over a five-year period, to define what action they had taken to minimize layoffs. Their findings are as follows:

- Hiring freeze   70%
- Restrict overtime   45%
- Retrain/redeploy   44%
- Switch to part time   22%
- Convert to consultants   11%
- Unpaid vacations   9%
- Shorter work week   9%
- Reduced pay   6%

Source: H. James Harrington, *The Down Side to Quality Improvement.*

MOC Project Plan for Process Redesign Phase II

Figure 6-15 presents a typical MOC project plan that is designed to support Phase II of a process redesign project.

Summary of MOC Activities in Phase II

Although Phase II lasts for about three weeks, a great deal of MOC activities must take place to prepare the organization to accept the

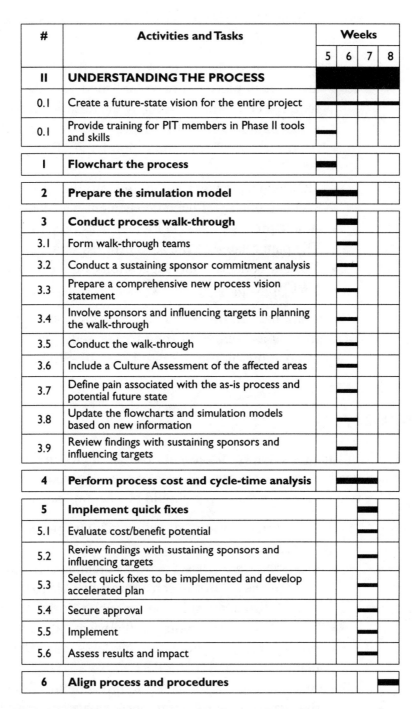

#	Activities and Tasks	Weeks			
		5	6	7	8
II	**UNDERSTANDING THE PROCESS**	■	■		
0.1	Create a future-state vision for the entire project	▬			
0.1	Provide training for PIT members in Phase II tools and skills	▬			
1	**Flowchart the process**	▬			
2	**Prepare the simulation model**	▬			
3	**Conduct process walk-through**		▬		
3.1	Form walk-through teams		▬		
3.2	Conduct a sustaining sponsor commitment analysis		▬		
3.3	Prepare a comprehensive new process vision statement		▬		
3.4	Involve sponsors and influencing targets in planning the walk-through		▬		
3.5	Conduct the walk-through		▬		
3.6	Include a Culture Assessment of the affected areas		▬		
3.7	Define pain associated with the as-is process and potential future state		▬		
3.8	Update the flowcharts and simulation models based on new information		▬		
3.9	Review findings with sustaining sponsors and influencing targets		▬		
4	**Perform process cost and cycle-time analysis**		▬	▬	
5	**Implement quick fixes**			▬	
5.1	Evaluate cost/benefit potential			▬	
5.2	Review findings with sustaining sponsors and influencing targets			▬	
5.3	Select quick fixes to be implemented and develop accelerated plan			▬	
5.4	Secure approval			▬	
5.5	Implement			▬	
5.6	Assess results and impact			▬	
6	**Align process and procedures**				▬

FIGURE 6-15. Typical MOC timeline plan for Phase II of process redesign project

drastic changes brought about by a process redesign project. Here are the highlights of the MOC activities completed in Phase II:

► Sustaining sponsors were classified by required commitment levels and plans were established to help them reach the required commitment level by the desired point in time. The targets' commitment to the change should be greatly increased.
► A correct vocabulary to support the MOC project was established.
► MOC concepts were integrated into the process walk-through.
► The personality of each department was defined.
► A new process vision statement was prepared.
► The pain related to the as-is process was completely defined.
► Targets' concerns and suggestions were compiled.
► MOC was applied to the PIT itself.

During Phase II, there should be a significant advancement in the MOC process as well as in the process redesign project. The PIT is now in a position to progress into Phase III--Streamlining the Process.

Summary

In Chapter 6 we've discussed how the MOC methodology should be used during the first two phases of a process redesign project. In these two phases, the following should be accomplished:

► The organization decides which processes should be redesigned.
► The organization assigns project teams called process improvement teams (PITs), which are responsible for developing a best-value future-state solution for each priority process.
► The PIT receives training in the basic MOC methodology.
► An as-is process simulation model is defined and documented, including measurement data.
► An MOC organizational structure is defined and each person in the structure is trained to perform his or her assigned tasks.

> ▸ A vision statement that defines the future-state process is pre-
> pared and discussed with the targets.
> ▸ The pain related to the present-state process is defined.

In Chapter 7 the PIT will apply MOC concepts while streamlining
the present process, developing a best-value future-state solution. A
future-state implementation team (FIT) will install the selected future-
state solution.

*A project is a lot like a three-legged stool, whose legs are process,
technology, and people. The project is only as strong as the weak-
est leg.*

References

Harrington, H. James, *Benchmarking Workbook* (New York: McGraw-Hill, 1997).

Harrington, H. James, *Business Process Improvement: The Break-through Strategy for Total Quality, Productivity, and Competitiveness* (New York: McGraw-Hill, 1991).

Harrington, H. James, *The Down Side to Quality Improvement*, Technical Report TR 92.001 HJH (San Jose CA: Ernst & Young LLP, 1992).

Harrington, H. James, and James S. Harrington, *Total Improvement Management: The Next Generation in Performance Improvement* (New York: McGraw-Hill, 1995).

Pritchett, Price, and Ron Pound, *The Employee Handbook for Organizational Change* (Dallas TX: Pritchett & Associates, Inc., 1995).

Pritchett, Price, and Ron Pound, *A Survival Guide to the Stress of Organizational Change* (Dallas TX: Pritchett & Associates, Inc., 1995).

7

Applying MOC to a Process Redesign Project—Phases III and IV

A process redesign approach will drive major organizational change.

Introduction

During Phase III, Streamlining the Process, the PIT will streamline the current-state process and develop a simulation model of the best-value future-state solution. When the executive committee approves the best-value future-state solution, a budget is prepared and a preliminary project plan is developed for implementing the future-state solution. This phase typically takes four to eight weeks to complete. Although Phase III is a highly technical phase, the impact of each change on the as-is process needs to be determined, in order to evaluate the way it will impact the targets and how the targets will react to this part of the total change. It's also a time when the PIT and sustaining sponsors need to continuously work to manage resistance to and build commitment for the changes to be implemented in Phase IV.

In Phase IV, a future-state implementation team (FIT) is formed. The FIT will prepare a final implementation plan, run the necessary pilot study, install the new process, and provide job-related training. From an MOC standpoint, this is where the real impact of the MOC program is measured. During Phase IV, the targets will go through the transformation stage and move into the future-state stage of the change process. By the end of Phase IV, the future-state process approved in Phase III becomes the current-state process. Basically, if the PIT has done a good job of MOC in Phases I, II, and III, during Phase IV the targets will be saying, "Let me show you how to make this work" instead of "Let me tell you why this will not work."

Phase III—Streamlining the Process

During Phase III of the process redesign project, the present process will be streamlined to reduce waste while reducing cycle time and making the process more effective. After the process is simplified, automation and information technology methods are applied to the new process to maximize the process's effectiveness, efficiency, and adaptability measurements.

Phase III is made up of five activities (see Figure 7-1):

► Apply the 12 streamlining tools.
► Perform a cost/benefits analysis.
► Select the best-value future-state solution.
► Obtain executive committee approval.
► Approve preliminary implementation plan.

Applying MOC to Phase III—Streamlining the Process

Now, let's look at the management of change activities that will be going on during the Phase III process. Typically, the Phase III process will take approximately four to eight weeks, depending on the complexity of the process being redesigned (see Figure 7-2). These are

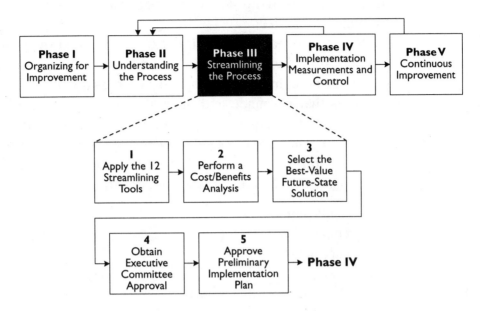

FIGURE 7-1. The five activities that make up Phase III

Phase III Activities	Week					
	9	10	11	12	13	14
1. Apply the 12 streamlining tools	▓	▓	▓	▓		
2. Perform a cost/benefits analysis		▓	▓	▓		
3. Select a FSS					▓	
4. Obtain executive committee approval						▓
5. Approve preliminary implementation plan					▓	

FIGURE 7-2. Phase III timeline chart

very key weeks in the MOC methodology. It's also a time when the PIT is very busy with the technical aspects of developing alternative future-state solutions and selecting the one that represents the best-value solution to the organization. It is very easy for the PIT members to get so wrapped up in designing the new process that they set aside their obligations to the MOC contents of the project plan. This is a sure formula for disaster.

Remember that in Phase I and II we provided the targets with a vision of how the new process would operate. Now, in Phase III, we need to be sure that we've designed a process that lives up to all of the promises that we made and implied when we presented the vision statement to the targets. It is also the time when the PIT must thoroughly understand and consider the process expectations of all of the process's stakeholders, so that the new process redesign lives up to these expectations. Typical stakeholders are:

- ▶ management
- ▶ employees
- ▶ suppliers
- ▶ customers
- ▶ stockholders (investors)
- ▶ the community in which the organization exists
- ▶ the employees' families

(Note: Review Figure 6-4 in Chapter 6 to see how the seven phases of the MOC methodology relate to Phases III and IV of the process redesign.)

Introduction to Applying MOC to Phase III

During the four to eight weeks of Phase III, the PIT develops the best-value future-state solution and the executive team approves it. Phase III is the second-longest phase cycle, even though there are usually no apparent changes taking place in the process. This is a period of uncertainty for all the people, both management and employees, who are engaged in the process. During this phase, the PIT will question many of the paradigms that the present process has been built upon. No one will know until the end of this phase what the new process will look like, how the organization will be structured, or which parts of the process will be outsourced. During this phase, the MOC activities need to assure everyone that the PIT is listening to their ideas and to help them prepare for the changes that will be required during Phase IV. There are a number of steps in the streamlining activities that can cause resistance to the change process if they are not managed correctly, including the following:

- Eliminate bureaucracy.
- Analyze non-value-added activities.
- Eliminate duplication.
- Simplify language.
- Restructure the organization.
- Use automation and mechanization.

In addition to these streamlining steps, the Managing Organizational Change activities will need to do the following:

- Communicate the as-is process pain and future process vision.
- Monitor sustaining sponsorship to prevent black holes from developing.
- Develop a change management plan to support the implementation of the best-value future-state solution.
- Upgrade the MOC Role Map diagrams to reflect new individuals and organizations added during the implementation phase.
- Evaluate the change agents' skill.

But the overriding MOC activity during this phase is a continuous effort to transform target resistance to support or commitment to the changes. The essential element is an effective two-way communication process, to help the targets express concerns, to elicit their active participation by welcoming and considering their suggestions, and to keep them informed about what is going on. Strengthening and maintaining sponsor commitment is also critical. The change agents, advocates, and sponsors who have sponsors reporting to them should reinforce sponsor commitment, since it is often subject to ebbs and flows due to other project commitments.

As the PIT starts Phase III, the future-state solution is uncertain, but it will evolve as the 12 simplification steps are applied to the as-is simulation model.

Managing Organizational Change and the 12 Simplification Steps

The way in which the 12 simplification steps are applied has a big impact on the way the change will be accepted by the targets. We will discuss the ones that have the biggest impact.

Eliminate Bureaucracy

The sustaining sponsors are the primary source of added bureaucracy. Bureaucracy is a key part of the way management controls businesses today and it often serves as a management security blanket. It is usually very hard for management to agree to drop bureaucratic activities, even when they cannot be justified. Each sustaining sponsor will be able to cite one or more instances when his or her signature saved the organization from getting into a problem. All of the sustaining sponsors should be introduced to the 12 simplification steps that will be used to streamline the as-is process. This will help them understand that all bureaucracy activities need to be cost-justified. This training is critical for keeping black holes from developing. It will also help prevent the sustaining sponsors from reacting negatively when they are required to cost-justify some of their personal activities and/or the activities of the departments they manage. Bureaucracy elimination is a cultural shock that often greatly upsets many managers. Top management needs to pave the way for this endeavor by communicating a strong desire to eliminate bureaucracy from every part of the organization.

Analyze Non-Value-Added Activities

No one wants to think that his or her activities are non-value-added, so be careful how you use this term. Tell a person that the job he or she has been doing so diligently for a number of years is a non-value-added activity and you're in for a fight. We've stopped using this term due to its negative impact on the change process. Use either "business-value-added" or "no-value-added" in place of "non-value-added." Still, be very careful when you use the term "no-value-added." People react just as negatively to the term "no-value-added" as they do to "non-value-added." We recommend limiting use of the term "no-value-added" to activities that even the employees doing the job would agree are no-value-added (e.g., movement, storage, and needless filing).

Eliminate Duplication

People keep duplicate records because they feel that a single database is not reliable or too hard to access or because they don't know about the other database. It is good practice to involve all the parties who maintain duplicate databases in determining how one database can serve everyone's needs. All the PIT needs to do is bring these parties together and facilitate the meeting. The PIT should let the individuals who are keeping duplicate records design the approach that will combine the databases.

Upgrade the Process

This step in the process-simplification cycle is directed at the equipment, facility, and layout of the work area. There are few things more personal to an individual than his or her work area. A flowchart may provide the PIT with an excellent view of the physical workflow, but it misses the whole social side of the business. The employees who will be occupying a work area should be involved in designing the area's layout and colors and selecting the equipment. When the user takes a position that one type of equipment is better than another, he or she will do everything possible to make that prediction a reality.

From the individual's standpoint, it can make a big difference whether the cabinet is to the right or left of the desk. Mary may want to sit beside Ruth because they fill in for each other during the lunch breaks to cover the phone. Joe wants to be located near Jane because Jane understands his job and helps him when he runs into a problem. Ruth does not want to sit near Jim because Jim talks too much and it causes her to make errors. If we put Ruth and Tom in the same area, we could eliminate one set of files.

Although we understand the need to standardize the work area, there's also a need to personalize it. We always go head to head with the office designer on this point. The office designer talks about "layout flow and harmony." We talk about establishing "personal activities islands." The question is, do you give everyone the same gray chair that costs $250 or do you allow everyone to have any chair that costs less than $250? The answer should come somewhere between these two extremes. Office designers tend to sacrifice office efficiency for office style. That's wrong. Why get all gray chairs when they will be almost totally covered up by people who wear different-colored clothes? Our studies indicate that the more you allow the employee to customize his or her work area, the more ownership he or she will have for making the new layout work. Remember that the average man or woman spends more time awake at work than at home.

Simplify Language

The language used in the documentation system is another place where the PIT may develop a great deal of resistance. Most people who write procedures are not good writers. They are usually process- or activity-related experts with good professional backgrounds. In college, they were taught how to write reports for highly technical professors so they could get A's. Typically, in that environment, brevity is not a virtue. As Rodney Dangerfield said in the 1986 movie, *Back to School*, when he picked up a two-inch-thick term paper that he'd paid someone to write for him, "It's too light. It feels like a C. Bulk it up and add a few multicolor graphs. Let's shoot for an A." With that type of background, it's often difficult for people to adapt their vocabulary and writing style to an environment where good writing is measured by how brief and understandable the document is to the people who use it.

Speak now or forever hold your peace."
—Everyman

It's important that the people selected to write procedures be well trained and understand the reasons for simplifying their writing. This can best be demonstrated by providing real examples. One way to measure the simplicity of a document is to have it read by someone who is at the same skill level as the people who will be performing the job but who is not acquainted with the process. Measure the length of time it takes the person to read the document and then have him or her explain the process and what needs to be done. Then, simplify the document and repeat the experiment with another person at the same skill level. The value of simplified language will soon become readily apparent. Most people, when they understand the value of simple writing, will be converted. A few will never make the transition. They should not be allowed to write procedures. The targets are more likely to accept your procedures if you keep the documentation simple and to the point. Use lots of pictures and short sentences. Minimize the use of words that are more than two syllables.

Use Automation and Mechanization

Applying information technology tools to the process provides many advantages to the organization—and many threats to the employees. Information technology (IT) has outrun many employees' skills in our businesses today. Often, the benefits touted by the information systems organizations are never realized. For example, in one office, everyone was provided with PCs to allow them to reduce the clerical support needed from six employees to three. One year later, two PC technicians were added to keep the PCs running, resulting in an increased cost because the salaries for the PC technicians were significantly higher than the salaries of the secretaries, let alone the additional time that was required for the staff to type their own correspondence rather than dictate it.

Information technology is a very important process improvement enabler, but it is often applied based upon the PIT's impression of what is state-of-the-art, not what is needed or what is in keeping with the targets' skills. Extreme care should be taken to ensure a good match between the technology and the skill level of the targets after they have been trained for that technology. To switch from one computer to another or from one program to another is a high-stress period for the targets and must be considered in managing change. This stress is minimized and, in many cases, even positively anticipated when the PIT is upgrading hardware or software. Be sure that the employees have a backup process to use when the IT system fails.

Don't let the techies drive your IT application. They have a tendency to put in complex IT systems that are more stressful for the target than helpful. The No. 1 rule in using IT solutions is "Keep it simple." Organizations in North America tend to take a simple process and make it overly complex by computerizing it. Compare, for example, Toyota's just-in-time system and the inventory control system used by General Motors.

Automation, on the other hand, presents a different problem. In this case, people are being replaced by machines. No one likes to be lose a job to a machine, even if the job is repetitive and monotonous. Great care should be taken to explain to the targets that the machines are freeing them up to do work that requires more skills and thought than their previous assignments.

Realign the Organization

The streamlining steps usually greatly simplify the process and reduce the number of people required to keep it running. As a result, many jobs are eliminated or combined, work product movement is reduced to a minimum, and activities that were previously performed in different locations in the organization are grouped together. This leads to changes in the organizational structure.

Organizational changes that affect the targets frequently diminish their ability to cope with the change. Employees in organizations that are doing a good management job will find reorganization particularly difficult. In these organizations, manager-employee relationships develop over time and the employees feel that the managers have a sincere interest in their careers and a good understanding of their abilities and accomplishments. The uncertainties and stress associated with being assigned to a new manager will last for upward of six months; if the new manager is not better than the old manager, the stress will last for years. We've consulted with an organization where the people are still saying, 10 years after a reorganization, such things as "They would not have done that to me if John was still my manager." Reorganization is often the straw that drives the targets into future shock. Great care should be taken to consider these stresses when the organizational structure is being defined and managers are being selected. When other process changes are already pushing targets close to future shock, it's best to keep the targets reporting to the same manager if possible. It's important to note that younger targets seem to handle organizational restructuring stress better than older employees.

Change-Resistance Assessment and Analysis Conducted During Phase III

This is an example of a change-resistance analysis that reflects the perceptions of Sales, Business Operations, and External Service organizations related to a specific process redesign project. Figure 7-3 shows the total degree of resistance.

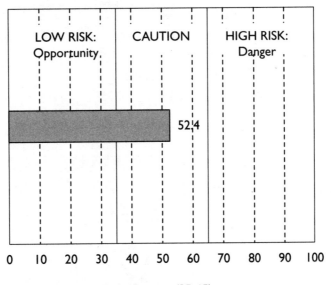

52.4 Moderate Risk–Caution (35-65)

FIGURE 7-3. **Total degree of resistance**

A resistance factor in this range is high enough that it should be considered a significant issue in predicting the success or failure of the change implementation. Target resistance will be a pivotal element in the project's outcome and therefore requires attention and resources in the planning and implementation steps. Figure 7-4 shows the resistance by individual assessment items.

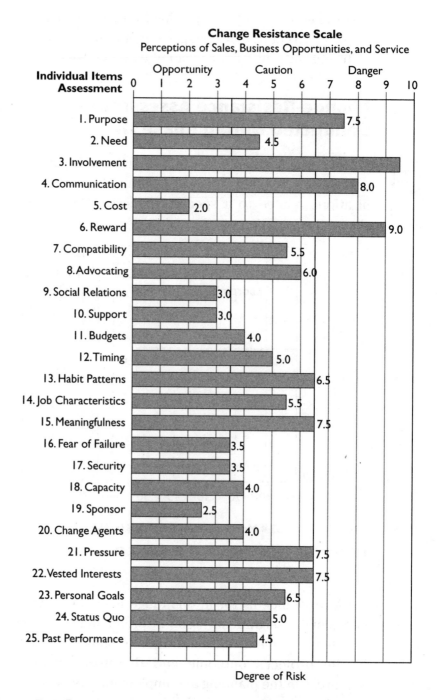

FIGURE 7-4. Degree of resistance by individual assessment items

An analysis of the individual items for Customer Service revealed the following enablers and barriers to the change. Any item scored in the Low Risk: Opportunity Range indicates a low level of resistance and a positive prognosis for successful implementation. The analysis also revealed a number of significant barriers to change that scored over 6.5, which warrant careful consideration. Any item that scored in this range indicates a high level of resistance and a negative prognosis for successful implementation. However, any score over 3.5 places the item in the danger zone and should not be ignored. The following is a listing of the perceived enablers or barriers of the change.

Enablers

5. **Cost** (score 2.0): the degree to which targets feel that the change has a physical, intellectual, or emotional cost.

19. **Sponsor** (score 2.5): the degree to which targets have a high level of trust and respect for the sponsor.

9. **Social Relations** (score 3.0): the degree to which targets perceive that relationships that are important will be improved or remain positive due to this change.

10. **Support** (score 3.0): the degree to which targets feel that organizational resources will be provided for this change implementation.

Barriers

3. **Involvement** (score 9.5): the degree to which the targets feel they have had input into planning this change.

6. **Reward** (score 9.0): the degree to which targets feel that there are adequate rewards for accomplishing the change.

4. **Communication** (score 8.0): the degree to which targets feel communication about the change has been made clear.

1. **Purpose** (score 7.5): the degree to which the targets feel the purpose of the change is clear.

Pain Management During Phase III

During Phase II, the PIT defined the pain related to the as-is process and prepared a future-state vision statement. During Phase III, the sustaining sponsor will be called upon to keep this data in front of the targets who report to him or her. The importance of this activity can not be overly stressed, because the targets will use this information to decide their level of support or resistance to the project. Even after the targets have committed to the change, it's important that the sustaining sponsors reinforce the targets' belief that the change will be beneficial. Team meetings, followed by one-on-one talks with the targets, should take place early in Phase III to discuss present (as-is) process pain and to provide a detailed understanding of the vision statement.

The sustaining sponsor or the change agent should estimate each target's position on the positive or negative response to the change model (see Chapter 2). The sustaining sponsor or change agent should then take appropriate action to help individuals who are not successfully moving through the model. We find it helpful for the change agent to explain these models to all of the targets so that they can better understand their emotions and help themselves through the model. Target training programs serve this purpose. If the change agent is performing this estimate, that does not relieve the sustaining sponsor of the responsibility for ensuring that his or her direct reports are at the correct point on the commitment continuum curve.

Using Career Planning to Decrease Resistance

During Phase III, the sustaining sponsor should work with his or her direct reports to develop an approach for creating career plans for each employee. The career plan is intended to define both long-term career objectives and interim work assignments leading to that objective. The plan will also define any education, training, or other special schooling or experience required so the employees are best qualified for new opportunities as they develop. In addition, this strategy has a number of other significant advantages:

1. It shows employees that management is interested in their personal welfare and is willing to invest in them.
2. It helps management understand employee goals, so that if a surplus occurs as a result of the project, managers can identify the best alternative assignments for each employee.

3. It helps employees accept the reality that the current state is always temporary, that new processes are inevitable, and that they have an obligation to improve their competencies and readiness to accept new opportunities and challenges.
4. It is an effective way to identify people who will benefit from a change in assignment if fewer people are required to operate the process.
5. This realization goes a long way toward breaking down the wall of resistance.

Keeping Black Holes from Developing During Phase III

During Phase III, the change advocates need to work very actively with sustaining sponsors to keep them building personal commitment to the project. Particular emphasis needs to be placed on the sustaining sponsors to ensure that black holes do not develop as they play a pivotal role in preparing the targets for Phase IV. The advocates should consistently monitor the sustaining sponsors' commitment progress and help them keep on schedule. During Phase III, the advocates, the process owners, and the managers of the sustaining sponsors should meet frequently to discuss the sustaining sponsors' progress along the commitment curve. They should jointly create a recovery plan for any sustaining sponsor who is not progressing as planned.

Future-State Solutions and MOC

As the PIT develops the future-state solutions, groups of targets should be used to validate those solutions by observing the simulation models in action and commenting on their feasibility. We find that these reviews by the people who will be using the process are very valuable. The employees can often point out gross errors and important improvement opportunities. When practical, physical models should be set up to allow the targets to physically operate the mock processes. We always try to include the influencing targets in these reviews. We like to end the session by having the targets do the following:

- ▶ Make suggestions on how the process could be improved
- ▶ Point out problems
- ▶ Point out things that should be added
- ▶ Point out things that concern them
- ▶ Rate their impression of the overall process as:
  1. worse than the present process
  2. same as the present process
  3. better than the present process
  4. much better than the present process
  5. great
- ▶ List how the new process would impact their present job assignment

Sustaining Sponsors' and Advocates' Involvement in the Best-Value Future-State Solution

Prior to meeting with the executive team, the PIT should present all of the future-state solutions to the sustaining sponsors and advocates, along with the PIT's recommendation of the best-value future-state solution. The purpose of these meetings is not only to keep the sustaining sponsors and advocates involved, but to make them part of the best-value future-state solution selection process. The PIT should ask each sustaining sponsor and advocate for his or her opinions about the various future-state solutions and any suggestions to further improve the future-state solutions. One of the advantages in having a simulation model for each future-state solution is that suggestions can often be added on the spot and the improvement impact can be calculated immediately. This allows ideas to be accepted or rejected on the spot. Usually, suggestions that don't improve the process's performance are rejected. It's important that this rule be established and understood by the sustaining sponsors and advocates at the very beginning of the meeting, so that they will not feel that the PIT is not listening to them.

We recommend that the sustaining sponsors and advocates on the executive team be provided with a private review and that the PIT generate a list of all of the questions and concerns expressed at this meeting. The PIT should then develop answers to these questions and concerns and review them with the sustaining sponsors and advocates before the executive team meeting. It's important that all the sustaining sponsors and advocates on the executive team be in complete accord with the PIT's recommendations before the executive team meeting. These allies will have a very positive impact on how smoothly the meeting runs and the results of the meeting.

For sustaining sponsors and advocates who are not on the executive team, private or group meetings can be held. This decision should be based upon the number of sustaining sponsors and their change-readiness status. If the PIT identifies sustaining sponsors with weak or inadequate commitment to the proposed best-value solution, it's

Sponsors are important in many areas

usually better to meet with them separately and provide them with some additional attention.

Immediately after the executive team approves the future-state solution to be implemented in Phase IV, the PIT should schedule a meeting with all of the sustaining sponsors and advocates who are not on the executive team, to review the details of the future-state solution and report the results of the executive team meeting. At that meeting, a plan should be developed on how and when the future-state solution will be shared with the targets. We believe that this feedback to all targets should occur within five working days of the executive decision.

Assessment of Change Agent

The change agents engaged in Phases I, II, and III should be reassessed to determine if they are now capable of handling the people side of the change as well as the technical and process side of the project. To do this, the change agents fill out the change agent questionnaires and the performance of each change agent is assessed by the project manager and his or her interfacing sustaining sponsors. The change agents who have reached the required balance of people, process, and technology should be considered for the implementation team or to participate in another process redesign or reengineering project. Managers should not give future assignments as change agent to any individual who has not reached the required level of organizational change performance.

Process Personality vs. Future-State Solution: Requirements

One of the considerations in defining the best-value future-state solution is the degree to which each future-state solution aligns with the personality (subculture) of the individual departments that make up the process. The future-state solutions that align with the personality of the present process have a far better chance of succeeding than the ones that are out of phase with it. To assess the alignment, the PIT will compare the Department Personality Identification Records that were developed in Phase II with the behavioral requirements for the specific departments involved in each future-state solution.

If the future-state solution makes heavy use of organizational realignment, exposure to failure is high. That does not mean that the process will not perform its intended task, but that it will be much more expensive to implement the change and take a lot longer to reach optimum performance. In developing our value proposition, we used to estimate what it would cost in time and dollars to reorganize a process departmental structure, then double it. After many overruns, we now multiply our estimated cost and time by 400%—and we still occasionally overrun. Restructuring the organization is far more expensive in stress, time, and dollars than most organizations realize.

Change-Management Readiness Assessment

The readiness of the people involved in the process to accept the future-state solution should be assessed by having all of them fill out a *Landscape Survey*. This is the form that was used to make the same type of assessment earlier in the process redesign cycle. By comparing the results of the two surveys, the PIT can determine how effective the management of change process has been to date. If the targets are still not ready to accept the change, a recovery plan needs to be included in the revised Phase IV MOC plan. If the targets have not reached the required commitment level, it may be necessary to put off implementing the new process.

Updating the MOC Plan to Support Phase IV

Figure 7-5 is a typical MOC timeline project plan to support Phase III of a process redesign project.

By the end of Phase III, the best-value future-state solution has been defined and approved. The PIT has accomplished its assigned task and will be disbanded after a preliminary implementation plan is developed. The project will then be turned over to a future-state implementation team (FIT) and the project enters into Phase IV. One of the PIT's last tasks should be to update the MOC plan to be in line with the implementation plan and the MOC assessments that were conducted during Phase III.

A very important consideration that must be addressed in the preliminary implementation plan is the make-up of the future-state implementation team (FIT). Any members of the FIT who do not have an interface with any of the targets (e.g., an employee who just writes code) can get by with very little understanding of the MOC methodology. There are very few of these types of assignments, however; most people who are involved in implementing the future-state solution must have an excellent understanding of the MOC methodology and how to work with the targets to help them accept the new process.

The PIT should be very careful when recommending people for the FIT, to ensure that they have the traits necessary to manage the human side of the change process. Priority should be given to people who have used the MOC concept successfully on other projects.

(Note: Review Figure 6-5 in Chapter 6 to understand which MOC assessments, planning tools, and training apply to Phases III and IV of a process redesign project.)

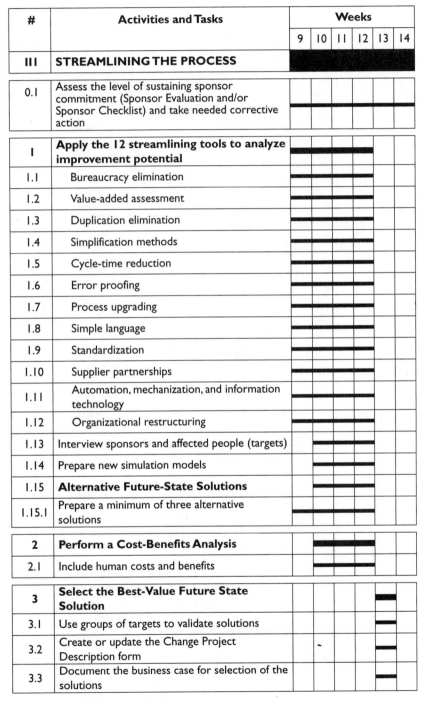

#	Activities and Tasks	Weeks					
		9	10	11	12	13	14
III	**STREAMLINING THE PROCESS**						
0.1	Assess the level of sustaining sponsor commitment (Sponsor Evaluation and/or Sponsor Checklist) and take needed corrective action						
1	**Apply the 12 streamlining tools to analyze improvement potential**						
1.1	Bureaucracy elimination						
1.2	Value-added assessment						
1.3	Duplication elimination						
1.4	Simplification methods						
1.5	Cycle-time reduction						
1.6	Error proofing						
1.7	Process upgrading						
1.8	Simple language						
1.9	Standardization						
1.10	Supplier partnerships						
1.11	Automation, mechanization, and information technology						
1.12	Organizational restructuring						
1.13	Interview sponsors and affected people (targets)						
1.14	Prepare new simulation models						
1.15	**Alternative Future-State Solutions**						
1.15.1	Prepare a minimum of three alternative solutions						
2	**Perform a Cost-Benefits Analysis**						
2.1	Include human costs and benefits						
3	**Select the Best-Value Future State Solution**						
3.1	Use groups of targets to validate solutions						
3.2	Create or update the Change Project Description form						
3.3	Document the business case for selection of the solutions						

FIGURE 7-5. Typical timeline project plan to support Phase III of a process redesign project

#	Activities and Tasks	Weeks					
		9	10	11	12	13	14
4	**Obtain Executive Committee Approval**						▬
4.1	Reaffirm initiating sponsor commitment to the project						▬
5	**Approve Preliminary Implementation Plan**					▬	▬
5.1	Assess the organization's capacity to assimilate the specific change proposed, using one or more of the following tools as applicable: Change Project Description form (detailed descriptions) When to Apply Implementation Architecture Landscape Survey Culture Assessment Predicting the Impact of Change Overload Index Implementation Problems Assessment Change History Survey					▬	▬
5.2	Update the Role Map document based on best-value solution impacts					▬	
5.3	Assess alignment of the infrastructure with desired behavioral objectives					▬	
5.4	Evaluate the level of teamwork required for successful implementation (Synergy Survey)					▬	
5.5	Identify infrastructure changes needed to reinforce the change					▬	
5.6	Identify advocates whose help will be needed during implementation					▬	
5.7	Analyze the effectiveness of prior communications					▬	
5.8	Update the communications plan					▬	
5.9	Identify the training needs of all affected targets					▬	
5.10	Develop a training plan to meet identified needs					▬	
5.11	Identify actual or potential resistance (Change Resistance Scale)					▬	
5.12	Include resistance mitigation activities in the plan					▬	
5.13	Identify actions to be taken by sponsors to maintain target commitment					▬	
5.14	Recommend members of the future-state implementation team (FIT)					▬	

FIGURE 7-5. (continued)

Summary of MOC Activities in Phase III

Although most processes are still being operated in the old manner, the targets are being prepared for the change. In terms of the MOC process, targets have moved out of the current stage into the transition state. They probably still have some fear about the future-state solution, because the exact impact on their personal assignment may not be defined in details until Phase IV, but they have been prepared mentally and emotionally to accept the change.

Phase IV–Implementation, Measurements, and Control

During Phase IV, the best-value future-state solution will be implemented and the appropriate measurement and control system will be established to support continuous monitoring of the BFSS. Phase IV consists of five activities (see Figure 7-6).

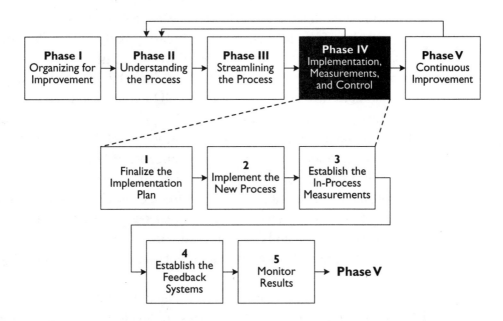

FIGURE 7-6. The five activities that make up Phase IV

MOC Activities Applied to Phase IV–Implementation

We concentrate on managing the factors that influence change rather than on managing the change itself. This mindset helps us identify the most significant elements affecting the outcome we're seeking and leveraging these elements to achieve it.
    —MICHAEL TOFOLO, VICE PRESIDENT OF LOGISTICS, BUENA VISTA HOME VIDEOS

It's during Phase IV that the organization's change management plan really pays off. If a good MOC plan was executed effectively during Phases I, II, and III, resistance from the affected personnel will be minimum in Phase IV. The difference between a well-implemented MOC plan and a poorly implemented one can be readily seen during Phase IV. If the MOC plan is poor, the employees' attitude will likely be expressed in such comments as "Just ignore it and it will go away." In contrast, a well-designed and well-implemented MOC plan results in comments such as "Can I be first?"

The implementation phase can vary from a few days to years, depending on the complexity of the best-value future-state solution. The complexity of the MOC process will vary greatly during this time period, depending on whether the employees just need to accept the new process or if they internalize the concept related to the new process. Let's look at how the MOC process will be applied during this phase.

This is the transition state—the time when targets will actually begin behaving in new ways. Up to now, much of our thinking about target resistance has been theoretical. Now, it becomes very real!

This phase will usually last longer than any of the prior phases, according to the complexity of the changes to be implemented. It's not unusual for full implementation of a process redesign and for establishing measurements and control to take from three to six months. This is the phase when it all comes together, when the plans developed for implementing the redesigned process and for managing the human impact of change are put to the test. The duration of this phase provides far more time than in earlier phases to develop and implement change plans. So, during this phase, seize the opportunity to build on foundations laid earlier, to make change plans more explicit, and to add detail not possible before the exact nature of the changes was determined.

Setting the Stage for MOC in Phase IV

The new process design has met all of its objectives. It has reduced costs by 40%, cycle time by 48%, and cycle-time variation by at least 60%. The number of people involved in the process has been reduced from 80 to 40. First-line managers have been reduced from eight to two and one of the two second-level managers has been eliminated. The San Jose and San Francisco offices have been combined. An information system is being installed to track each transaction as it moves through the process. This will provide performance data related to each employee's activities. Transactions that are set on a desk for a time that exceeds the two-sigma limit of the normal distribution will be highlighted to that employee. In other words, when an item enters an activity and is not processed within the maximum time, the time within which 95% of the items are processed, the employee is notified.

For example, if 95% of the orders are entered into the computer database within six hours, any order that is not entered within six hours is highlighted to the employee, so that he or she can find and process it immediately. If the delay exceeds the three-sigma limit, the employee's manager will be notified and he or she will be required to submit a corrective-action report. All employees will be provided with voice-activated computer programs so that keyboards will be unnecessary. This will mean that each employee will be provided with a soundproof cubicle as a work station. The new office will be located in San Francisco, which means that the organization will have to pay relocation expenses (moving and home guarantee) for any employee transferred from San Jose to San Francisco. This averages about $40,000 per employee.

MOC Applied to Phase IV, Activity 1–Finalize the Implementation Plan

During Phase III, both the implementation plan and the change management plan were updated to the extent possible based on the facts known at that time. During the final review and approval process, it's almost certain that modifications will have been made to the future-state solution or that details will have been made more explicit as questions were raised and resolved.

A more detailed future-state solution implementation plan will provide the information necessary to prepare a detailed future-state solution implementation plan (FSIP). This is the time to look at each activity within the new implementation plan and ask these questions:

- ▶ What has been added or modified?
- ▶ What are the MOC implications of those changes?
- ▶ Have those implications been adequately covered in the prior MOC plan?
- ▶ What additional change activities are needed to ensure successful implementation?

Frequently the FIT will have some members who have not been on the PIT working the project from its inception. The FIT is often made up of people highly skilled in implementing future-state solutions rather than in designing process improvements. For example, the FIT might have programmers, industrial engineers, or subcontract experts temporarily assigned to ensure implementing the new process design effectively. The PITs are usually made up of sustaining sponsors or other people who understand the process. The FIT is made up of people who can change the environment for the process.

Sometimes the mix of skills needed makes it appropriate to form an entirely new team. In either case, you will need to revisit the new team's training needs in order to bring the new people up to speed on change principles, tools, and the MOC components of the project plan that they will implement during this phase.

In further refining the implementation plan, consider also the optimum sequence of activities. Change implications can influence that sequence. If significant resistance is anticipated, weigh carefully both the speed of implementation and the decision whether to pilot in a limited area or to implement fully. If readiness has not been assessed before this phase or if there are signs of resistance, conducting a Landscape Survey before initiating implementation is good insurance against a false start. The results of such analysis can help the team decide where to begin the implementation, how much change to introduce, and at what pace.

Before deploying the implementation, take a fresh look at what pace of change the organization is ready to accommodate. What other changes have occurred since the project began? How much can the organization take on at once? Which changes will best lay a foundation for the rest of the changes needed?

Look for those groups most likely to implement effectively, minimize resistance, function as internal advocates for other groups, and maximize learning. An investment made now in thoughtfully planning implementation can yield significant returns in the speed and effectiveness with which the entire organization assimilates the change.

In the updated change management plan, pay particular attention to those aspects of the organizational infrastructure that must be in alignment with the future-state solution if it is to be fully implemented. Wherever new behaviors are required, look at the current performance management system to see if it truly supports and reinforces the desired behavior. It's not at all uncommon to see new process designs that place increased emphasis on collaborative or team-oriented behavior, while the reward or recognition system continues to reinforce individual rather than team performance.

Think back a decade to the time when Magic Johnson frequently received the MVP award in the NBA. His recognition came not so much for points scored or rebounds as it did for his extraordinary number of assists. When Michael Jordan joined the NBA, his coach admitted that Michael had all the talent, physical skills, and knowledge of the game and he could do little to improve his play. Instead, the coach focused on developing Michael's leadership skills—the crucial component that he was lacking to become a total player. It is the rare business that has figured out how to reward its MVPs for helping others.

Education, training, and development are key in the alignment of organizational infrastructure. The implementation of new processes frequently requires new skills; concerns or resistance frequently arise when employees worry about their ability to master those new skills and about some of their old skills becoming obsolete. Any implementation plan must include identifying new skills required and providing comprehensive education, training, and development.

Before the start of implementation activities, one last check is needed. Do you have enough qualified and competent change agents to ensure successful implementation? A final *Change Agent Evaluation* should be conducted; those who are unable to carry out their crucial role and manage both the human and technical aspects of the change should be further trained or reassigned to a less critical role.

The Role Map diagram usually needs to be completely redesigned. In this case, 50% of the sustaining sponsors have been eliminated. Additional technical people have to be added to the FIT who often play change agent roles in addition to their technical roles. Some of the advocates are no longer needed because the person they supported is no longer on the Role Map diagram. In addition, new sustaining sponsors are added, making it necessary to assign new advocates to them.

Special MOC Plan Consideration

Let's take a look at the change considerations that result from the new process design we presented earlier as an example. Here are some of these human stress factors:

- ▶ What are we going to do with the excess people?
- ▶ How do we select which people stay with the process?
- ▶ How do we keep our best people from leaving?
- ▶ What impact does the relocation have on the employees?
- ▶ What impact does the relocation have on the employees' families?

- ▶ What impact will the individual measurement system have on the employees?
- ▶ How much stress is involved in taking away the computer keyboard and replacing it with the voice-activated system?
- ▶ What is the emotional impact of working in a soundproof cubicle?
- ▶ What are the desired behavioral patterns related to the new process?
- ▶ How will the reward system be changed to reinforce the desired behavioral patterns in a new process?
- ▶ How do you retrain the excess managers to be able to handle staff roles?
- ▶ Do you need to implement a technical vitality program?
- ▶ Should you reverse the decision to locate in San Francisco?
- ▶ Would the people in San Jose be more supportive of the change if the process were located in their city?
- ▶ Which location has more change activities going on now or in the near future?
- ▶ Which location has more people who technically competent to support the change so that the change will have less emotional impact upon them?

It's easy to see that each of these points requires preparing a separate action plan as part of the future-state solution MOC implementation plan. Probably the point to be addressed first is what you are going to do with the excess sustaining sponsors, because they have already seen the future-state solution and know that their jobs may be eliminated. Each is likely wondering, "Will I be a survivor or a victim of the process redesign project?" At this point, everyone feels like a probable victim and hopes to be a survivor. No one performs well in this situation. Everyone is trying to look good and make the others look bad. It's a bad situation.

The first thing is to define who will be the survivors. Then the executive team needs to analyze the personal characteristics of the victims, to decide what the options are for them. For example,

- ▶ Are any of them close to retirement?
- ▶ Are any other management jobs open that any of them can fill?
- ▶ Are there staff jobs that any of them can be trained to fill?
- ▶ Would any of them make good salespeople?
- ▶ Would an early retirement program attract any of them?
- ▶ Would sweetening the early retirement program with the budgeted $40,000 for relocation make it more attractive?
- ▶ If we have to let some of the sustaining sponsors go, how do we do it?
  1. Let the latest hired go first?
  2. Let the youngest go first?
  3. Let the poorest performers go first?
  4. Let the ones with the least potential go first?

We recommend that you communicate these types of decisions and options right away, to give the survivors a sense of security and allow the other sustaining sponsors to start adjusting to their situation. Just knowing puts the worry behind them and they can start to plan for the future. Because all of the sustaining sponsors will still function in their present jobs for a while, those who will be leaving will have some time to adjust, to make other arrangements, to look for other situations that may be better for them, from their standpoint. We believe that honesty is the best policy. Where better to start than with your management team that has served you so faithfully over the years?

The MOC and/or the human resource parts of the project future-state implementation plan must systematically address each of the special human stress factors caused by the specific future-state solution in a very complete manner. Due to the specific nature of these plans, we will not discuss each of the stress factors previously presented. The single example should provide you with a typical approach to addressing these stress factors.

MOC Applied to Phase IV, Activity 2–Implement the New Process

Bill Trahant, partner at Coopers & Lybrand L.L.P., stated in *Management Review*, September 1997 ("12 Principles of Organizational Transformation"), "Too many changes flounder today because the company tries to change its employees' beliefs, values, and work schedules, rather than change people's everyday behavior on the job. Stress new ways of working in your organization, communicate with people frequently, and reinforce work expectations with the right kinds of policy and procedures."

The beginning of actual implementation is, of course, the time when all the theory and the planning for change come to fruition. This is the time when people are confronted with the reality that their world is actually changing, not sometime, not perhaps, but here and now. It's crucial to implement the plans fully and on time. There's a substantial risk that those responsible for implementing the new process focus so much on the technical aspects of the change that they neglect the people issues. It's important that selected members of the implementation team maintain a focus on timely implementation of the change aspects of the plan.

The future-state vision that was prepared in Phase I or II is now replaced with a future-state process specification. The vagueness of the vision statement has yielded to specifics. Before the implementation plan was finalized, the transformation pain could not be identified. Now the project implementation plan defines the timeline and the activities that will drive the transformation.

Communications about the future-state process specification, the implementation plan, and the business case supporting it must be maintained throughout this phase. The full impact of the change may not have been evident to people when they heard those messages earlier in the project; this is the time to reinforce them so that no one loses sight of the reasons behind the change.

Whenever possible, use simulation models, prototypes, mockups, examples of the new process, and conference room pilots, to show the changes in terms that are clear and easy to understand. Walk people through the model process and provide plenty of time and opportunity for them to ask questions, make suggestions, and communicate their issues and concerns. When the people most affected have become comfortable with the change, they can become very powerful allies in helping others. It can be a very effective strategy to use a conference room pilot, even when one is not required for technical or design reasons, to give large numbers of targets an opportunity to experience the changes in a safe environment and to create vocal supporters.

Create focus groups of targets and hold "town meetings" periodically to discuss the changes and the issues that may be of concern to the larger population. Use these groups to identify potential solutions for presentation to the FIT.

Proper attention to sustaining sponsors is also critical during this transition period, to prevent the emergence of new "black holes." When the planning has been completed and the new process is becoming operational, there's a risk that sponsors may become either distracted by other priorities or so focused on making sure the new process succeeds that they fail to notice important signs of target reactions. It is a time for vigilance. The implementation team members should maintain frequent contact with sponsors, both giving and receiving feedback on the progress of the implementation.

Because it takes a long time to implement many of the future-state processes, a number of assessments may be conducted to measure the change in attitude and ability of the people involved in the change. Often, the same assessments may be repeated at scheduled intervals, such as every three months. It may be necessary to alter the entire new process implementation plan if support for the change does not reach the required level or other matters distract from the support. These conditions often call for MOC corrective action plans to minimize the risk of failure.

While the change is being implemented and the targets are going through the transformation stage of the change process, it's extremely important that the sustaining sponsors, change agents, and advocates spend a lot of time with the targets, reading both their verbal and their nonverbal communications. For changes that are as complex as are most process redesign projects, few MOC implementation support plans are so well defined during Phase II, Activity I that they don't need to be upgraded as new, unexpected concerns are identified that affect the targets.

MOC Applied to Phase IV, Activity 3—Establish the In-Process Measurements

We mentioned during our discussion of Phase I, Activity 7—Establishing Measurements and Goals, that establishing new measurements frequently causes resistance and becomes a change issue itself. In organizations that have done little measuring in the past or have used measurement data to attack people, the very idea of new measures can strike fear into the hearts of the most dedicated employees. Resistance can be reduced by involving the employees in initiating the new measures. Wherever possible, use self-measurement or measurement that flows directly from the process; either is far more acceptable than measurement by others. Also, focus on the fact that it's the process that is being measured, not specifically the person operating the process.

The measurement system must include all the key total-process measurements for effectiveness, efficiency, and adaptability. This will allow the process owners to ensure that improvements that are made later on in the project do not suboptimize the total process.

Accurate data can help identify trouble spots in the process or opportunities to make the process more effective or more efficient; when the team properly understands the data and acts appropriately, it can improve the lot of the process operator. Include verification and validation processes to ensure that the right data are being collected and that the data are fair and accurate.

Finally, measurement systems should include an appropriate balance between the process and outcomes. Each is important, but for different reasons. Measurement of the process enables continuous improvement and optimization of the way in which the product or service is designed, produced, or delivered. Measurement of outcomes is the test of whether the improvements in the process are producing their desired results.

Now, let's consider the future-state solution that we discussed earlier in this phase. In this case, the simulation model is used to track individual transactions through the process, thereby providing data not otherwise available on backlog and wait time. Data will measure the average time a transaction is on each person's desk and define the normal distribution of the desktop cycle time for each employee. These are powerful data that can be used to improve the process or to identify individuals who are performing poorly. In addition, any transaction that falls outside of the process's negative three-sigma (-3σ) distribution is automatically brought to the attention of the manager so that he or she can take immediate corrective action. Although this data system provides an excellent way to increase customer satisfaction, it is also a cannon pointed at each target's head, ready to go off if he or she relaxes. In most cases, these support personnel have never been subjected to a variable type measurement system.

You can be sure that the poor performers will strongly resist this type of data system. The best performers may also resist the data system, because it can provide more control over their activities than they would like. Usually everyone will not object outwardly to being measured, but inwardly and among themselves they will express strong opinions. To management they may state the measurement system is unnecessary, that they will get the work out without this additional record keeping. The truth of the matter is that the work does not get out, that transactions are misplaced, that cycle time per transaction varies a lot, and that the data system is needed. The challenge for the FIT is to get the targets to accept the new data system, because if the targets do not provide the input data, the new data system is sure to fail.

To overcome this problem, the FIT will need to use pain management concepts. The team members first need to surface the pain related to the present processes as viewed by both the targets and management. They then need to define how the data system will be used when the future-state process is installed. To minimize the pain related to the future-state process, they need to minimize the effort required to collect the additional data. Typically, a mark sense scanning system is used to document the transaction movement between desks. The sustaining sponsors should then have the FIT set up a conference room pilot so that the targets can see the data system in action. After demonstrating the system to the targets, arrange for the targets to operate the system themselves. The sustaining sponsors should then hold a brainstorming session that uses a force field analysis technique to develop the pros and cons of the new system. If the pros do not outweigh the cons, the FIT needs to work on eliminating the negative impacts to the point that the positive impacts are greater than the negative impacts. Or, drop the concept.

MOC Applied to Phase IV, Activity 4—Establish the Feedback Systems

Measurement without a feedback system is always a no-value-added activity. Regular feedback of the data, in a forum that allows people to discuss its validity and opportunities for improvement, will help them accept and use the data and the measurement process itself. Be sure that the data are used to identify root causes of problems or evaluate and improve the process, not to point fingers or assess personal blame.

The simulation model, when used to track individual transactions, will provide feedback to the individual to help prioritize work. It can also notify management of overdue transactions, so that managers can address potential problems created by exceptionally heavy workloads or insufficient personnel before they impact customer delivery.

Feedback of the data obtained should be:

▶ **Prompt**—the value of data decreases with time
▶ **Frequent**—so that employees develop habit patterns of responding to data
▶ **Accurate**—faulty data are quickly ignored or disregarded
▶ **Useful**—something the recipient can do something about, providing data that will empower the operator to make recommendations or improvements

MOC Timeline Project Plan for Phase IV of a Process Redesign Project

Figure 7-8 is a typical MOC timeline chart that would be developed to support Phase IV of a process redesign project.

Sometimes I get the feeling that the whole world is against me, but deep down I know that's not true. Some of the smaller countries are neutral.

— ROBERT ORBEN

MOC Results in Phase IV

At the end of Phase IV, the impact of the MOC activity on the project can be measured. The *Landscape Survey* will help with this task. The question to ask is "Was the project completed on schedule, within budget, and did it produce the desired results?" If the answer is "Yes" to all three of these items, then the MOC part of the project was probably a success. If the answer to any one of these items is "No," then the MOC part of the project is a failure. Of course, there are other, secondary measures of the success of the MOC part of the project. Typical other measurements are:

▶ the degree of resistance to the change
▶ the degree of commitment that the targets have to the change
▶ how successful the targets consider the project

Summary

During this chapter, we've discussed the streamlining and implementation phases (III and IV) of the process redesign methodology down to the task level. At the end of each of the two phases, we discussed in detail the Managing Organizational Change activities that took place during that phase. As a result of understanding this chapter, you should be able to apply the management of change methodology to a process redesign assignment and have a good understanding of how to

apply MOC to any performance improvement opportunity or major project.

Change within us starts before we are born and continues after we die. Why try to fight it while we are alive?

#	Activities and Tasks	Weeks			
		15	16	17	18
IV	**IMPLEMENTATION, MEASUREMENTS, AND CONTROL**	▬			
0.1	Assess the level of sustaining sponsor commitment (Sponsor Evaluation and/or Sponsor Checklist) and take corrective action where necessary	▬▬			
0.2	Form the future-state implementation Team (FIT)	▬			
0.3	Assess change knowledge of FIT members	▬			
0.4	Assess change agent competency to facilitate Phase IV implementation (Change Agent Evaluation)	▬			
0.5	Conduct training as needed in both technical skills and MOC skills	▬▬			
0.6	Complete a change project description	▬▬			
1	**Finalize the Implementation Plan**		▬▬▶		

1.1	Review the implementation plan, revise and update:
	  Verify all prior plan activities
	  Add any new activities identified by the FIT members
	  Detail the plan to the task level
	  Assess MOC implications of any changes to the plan
	  Identify the individual responsible for each activity and task
	  Refine the timetable for completion of each activity and task
	    and assess the cumulative impact of the change timetable
	  Update the Role Map diagram and use it to drive
	    implementation
	  Update and implement the communications plan
	  (Organizational Change Implementation Plan and/or
	  Implementation Plan Evaluation)
			▬▬▶		

2	**Implement the New Process**		▬▬▶		
	Secure the involvement of sponsors, advocates, and target advocates		▬▬▶		

	Deliver required training for all targets
	  technical or job skills
	  MOC or resilience competencies
			▬▬▶		

	Implement the planned changes to the infrastructure		▬▬▶		
	Communicate the future-state process specifications		▬▬▶		

FIGURE 7-8. Typical MOC timeline project plan for Phase IV of a process redesign project

#	Activities and Tasks	Weeks			
		15	16	17	18
2 (cont'd)	Provide simulation models of new processes when feasible		→————→		
	Implement the planned changes to the process		→————→		
	Update simulation models		→————→		
	Provide rewards and recognition for adopting new required behaviors		→—————→		
	Implement plans for removing excess people (sponsors and targets)		→—————→		
	Maintain frequent contact with sponsors to prevent new "black holes"		→—————→		
3	**Establish In-Process Measurements**		→————→		
	Include both in-process and outcome measurements		→————→		
4	**Establish the Feedback Systems**			→———→	
	Create focus groups to solicit feedback			→———→	
	Conduct "town meetings" for collecting feedback			→———→	
	Conduct an Implementation Problems Assessment			→———→	
5	**Monitor Results**			→———→	
	Analyze effectiveness of communications			→———→	
	Track process measurements against goals			→———→	
	Include tracking of human as well as process metrics (Landscape Survey and/or Overload Index)				→——→
	Initiate MOC tracking				→——→

FIGURE 7-8. (continued)

CHAPTER

8

Applying MOC to an SAP R/3 Project

**In many organizations the technology has outrun employees'
readiness to accept and use it.**

Introduction

In this chapter, we will review a typical SAP R/3 installation application to see how MOC supports this type of software project. SAP—Systeme Anwendungen Produkte in der Datenverabeitung, a.k.a. Systems, Applications and Products in Data Processing—was founded in 1972 and is based in Waldorf, Germany. Today, more than 7,500 customers in over 90 countries use SAP to manage their financial, manufacturing, sales and distribution, and human resource functions.

We selected an SAP R/3 project because it is one of today's most popular approaches to upgrading business processes in all parts of the organization and the upgrade cost often exceeds $10 million. Data indicate that more than 60% of the SAP programs fail to meet their projected improvement targets and that more than 30% of the SAP programs are dropped before they are implemented. We believe that with the effective use of MOC methods these failure rates can be greatly reduced.

275

The most common SAP products are the enterprise application suites, R/2 and R/3. R/3 applications are open client/server systems. Customers have the option of installing the core system and one or more of the functional components or purchasing the software as a complete package. At R/3's core are powerful programs for accounting and controlling, production and materials management, quality management and plant maintenance, sales and distribution, human resource management, and project management. R/3 is a software product that unlocks the path to effective organization units and to new IT structures with the ability to continuously adapt to a dynamic market and to competitive changes. With its integrated processes for handling enterprise processes, R/3 holds considerable potential for redesigning conventional structures and organizational methods. R/3 enhances performance by redesigning core business processes to revitalize and optimize them. For multi-enterprise business processes, R/3 covers organizations and their vendors, customers, and banks.

It is easy to see that SAP R/3 projects often are very complex and have a major impact on the way an organization is managed. As a result, there are very few SAP R/3 projects that should not make effective use of the MOC methodology. The magnitude of the changes driven by SAP projects causes resistance to the SAP project in most of the people who will be affected by the changes. To succeed, the SAP team needs to help the targets move from resistance to a supportive attitude. We need to change the attitude of every target from "It can't be done" into "We will get it done." That's what we mean by changing resistance into support. To make this transformation, we need to do the following:

- ▶ Prepare a future-state vision.
- ▶ Define the panic related to the current state.
- ▶ Develop a what-if scenario.
- ▶ Understand the reasons for resistance.
- ▶ Respect those who resist.
- ▶ Tell the truth.
- ▶ Listen intently.
- ▶ Look for win/win solutions.

- ► Walk a mile in the targets' shoes.
- ► Align the change with the organizational culture.
- ► Involve the targets in the change process.
- ► Don't move too fast.
- ► Define rewards for change.
- ► Sell the idea.
- ► Provide training.
- ► Keep everyone informed.
- ► Understand problems with past changes.
- ► Get people talking about the change:
  - Town meeting
  - Small focus groups
  - Department meetings

A typical SAP R/3 project is made up of the following 11 phases, as charted in Figure 8-1.

Phase I—Project Start-Up and Preparation

- ► Define project charter.
- ► Develop value proposition.
- ► Establish project-management infrastructure.
- ► Clarify scope of organizational change.
- ► Develop project plan.
- ► Kick off project.
- ► Monitor and control project.

Phase II—Current-State Analysis

- ► Document current information system environment.
- ► Document current business processes and organization.
- ► Review and approve current-state analysis stage.

Phase III—Future-State Scoping

- ► Establish business system vision.
- ► Define initial gap solutions.
- ► Establish initial deployment plan.
- ► Review and approve future-state scoping stage.

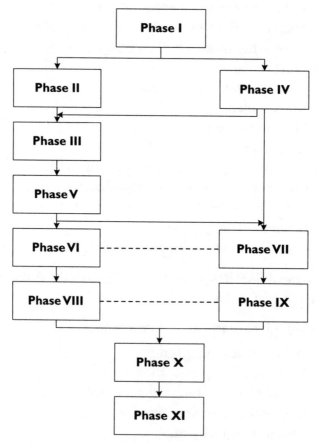

FIGURE **8-1.** The 11 phases that make up a typical SAP R/3 project

Phase IV—Infrastructure Initialization

- ▶ Establish development instance and procedures.
- ▶ Conduct project team training.
- ▶ Define development standards.
- ▶ Review and approve infrastructure-initialization stage.

Phase V—Analysis and Prototyping of Business Transactions

- ▶ Identify business transactions.
- ▶ Develop SAP R/3 prototyping scripts.
- ▶ Gather SAP R/3 configuration requirements.

▶ Configure business transactions in SAP R/3.

▶ Execute SAP R/3 prototyping scripts and develop procedures.

▶ Review and approve analysis/prototyping business transaction stage.

Phase VI—Gap Solutions Development

▶ Design interface.

▶ Design bolt-ons.

▶ Design SAP R/3 modifications.

▶ Design implementation of additional SAP R/3 modules.

▶ Design altered business transactions.

▶ Design reports.

▶ Build and test interfaces.

▶ Build and test bolt-ons.

▶ Build and test SAP R/3 modifications.

▶ Implement and test business transaction alterations.

▶ Build and test reports.

▶ Integrate test gap solutions.

▶ Review and approve gap solution development stage.

Phase VII—Infrastructure Deployment

▶ Design data conversion.

▶ Build and test data conversion applications.

▶ Establish test instance and procedures.

▶ Design system test.

▶ Migrate to test instance.

▶ Establish production instance and procedures.

▶ Review and approve infrastructure development stage.

Phase VIII—User Procedures and Training Development

▶ Develop user procedure manuals.

▶ Schedule training and develop materials.

▶ Conduct user training.

▶ Review and approve user procedures/training development stage.

Phase IX—System Testing

▶ Perform functional consolidation tests.
▶ Perform performance tests.
▶ Perform acceptance tests.
▶ Review and approve system testing stage.

Phase X—Solution Deployment

▶ Migrate to production instance.
▶ Implement customer strategy.
▶ Review and approve solution deployment stage.

Phase XI—Project Review and Assessment

▶ Review project performance.
▶ Close down project.

Figure 8-2 overlays in time sequences the 11 SAP phases with a typical four-phase software development project cycle:

▶ Design phase
▶ Build phase
▶ Test phase
▶ Deploy phase

SAP Phases	Phases of Software Development			
	Design Phase	Build Phase	Test Phase	Deploy Phase
I	✓			
II	✓			
III	✓			
IV	✓			
V	✓	✓		
VI		✓		
VII		✓	✓	
VIII			✓	
IX			✓	✓
X				✓
XI				✓

FIGURE 8-2. The 11 SAP phases compared with a typical four-phase software development project cycle

The following is a list of high-level activities performed in each of the four phases of a typical software development and implementation project and some of the key MOC outputs from the activities.

Phase I—Design Phase

Description of High-Level Activities	Work Products/Deliverables
Design phase and life cycle project plans developed	• Approved MOC Project Plans • Project-ready MOC Team Members
MOC strategy and approach developed	• Approved MOC Strategy and Approach
MOC Team activities planned and executed	• Finalized MOC Process
Follow the Work planning activities conducted	• Follow the Work plans and timelines
Proof of Concept materials developed and event coordinated	• Proof of Concept materials and successful event
Stakeholder Profile information collected and stored	• Populated Organizational and Individual Readiness Change Database • Approved activity design scripts
Stakeholder Profiles developed	• Initial Stakeholder Profiles • Refined and Finalized Stakeholder Profiles
Stakeholder Profile strategies developed	• Profile Strategy template • "Straw-Man" Profile Strategies • Finalized Profile Strategies

Phase II—Build Phase

Description of High-Level Activities	Work Products/Deliverables
Build phase and life cycle project plans reviewed and refined	• Refined MOC work plan
MOC Team activities continued	
Follow the Work enrollment activities conducted	
Sponsor/Advocate/Change Agent tactical plans developed	• Sponsor/Advocate/Change Agent tactical plans • Change Role Map diagram
Deployment Coaches and Managers oriented, trained, and educated for the change management aspect of their job	• Deployment Coaches' and Managers' orientation materials

Deployment Coaches and Managers supported in organization assessment and development of tactical plans	• Tools and techniques to support the organization assessment and development of tactical plans

Phase III—Test Phase

Description of High-Level Activities	Work Products/Deliverables
Test phase and life cycle project plans reviewed and refined	• Refined MOC work plan
Refined MOC work plan	• Follow the Work offer
Sponsor/Advocate/Change Agent tactical plans executed	• Various
Deployment Coaches and Managers supported in the development and execution of tactical plans	• Tools and techniques to support the execution of tactical plans

Phase IV—Deploy Phase

Description of High-Level Activities	Work Products/Deliverables
Deploy phase and life cycle project plans reviewed and refined	• Refined MOC work plans
Sponsor/Advocate/Change Agent tactical plans executed	• Various
Deployment Coaches and Managers supported in the execution of tactical plans	• Tools and techniques to support the execution of tactical plans

Due to the complexity of a typical SAP project, we will not discuss each of the 11 SAP phases and how the MOC process relates to them. We will only define how the MOC process relates to the four phases of the software development project plan schedule. We will also leave out much of the detail that was discussed in the previous chapters. You will note as well that the software profession has developed its own MOC terms, even though the approach is the same as for all other projects.

Figure 8-3 compares the four phases of the software development cycle and the seven phases of the MOC methodology.

	Software Development Phases			
MOC Phases	**I–Design**	**II–Build**	**III–Test**	**IV–Deploy**
Phase I–Clarify				
Phase II–Announce				
Phase III–Diagnose				
Phase IV–Plan				
Phase V–Implement				
Phase VI–Monitor				
Phase VII–Final Evaluation				

FIGURE 8-3. The MOC phases compared with a typical four-phase software development project cycle

Introduction to Using MOC to Support SAP Projects

Organizations can't wait until the SAP team is ready to implement a change before they prepare the targets to accept the change. All too often projects are completed and the project team disappears to wait for the storm to blow over. This approach leads to heartbreaks and failures. It's like Pete Silas, chairman and CEO of Phillips, puts it, "We can't wait for the storm to blow over. We've got to learn how to work in the rain."

Any organization that is embarking on a project to make its business processes more competitive through the use of SAP software programs needs to establish a foundation for continuous process change. SAP programs have three goals:

1. to redesign processes to leverage SAP best practices where appropriate
2. to develop the capability to react quickly, effectively, and economically to changing business requirements

3. to realize cost savings as a result of standardized technology and business processes.

One of the keys to realizing the benefits of this initiative is to proactively identify stakeholders who will be impacted significantly by the changes associated with the SAP implementation. Once stakeholders are identified and the implications of the changes upon these groups are assessed, tailored strategies and tactical activities encompassing training and education, communication, and end-user involvement are developed. To help ensure a single approach to managing the change, the MOC methodology, communication, and performance solutions teams are structurally integrated within a group called organizational and individual readiness (OIR). The OIR is part of the total SAP project team.

Team Mission

As a result of this integrated approach, the mission of the MOC team is identical to the overall OIR mission: "By gaining an understanding of employee needs, the team will facilitate the individual and organizational transition while enabling employees' capabilities. It will accomplish this by using appropriate mechanisms and just enough effort."

Goals

One way the MOC team supports the employee systems project is by identifying impacted stakeholders and developing stakeholder profiles that summarize the changes to each of the groups. Comprehensive strategies and tactics are developed to manage the change, minimizing disruption of daily operations and generally facilitating a smooth transition to the new environment.

Objectives

Ensure that each stakeholder group receives the appropriate type and level of change management intervention to:

▶ Provide a necessary level of commitment to and understanding of the project, as measured by a survey of stakeholders

▶ Minimize productivity losses and disruption of daily operations, as measured by a survey of supervisors

This part of this chapter will:

1. Provide an overview of the MOC strategy
2. Describe an approach for implementing the strategy
3. Describe the high-level stages and work products needed to execute the approach
4. Present a high-level timeline that illustrates when key activities in the approach will occur.

MOC Strategy for an SAP Project: Overview

This section summarizes the overall MOC strategy for an SAP project. There are four core concepts that shape the overall MOC strategy: stakeholder profiles, commitment continuum, profile strategies, and integration with other project teams.

Stakeholder Profiles

The fundamental concept of the MOC strategy revolves around the idea of stakeholder profiles. These profiles will be created based on how changes driven by the implementation affect groups of stakeholders throughout the organization. There are two categories of stakeholder profiles: sponsor/advocate/change agent profiles and target profiles. These are the same names used in the basic MOC methodology, but in applying them to software development, special emphasis is placed on the targets.

Commitment Continuum

Another important concept within the MOC strategy is the concept of the commitment continuum that was detailed in Chapter 2. Every member of a stakeholder profile needs to achieve a certain level of commitment to the SAP project to make it successful. The level of commitment needed varies by how stakeholders will be affected by the changes or what they will be asked to do to effect change. Never invest in getting more commitment than is necessary to implement the SAP projects.

Profile Strategies

Strategies and tactical activities will be developed for the stakeholder profiles to move each of the groups toward the necessary level of commitment.

Integration with Other Project Teams

It is extremely important that the MOC Team coordinate and integrate its efforts with other project teams, particularly deployment coordination, the functional teams, and the other teams within the OIR group.

MOC will integrate with the functional teams to identify and understand changes caused by the implementation of SAP. Each MOC member will serve as a liaison to one of the functional teams (working with other OIR team members), with the responsibility of:

1. Reviewing and understanding each of the activity design scripts developed by his or her functional team;
2. Signing off on these scripts after ensuring that all information necessary from a deployment perspective is included;
3. Entering the information into an OIR database; and
4. Developing ongoing relationships with members of the assigned functional team to ensure access to subject matter experts as the project progresses.

The deployment coordination (DC) team will implement, through the deployment infrastructure, the OIR stakeholder profile strategies. The deployment infrastructure, at a high level, consists of deployment coaches, who will work with deployment managers from the target organizations to develop customized tactical plans that fit the various target organizations. Prior to the development of these tactical plans, an organizational assessment will be conducted to determine which strategies will be appropriate for each field organization. The deployment managers, coached and guided primarily by the deployment coaches, will be responsible for assessing their organizations and developing tactical plans to ensure a successful deployment. The deployment coaches and MOC team members will work closely with these deployment managers, coaching and guiding their efforts throughout these activities.

Finally, it is critical that the efforts of the three areas of the OIR team be coordinated. At the heart of a successful integrated OIR strategy are the stakeholder profiles and where these profiles need to fall along the commitment continuum. The levers to move them along the continuum—communication, training/education, and involvement—will be supplied by the communication, MOC, and performance solution teams. Figure 8-4 integrates the efforts of the three OIR subteams around the stakeholder profiles and commitment continuum to ensure a collaborative solution targeted at providing the information, understanding/commitment and the skills to perform using the employee systems solution.

MOC Approach Applied to SAP Projects

Parameters of Profile Strategies

The overall MOC approach, and the stakeholder profile strategies in particular, must fit within overall project parameters. The project's mission, vision, and operating principles will be used to create a framework within which all change management strategies and tactical plans must exist and all change management decisions will be

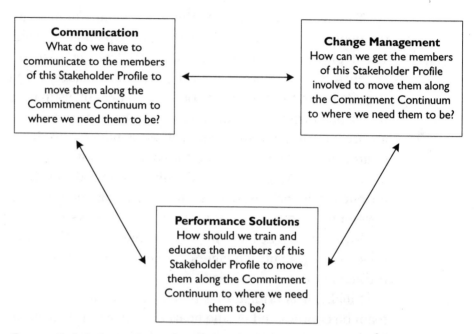

FIGURE 8-4. Integration of communication, MOC, and performance solution teams

made. Furthermore, the OIR team's mission will ensure that just enough effort is exerted to successfully implement the strategies.

The following are typical examples of project mission, vision, and operating principles statements.

Employee Systems Project Mission

▶ To successfully deploy SAP for release 2 by June 30, 2001.

Employee Systems Project Vision

▶ Implement an enterprise-wide HR/payroll system reflecting simplified and common processes and practices that drives economic benefits to the business and leverages enterprise self-service to establish end-user accountability for their own data.

Employee Systems Project Operating Principles

The following are typical operating principles that would be prepared by the project team:

▶ Spend 80% of effort on critical business functions and 20% on the "nice to haves."

▶ If the standard SAP functionality meets 80% of our business needs, use it.

▶ No modifications to SAP unless required by laws, regulations, or contracts.

▶ Strive to simplify/standardize everything.

▶ Priorities are time (first), budget (second), and functionality (third).

▶ Represent the team with one voice.

▶ Use team model for implementation and project management.

▶ Quickly raise and resolve issues.

▶ If it doesn't contribute towards the June 30, 2001 implementation, don't do it.

▶ Provide a proposed solution when raising issues.

▶ Don't make decisions in a vacuum.

OIR Team Mission

By gaining an understanding of employee needs, we will facilitate the individual and organizational transition while enabling employees' capabilities. We will accomplish this by using appropriate mechanisms and just enough effort.

Inputs

To develop the stakeholder profiles, information will be gathered from a variety of sources, described below. Members of the OIR team will compile this information in a change database designed by the OIR team to allow the compilation and sorting of change implications. Members of the OIR team will review and analyze the information and create the stakeholder profiles. The following are typical information sources.

Activity Design Scripts

Activity Design Scripts—Define what the activity will look like after the SAP project has been implemented.

The activity design scripts developed by the functional teams are the primary information sources used to capture change implications in the stakeholder profiling process. A member of the OIR team will be assigned to each functional team as a liaison, with responsibility for reviewing that team's activity design scripts, understanding the change implications to the organization, and entering that information into the change database. A formal deployment activity design script sign-off process ensures that information important to the deployment team is being captured in the scripts.

Functional Teams

Functional team members serve as another important source of input by clarifying, enhancing, and explaining information in the activity design scripts. The OIR liaisons develop ongoing relationships with the functional team members to better understand the activity design script information. This established relationship helps to ensure that the functional team members are available as subject matter experts as the iterative process of reviewing and refining the information begins.

Focused Organizational Assessment

After the stakeholder profiles and strategies have been developed, an organizational assessment will be conducted within each organization (defined by deployment coordination) to determine which profiles and strategies apply to a given organizational unit. The organization assessment will be conducted by a deployment manager, with assistance and guidance from a deployment coach and members of the deployment coordination and OIR teams.

Deployment Managers/Coordinators

Through the deployment infrastructure, the deployment managers and coordinators will validate the profile strategies and contribute to them as appropriate. They will also conduct the organization assessment and use the information to customize the profile strategies to develop tactical plans.

Leadership Team

The leadership team (project management team) will serve as an important source of input by reviewing the stakeholder profile strategies and suggesting modifications/enhancements as appropriate.

Dimensions

Dimensions—Define how individuals or groups will be affected by the change.

A number of dimensions are identified and documented from a preliminary assessment of the activity design scripts, initial interviews with functional team members, and initial interviews with members of the deployment team. These dimensions serve as the primary tool to differentiate among the effects of the change on various groups and subsequently segment these groups into stakeholder profiles.

An electronic worksheet should be developed to provide a front-end into the OIR changes database for OIR liaisons to input information from the activity design scripts.

The OIR liaison entering the change into the OIR database provides information across the dimensions regarding the individuals or groups that may be impacted by the change.

Applicable Customers—External customers that will be impacted by the SAP project.

Role

Role—A description of task(s) bundled into a logical grouping and performed by one or more jobs/positions. (Multiple roles can be associated with any given job/position.)

This dimension will serve to identify all roles that will be affected by a change. A preliminary list of roles will be populated in the database and the liaison will review the roles to see if every role that is impacted is on the list. If not, the liaison will add any missing role.

Type of Employee

Further refinement for each role selected will include categorization of that role as performed by employees who are exempt management, nonexempt management, supervisor, and/or nonexempt nonmanagement. The operating definition of "supervisor" will be any employee who has one or more direct reports.

Organizational Unit

Organizational Unit—A discrete entity made up of one or more jobs/positions that utilizes distinct functionality to achieve a specific purpose.

This dimension will serve to identify all organizational units that will be impacted by a change. A preliminary list of organizational units will be populated in the database and the liaison will review them to see if every organizational unit that is impacted is on the list. If not, the liaison will add any missing organizational unit.

Impact Significance

Each change will be evaluated on the level of impact—high, moderate, or low—on the affected role, type of employee, or organizational unit.

Changes that impact different groups differently will be described in a Notes section of the worksheet.

Perception

Each change will be evaluated on how it will be perceived by the impacted role, organizational unit, or type of employee—as positive, neutral, or negative. Changes that are perceived differently by different groups will be described in the Notes section of the worksheet.

Stakeholder Profiles

A stakeholder profile is a grouping of individuals, roles, positions, jobs, or organizational units (whichever unit is appropriate to a given change) affected in a similar manner by the changes caused by the deployment of SAP. Creating these profiles makes it possible to form a strategy for best managing the change for each grouping.

Stakeholder profiles will be developed by the OIR team, after careful review and analysis of the information gathered from the inputs, particularly the activity design scripts. These stakeholder profiles will illustrate how each stakeholder group will affect the change or be affected by the change, depending on the profile category. The major output of the stakeholder profiles is customized strategies and tactical activities tailored for each profile to move that profile toward the appropriate location on the commitment continuum. As stated previously, there are two categories of profiles, sponsor/advocate/change agent profiles and target profiles.

The roles are often pictured by creating a role map diagram in which the following roles are assigned to individuals:

- ▶ Initiating Sponsor
- ▶ Sustaining Sponsor
- ▶ Change Sponsor
- ▶ Change Agent
- ▶ Target
- ▶ Advocate

Often one individual will wear more than one hat at different points in the project.

Commitment Continuum

Every stakeholder profile needs to achieve a certain level of commitment to the employee systems project to make it successful. The level of commitment needed varies by how stakeholders will be affected by the changes or what they will be asked to do to effect change.

The OIR team, with input from other sources, will estimate how committed each of the stakeholder profile groups needs to be to ensure a successful implementation:

- ► at the beginning of the Build Phase
- ► at the beginning of the Test Phase
- ► at the beginning of the Deploy Phase.

The desired placement of each stakeholder profile along the commitment continuum prior to each phase of the project will be used to guide and develop involvement, communication, training/education strategies, and tactical activities for each of the stakeholder profiles and to ensure that an appropriate amount of effort is expended on each of the groups.

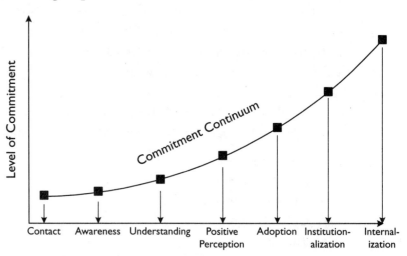

FIGURE 8-5. Commitment continuum

Profile Strategies

Profile strategies and tactical activities will be different for the two categories of profiles.

Sponsor/Advocate/Change Agent Profiles

Sponsors, advocates, and change agents will be treated first as targets, to build commitment for the project. As with target profile strategies, "key events" will be designed to move them along the commitment continuum.

The focus of these profile strategies for this group, however, will be activities that the sponsors, advocates, and change agents will execute to move their organization to the desired location along the commitment continuum. The strategies will be developed recognizing that the people in this group will be in the process of accepting the change at the same time as they will have to be championing the change. Support for this critical group will be provided by the project manager and the deployment team as the members of this key group perform their role.

Each sponsor/advocate/change agent profile strategy will include the following:

- ▶ **Stakeholder Profile Name**
- ▶ **Description of the Stakeholder Profile**—Defining characteristics of this group
- ▶ **Involvement Strategy**—Strategy for getting these stakeholders involved, aware, and educated regarding their role in the change process
- ▶ **Key Activities with Timeline**—A high-level tactical translation of the involvement strategy, including five or six key events and/or milestones for this group.

Target Profile

Target profile strategies are designed to move each target profile group to wherever it needs to be on the commitment continuum prior to deployment. The target profile strategies are designed to build commitment along the continuum over time. The design of the strategies is based upon the training/education, communication, and involvement that the target stakeholder profile group will need in order to reach the proper level of commitment to the change. Target profile strategies will be executed primarily through the deployment infrastructure, with assistance and guidance from the MOC team. Primary responsibility for the execution of some target profile strategies (those involving target groups falling outside the deployment infrastructure) will belong to the MOC team. The target strategy template can be seen in Figure 8-6.

Target Strategy Template

Profile Name

XXX

Significant Changes That This Group Will Experience

- XXX
- XXX
- XXX

Profile Description

XXX

Involvement Needs 1. 2. 3.	**Communication Needs** A. B. C.	**Training/Education Needs** I. II. III.

Key Activities with Timeline for Involvement, Communication, and Training/Education Strategies

I				A		B					II				C		
Design				Build					Test						Deploy		
I	2	3	4	5	6	7	8	9	10	11	12	13	14	15	16	17	18
Months																	
				2		3		I							III		

FIGURE 8-6. Target strategy template

Each target profile strategy will include the following:

► **Stakeholder Profile Name**

► **Description of the Stakeholder Profile**—Defining characteristics of this group

► **Significant Changes That This Group Will Experience**—Changes that will cause members of this stakeholder group to modify their beliefs, attitudes, behaviors, skills, or knowledge base

► **Involvement Needs**—Strategy for getting these stakeholders involved in the change process at the appropriate level

► **Communication Needs**—Strategy for communicating to this stakeholder group at the appropriate level

► **Training/Education Needs**—Strategy for educating and training this stakeholder group at the appropriate level

► **Key Activities with Timeline**—A high-level tactical translation of the identified involvement, communication, and training/education needs, including five or six key events and/or milestones for this group.

The strategies and key activities developed for each of the types of stakeholder profiles reflect a holistic approach, joining the activities of the MOC, performance solutions, and communication teams into one integrated solution.

Tactical Plans

After the strategies and tactical activities have been defined for each of the stakeholder profiles, execution will begin. This will occur differently for the two categories of profiles.

For the sponsor/advocate/change agent profiles, the OIR team will have primary responsibility for executing the tactical activities, including communicating to, educating, and involving the individuals within those profiles. Some of these activities will be conducted in the field organizations through the deployment infrastructure. However, primary ownership for enrolling the sponsors, advocates, and change agents resides with the OIR and deployment coordination teams.

For the target profiles, the deployment managers will be responsible for reviewing the profile strategies and activities that have been developed, customizing these strategies and activities to fit their own organizations, and developing and executing tactical plans to ensure a successful deployment. These deployment managers will have primary ownership of the tactical plan development and execution, yet will be guided and assisted by members of the deployment coordination and OIR teams and, most notably, by the deployment coaches.

Feedback

Formal feedback processes should be put in place to ensure that the overall MOC strategy and approach, as well as the customized stakeholder profile strategies and tactical activities, are working. Some of the mechanisms to collect feedback from end users could be:

- ▶ Evaluations from live demonstrations, such as Proof of Concept or Day-in-the-Life Scenario presentations for specific roles and job titles.
- ▶ The linkage between the deployment infrastructure (deployment coaches, managers, and coordinators) and the OIR and deployment coordination teams. This linkage will ensure that information from the operating units is gathered and channeled back to the deployment team.
- ▶ The linkages between the OIR and the functional teams (OIR liaisons to the functional teams and functional team liaisons to OIR, starting in the Build Phase of the project). These linkages will ensure that information gathered in the field is channeled back to the functional teams during the Build and Test Phases.
- ▶ Widely known and distributed phone and electronic access providing a linkage from the field directly to the project team.

Commonly accepted evaluation tools (such as electronic and manual surveys) and questionnaires will be developed by the MOC team to support the feedback channels described above.

MOC Schedule to Support an SAP Project

Figure 8-7 is a schedule to support a typical 18-month SAP project that progresses through four phases—Design, Build, Test, and Deploy.

	Months																	
	1	2	3	4	5	6	7	8	9	10	11	12	13	14	15	16	17	18
	Design				Build					Test						Deploy		
1. MOC approach developed	▬																	
2. Activity Design Script Deployment Section developed and rolled out to Functional Teams	▬																	
3. Script Sign-off Process for Deployment developed and rolled out	▬																	
4. Proof of Concept Event held	▬																	
5. OIR Database developed		▬																
6. Dimensions Defined for Stakeholders		▬																
7. Front-end Electronic Worksheet developed for Database		▬																
8. Activity Design Scripts reviewed and approved		▬																
9. Changes filtered out and entered in OIR database		▬																
10. Stakeholder Profiles Development initiated			▬															
11. Database complete. Stakeholder Profiles finalized				▬														
12. Profile Strategies Development initiated				▬														
13. MOC tools developed for Business Champion Kick-off				▬														

FIGURE 8-7. Typical MOC/SAP schedule

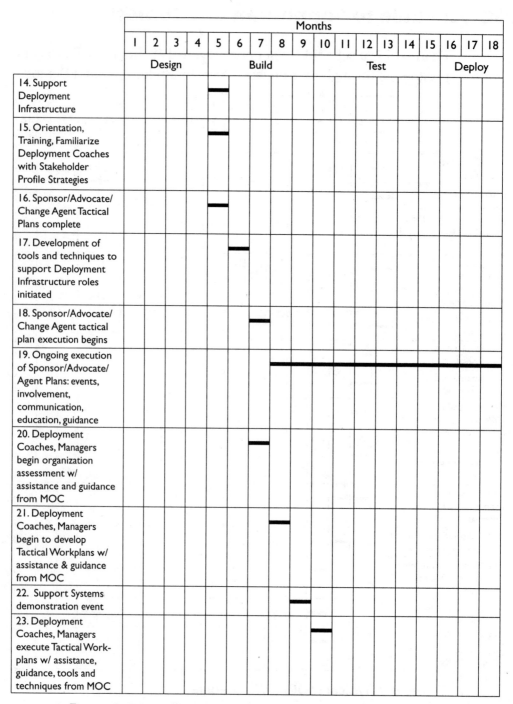

Figure 8-7 (continued)

	Months																	
	1	2	3	4	5	6	7	8	9	10	11	12	13	14	15	16	17	18
	Design				Build					Test						Deploy		
24. Ongoing assistance and guidance in Execution of Deployment Infrastructure Plans										▬	▬	▬	▬	▬	▬	▬	▬	▬
25. Day-in-the-Life Scenarios developed Presentations initiated											▬	▬						

FIGURE 8-7. (concluded)

MOC Assessments, Planning Tools, and Training Used During an SAP Project

Figure 8-8 is a partial list of MOC assessments, planning tools, and training that could be used during an SAP project.

Summary

A high percentage of Ernst & Young LLP management consulting efforts relate to helping clients install and update their information systems. Jay C. Juliussen, partner of E&Y in charge of Business Transformation Management Services, wrote in a letter to E&Y management consultants May 1999, "Historically our clients' view of change management was tactical. They associated the change management services with specific projects. Organizations now see that the ability to effectively manage transformation as mission-critical and a strategic necessity. It must be built into how they manage their business if they want to be the industry drivers and not industry roadkill. The change management concept is not something we need to push. It is an issue most of our clients bring up without any prompting."

	MOC Assessments, Planning Tools, and Training	Software Development			
		I	II	III	IV
I.	Adaptation Capacity Audit	✓		✓	
2.	Change Agent Evaluation	✓		✓	
3.	Change Agent Selection Form	✓			
4.	Change History Survey	✓			
5.	Change Knowledge Assessment			✓	
6.	Change Project Description Form	✓	✓	✓	✓
7.	Change Resistance Scale			✓	
8.	Coaching Styles Inventory and Guide		✓	✓	
9.	Communicating Change: Announcement Plan	✓	✓	✓	
10.	Communicating Change: Constituency Analysis	✓	✓	✓	
11.	Communicating Change: Project Analysis		✓	✓	
12.	Communicating Change: Statement Development		✓	✓	
13.	Communicating Style Survey and Guide		✓	✓	
14.	Culture Assessment	✓	✓		
15.	Culture Audit		✓	✓	
16.	Expectations for a Successful Change Project	✓	✓		
17.	Focus Groups Tools*			✓	✓
18.	Force-Field Analysis*			✓	✓
19.	Implementation Plan Advocacy Kit				✓
20.	Implementation Plan Evaluation				✓
21.	Implementation Problems Assessment	✓			
22.	Individual Error Rate Measurements*				✓
23.	Influence Style Survey and Interpretation Manual	✓			✓
24.	Landscape Surveys			✓	✓
25.	MOC Training for Sponsors, Agents, Targets, and Advocates	✓	✓		
26.	Organization Change Implementation Plan (OCIP)			✓	✓
27.	Overload Index	✓		✓	

FIGURE 8-8. The MOC assessments, planning tools, and training in the software development cycle (continued on page 303)

	MOC Assessments, Planning Tools, and Training	Software Development			
		I	II	III	IV
28.	Pain Management Strategies: Sponsor	✓	✓	✓	✓
29.	Pain Management Strategies: Target			✓	✓
30.	Personal Power Survey		✓		✓
31	Personal Resilience Questionnaire and Profile				✓
32.	Postmortem*				✓
33.	Predicting the Impact of Change			✓	
34.	Preliminary Implementation Plan		✓	✓	
35.	Process Modeling*		✓	✓	
36.	Process Walk-through Checklist*	✓	✓	✓	
37.	Rewards and Recognition Tools*	✓			✓
38.	Role Map Application Tool	✓	✓	✓	
39.	Senior Team Value for Discipline	✓			
40.	Simulation Modeling*			✓	
41.	Sponsor Checklist	✓		✓	✓
42.	Sponsor Evaluation	✓		✓	
43.	Synergy Survey		✓	✓	
44.	When To Apply the MOC Methodology	✓		✓	
* Use of this tool is not limited to the MOC Methodology					

FIGURE 8-8. (continued)

To realize the full value of any SAP project, it is absolutely mandatory to have an effective MOC program integrated within the SAP project. All too often SAP projects have failed to reach their promised potential because the project team focused its effort on changing the process through the effective use of technology without placing equal effort on preparing the employees and management to embrace the new process and equipment.

According to a Bain & Co. survey reported in *Fortune*, Sept. 7, 1998 ("What's Today's Special at the Consultants' Cafe?"), "[Management] tool usage is high across all industries and in all countries, with the average respondent using 13 of the top 25 tools. Yet 77% of executives report that tools promise more than they deliver, and even highly rated tools vary widely in their ability to improve financial results, customer equity, and competitive advantage."

I believe that the shortfall between promised results and actual results is largely because the change was not managed well.

Application Examples

We have provided you with the process, but will it work in real life? Let's look at where Ernst & Young LLP has applied the change management concepts and the results that were obtained.

We have successfully implemented solutions that range from accelerating new product development while streamlining billions from the process at a major automotive manufacturer, implementing new shared services and integrating one of the largest health care systems in the country, and integrating one of the largest telecommunication companies after an announced merger and working with that company currently to enable an even larger integration.

We worked with a major chemical manufacturer in the implementation of a total enterprise solution that represents the most extensive SAP implementation to date. The changes touched all areas of the business, including the financial and controlling processes, plant maintenance, and realignment and optimization of its internal as well as customer-facing supply chains.

The following describes the highlights of the people and organizational work done in support of implementation:

▶ Development and deployment of a People Enabler Strategy to support the implementation: definition of the scope of change and its impact on people, definition of competency architecture aligned with the SAP and work process solution, and assessment of the level of alignment between the HR practices and the objectives of the change

▶ Development and deployment of a change readiness strategy: stakeholder mapping, leader alignment strategy, organizational strategy

- Securing leadership sponsorship and active change leader roles prior to and during deployment through a leader alignment cascade process
- Developing and deploying "Organizational Alignment" sessions to serve as orientation, and more detailed communication forums for employees

▶ Overall communication planning

▶ Facilitation of mapping "end to end" transitional and new work processes

▶ Planning of a conference room pilot to demonstrate SAP functionality, new work processes, and roles

▶ Enterprise-wide restructuring, including design and supporting business case development

▶ Tactical organization redesign, including structure, new role definitions and descriptions, competency identification, key metrics, and individual performance measures

▶ Development of job-mapping process and Access database tool to collect current-state information on jobs and tasks and map to future-state jobs designed as part of the SAP solution definition

▶ Development of a work process owner structure to ensure consistent implementation and ongoing management of common work processes across business units

▶ Documentation of new decision-making process to support new process design (determining who needs to be involved and drawing up a charter for new decision-making forums and accountabilities)

▶ Documentation of HR processes to be used during implementation and on an ongoing basis to support the change objectives: selection, performance management

> ▸ Intensive end-user training that encompasses Web-based, role-based, and leader-led instruction

Results and Value Added

> ▸ Understanding, commitment, and competence needed by leadership team to drive the effort under tight timeframes and technical challenges
>
> ▸ New organization that will be better aligned to enable new, common work processes across the enterprise—and at significantly less cost to the business in terms of number of leadership roles, layers, and staffing, as well as inventory optimization
>
> ▸ More data-oriented process, which accelerated decision making through high-quality information to map current personnel to future roles, a mapping process that allows more targeted, role-based training
>
> ▸ New, more targeted performance measures—with clear accountabilities throughout the business

MOC change often increases the return on investment by as much as 30%.

APPENDIX A

Glossary

Activity Design Scripts: Define what the activity will look like after the SAP project has been implemented.

Adapt: To recover from a significant disruption in expectations. This is accomplished when new expectations are developed that allow people to succeed in an unfamiliar environment.

Adaptability: The flexibility of the process that handles future demands, changing customer expectations, and today's individual special customer requirements. It is managing the process to meet today's special needs and future requirements.

Advocates: The individuals or groups that want to achieve a change but lack the power to sanction it.

Applicable Customers: External customers that will be impacted by the SAP project.

Benchmarking: A systematic way to identify, understand, and creatively evolve superior products, services, designs, equipment, processes, and practices to improve the organization's real performance by studying how other organizations are performing the same or similar operations.

Best-Value Future-State Solution (BFSS): A solution that results in the most beneficial new item as viewed by the item's stakeholders. It is the best combination of implementation cost, implementation cycle time, risk, and performance results (e.g., return on investment, customer satisfaction, market share, risk, value added per employee, time to implement, cost to implement).

Black Hole: A condition in which one or more managers fail to fulfill their sponsor responsibilities, such as by withholding or distorting information so that it doesn't get passed on to the rest of the organization.

Business Process Improvement (BPI): The breakthrough methodologies used to improve individual processes, which include process redesign, process reengineering, benchmarking, restructuring, and major software projects like SAP.

Change Agents: The individuals or groups responsible for making the change.

Change Facilitator: The individual who leads and directs the change management activities for a project. He or she provides the just-in-time MOC training and change management guidance to the PIT, sponsors, and others requiring that level of training. The change facilitator can be viewed as a "black belt" change agent. Often internal or external consultants serve as the change facilitators.

Communicating Style: Manner or characteristic mode of interaction among people. A specific style suggests a frame of reference. The basic frames of reference are thinker, sensor, feeler, and intuitor.

Comparative Analysis: The act of comparing a set of measurements with a set of similar measurements for a similar item.

Control: The extent to which individuals can direct or at least anticipate outcomes in a change process.

Corporate Culture: The beliefs, behaviors, and assumptions shared by individuals within an organization. Includes such things as procedures, values, and unspoken norms.

Department Improvement Team (DIT): Group made up of employees who report to the same manager, formed to train the department members to solve problems that impact the department's operations and to improve processes within the department.

Desired Future State: This state results from vacating the current state and integrating the new behavior patterns required by a change. The desired future state represents full achievement of the objectives of the change.

Dimensions: Define how individuals or groups will be affected by the change.

Direct Control: The ability to dictate outcomes.

Dysfunction: Any change-related action or feeling that diverts resources away from meeting productivity and quality standards.

Effectiveness: The extent to which the output of a process or subprocess meets the needs and expectations of the customers. A close synonym of effectiveness is quality. Effectiveness is having the right output at the right place at the right time at the right price. Effectiveness impacts the process's direct and indirect customers.

Efficiency: A measure of the resources (human, money, cycle time, etc.) that a process consumes in order to produce its output. A close synonym of efficiency is productivity.

Enabler: A technical or organizational facility/resource that makes it possible to perform a task, activity, or process. Examples of technical enablers are personal computers, copying equipment, decentralized data processing, voice-response acceptance, etc. Examples of organizational enablers are self-managed work teams, virtual departments, network organizations, and education systems.

Execution Costs: The expense of identifying what to do—which you may figure into the cost associated with how the human aspects of change will be managed, the lost efficiency (productivity and quality) that typically occurs when resources are focused away from day-to-day operations to project implementation, and the price of any new infrastructure required to maintain the BPI solution (e.g., technology, people, and training).

Fast Action Solution Technique (FAST): A breakthrough approach that focuses a group's attention on a single process for a one- or two-day meeting to define how the group can improve the process over the next 90 days. Before the end of the meeting, management approves or rejects the proposed improvements.

Frame of Reference (FOR): A compatible set of ideas, theories, beliefs, feelings, values, and assumptions that allows meaning to be applied to a person's experience. FOR is an unconscious model for comprehending reality.

Future Shock: The point at which no more change can be accommodated without the display of dysfunctional behaviors.

Future-State Implementation Team (FIT): Group of people who are assigned to refine, document, install, and provide training related to the future-state process.

Future-State Solution (FSS): A combination of corrective actions and changes that can be applied to an item (process) being studied to increase its performance and its value to the stakeholders.

Human Due Diligence (HDD): Gathering information, planning, and engaging in actions related to the impact that change is having or will have on an organization's human capital.

Indirect Control: The ability to at least anticipate outcomes.

Influencing Targets: A nonmanagement member of a group who sways other members of the group as a result of the trust and respect that they have for that person.

Major Change: A perceived departure from what was expected. Change is disruptive when a large gap exists between what was expected and what was experienced.

Managing Organizational Change (MOC): The disciplined application of a comprehensive set of structured procedures for the decision-making, planning, and execution phases of the change process. It does not focus on what is to be changed.

Negative Analysis: The act of looking at an activity and defining things that could cause the activity to fail.

Nimbleness: The ability for an organization to consistently succeed in unpredictable, contested environments by implementing important changes more efficiently and effectively than its competitors, thereby maintaining its desired return on change (ROChg).

Organization: Company, corporation, firm, enterprise, or association or any part thereof, whether incorporated or not, public or private, that has its own function and administration (source: ISO 8402, 1994).

Pain: A critical mass of uncomfortable information about staying in the status quo that justifies suffering through the transition state while moving toward the desired state.

Present State: The status quo, the established patterns of expectations. It is characterized by relative stability and familiarity. It represents a dynamic equilibrium that continues indefinitely until a force disrupts it. As the rate of change increases, the present state shifts from stasis into fluidity.

Process Improvement Team (PIT): A group of individuals, usually from different functions, assigned to improve a specific process or subprocess. They design the best-value future-state solution using methodologies such as process redesign, process reengineering, and process benchmarking.

Process Redesign: A methodology used to streamline a current process with the objective of reducing cost and cycle time by 30% to 60% while improving output quality from 20% to 200%.

Process Reengineering: A methodology used to radically change the way a process is presently designed by developing an independent vision of how it should perform and using a group of enablers to prepare a new process design that is not hampered by the present process paradigms.

Program: A group of related projects managed in a coordinated way. Programs usually include an element of ongoing activities.

Project: A temporary endeavor undertaken to create a unique product or service.

Project Management: The application of knowledge, skills, tools, and techniques to project activities in order to meet or exceed stakeholders' needs and expectations for the project.

Project MOC Implementation Team (CIT): Person or group responsible for developing and implementing the MOC plan for the project.

Remedy: The actual behaviors needed to achieve the desired future state on time and within budget. A BPI solution is a good example.

Resilience: The ability to absorb high levels of disruptive change while displaying minimal dysfunctional behavior.

Resistance: Any thought or action directed against a change. Some level of resistance should be expected in any major change.

Return on Change (ROChg): An objective measure of goal attainment, given the resources invested in your project activities. ROChg is derived by dividing the yield from a project by the implementation cost of that effort.

Risk Areas: Any class of activities or lack of activities that reduce the probability of successful project implementation. Examples include resistance, change knowledge, project overload, and implementation skills and techniques.

Role: A description of task(s) bundled into a logical grouping and performed by one or more job / positions. (Multiple roles can be associated with any given job / position.)

Role Map Diagram: The graphic representation of the key people, influential relationships, political realities, and organizational structures that are integral to the success of a major change.

Set Context: Clarify how a BPI effort fits with the organization's business strategy.

Sponsor: An individual or group with the power to sanction or legitimize the project.

Stakeholder: An individual or group of individuals or organizations with a common interest. Stakeholders of an organization typically are the customers, the owners, the employees, the employees' families, the suppliers, management, and society. Stakeholders are sometimes called interest partners or interested parties.

Status Quo: Same as present state.

Strategic Change: Any change that has a significant impact throughout an organization.

Synergy: Individuals or groups working together in a manner that produces a greater total effect than the sum of their individual efforts, generates more benefits to the organization than the amount of resources consumed, promotes a higher future shock threshold, and requires fewer adaptation resources to change.

Targets: The individuals or groups affected by the change.

Transition State: The phase during which people no longer behave as they did in the past, but are not yet fully "set" in the new pattern. They disengage from the status quo. The dynamic equilibrium of the present state has been disrupted, but the desired or future state has not yet been reached completely.

Yield from Effort: A measurement of movement toward achieving the project's objectives. ("Movement" refers to the difference between the status of the organization before implementation of the initiative and its status after implementation.)

MOC Timeline Chart for a Total Process Redesign Project

#	Activities and Tasks	Weeks									
		-6	-5	-4	-3	-2	-1	1	2	3	4
I	**ORGANIZING FOR IMPROVEMENT**	■	■	■	■	■	■	■	■	■	■
1	**Evaluate the Applicability of BPI**	■	■	■	■						
1.1	Prepare the overall business case for BPI (identifying the cost of the status quo and defining the burning platform)	■									
1.2	Create a future-state vision for the entire project	■									
1.3	Assess the organization's capacity to assimilate new change using one or more of the following tools as applicable: Change Project Description form (initial high-level descriptions) When to Apply MOC Methodology Predicting the Impact of Change Adaptation Capacity Audit Overload Index Implementation Problems Assessment Change History Survey		■	■							
1.4	Assess the MOC knowledge and skills of the executive team, using one of more of the following tools as applicable: Personal Resilience Questionnaire Personal Power Survey Influence Style Survey Communicating Style Survey Change Knowledge Assessment Sponsor Evaluation Sponsor Checklist Senior Team Value for Discipline		■	■							

#	Activities and Tasks	Weeks									
		-6	-5	-4	-3	-2	-1	1	2	3	4
1.5	Conduct MOC awareness and training as needed to close gaps found		▬								
1.6	Appoint the BPI champion		▬								
1.7	Ensure initiating sponsor and BPI champion understanding and commitment to MOC			▬							
1.8	Draft and release high-level communications about the BPI project being initiated, the business case requiring it, and the future-state vision			▬							
2	**Define Critical Business Processes**					▬					
2.1	Identify the process and criteria for the prioritizing and selecting processes					▬					
2.2	Evaluate such change-relevant factors as: The extent of expected disruption (Predicting the Impact of Change) The change capacity of people involved in the process Past history of changes (Implementation Problems Assessment) The sub-culture of each process (Culture Assessment) Assess extent and probability of resulting work force reductions Other changes that would affect people involved in each process					▬					
2.3	Select the critical business processes that will be targeted for BPI					▬					
2.4	Select the BPI methodology that will be applied to each					▬					
2.5	Prioritize the sequence with which BPI will be applied					▬					
2.6	Create a future state vision for each selected process						▬				
2.7	Set improvement objectives for each selected process						▬				
2.8	Establish a policy and strategy for dealing with workforce reductions						▬				
3	**Select the Process Owners and Executive Sponsors**						▬				
3.1	Define needed roles and responsibilities						▬				
3.2	Create change role behavior requirements						▬				
3.3	Confirm the role and commitment of the initiating sponsor						▬				

#	Activities and Tasks	Weeks									
		-6	-5	-4	-3	-2	-1	1	2	3	4
3.4	Evaluate the change capacity and knowledge of potential owners/ sponsors						▬				
3.5	Select a process owner for each process						▬				
3.6	Select an executive sponsor for each process						▬				
3.7	Create project infrastructure (steering committee, project management)						▬				
3.8	Provide MOC training for process owners and sponsors						▬				
4	**Define Preliminary Boundaries**							▬			
4.1	Define the preliminary scope of each process / project							▬			
4.2	Create a preliminary Role Map diagram							▬			
4.3	Create preliminary communications about the project							▬			
5	**Form and Train the Process Improvement Team**							▬	▬		
5.1	Define required team member competencies, skills, resilience, etc							▬			
5.2	Process owner block diagram each process to the department level							▬			
5.3	Meet with each affected department manager							▬			
5.4	Select a PIT team member from each affected department							▬			
5.5	Select additional PIT team members as needed (experts, customers, etc.)								▬		
5.6	Select a change facilitator if warranted by the magnitude of the change								▬		
5.7	Create a PIT charter								▬		

5.8	Identify PIT member's existing skills and competencies, etc. using
	    Sponsor Evaluation
	    Change Knowledge Assessment
									▬		

5.9	Create a training plan to close the gap								▬		
5.10	Conduct training and assess results								▬	▬	

#	Activities and Tasks	Weeks									
		-6	-5	-4	-3	-2	-1	1	2	3	4
6	**Box In the Process**										▬
6.1	Clarify process/project scope--what is included and excluded?										▬
6.2	Update the Role Map diagram based on updated scope information										▬
6.3	Update the communications plan based on updated scope information										▬
6.4	Implement the communications plan										▬
7	**Establish Measurements and Goals**										▬
7.1	Determine the metrics to be applied to the process/project										▬
7.2	Establish goals for each metric										▬
7.3	Create a project-specific change management data base										▬
8	**Develop Project and Change Management Plans**										▬
8.1	Create or update the project mission statement										▬
8.2	Clear statement of the business case (the burning platform)										▬
8.3	Develop a set of PIT operating guidelines										▬
8.4	Create Individual member assignments										▬
8.5	Incorporate the Process Measurements established in Activity 7										▬
8.6	Incorporate the improvement goals for each process metric										▬
8.7	Identify key barriers										▬
8.8	Incorporate the current version of the Role Map diagram										▬
8.9	Evaluate the extent, causes and sources of potential resistance										▬
8.10	Create preliminary plan for Phases II and III										▬
8.11	Set timetables for completion of Phases II and III										▬
8.12	Identify resource requirements										▬
8.13	Assess the plan using the MOC Implementation Plan Evaluation										▬
8.14	Communicate the plan to affected employees										▬

#	Activities and Tasks	Weeks			
		5	6	7	8
II	**UNDERSTANDING THE PROCESS**	■■■■■■			
0.1	Create a future-state vision for the entire project	▬▬			
0.1	Provide training for PIT members in Phase II tools and skills	▬			
1	**Flowchart the process**	▬			
2	**Prepare the simulation model**	▬▬			
3	**Conduct process walk-through**		▬		
3.1	Form walk-through teams		▬		
3.2	Conduct a sustaining sponsor commitment analysis		▬		
3.3	Prepare a comprehensive new process vision statement		▬		
3.4	Involve sponsors and influencing targets in planning the walk-through		▬		
3.5	Conduct the walk-through		▬		
3.6	Include a Culture Assessment of the affected areas		▬		
3.7	Define pain associated with the as-is process and potential future state		▬		
3.8	Update the flowcharts and simulation models based on new information		▬		
3.9	Review findings with sustaining sponsors and influencing targets		▬		
4	**Perform process cost and cycle-time analysis**		▬▬▬		
5	**Implement quick fixes**			▬	
5.1	Evaluate cost/benefit potential			▬	
5.2	Review findings with sustaining sponsors and influencing targets			▬	
5.3	Select quick fixes to be implemented and develop accelerated plan			▬	
5.4	Secure approval			▬	
5.5	Implement			▬	
5.6	Assess results and impact			▬	
6	**Align process and procedures**				▬

#	Activities and Tasks	Weeks					
		9	10	11	12	13	14
III	**STREAMLINING THE PROCESS**	██	██	██	██	██	██
0.1	Assess the level of sustaining sponsor commitment (Sponsor Evaluation and/or Sponsor Checklist) and take needed corrective action	▬	▬	▬	▬	▬	▬
I	**Apply the 12 streamlining tools to analyze improvement potential**	▬	▬	▬	▬	▬	
1.1	Bureaucracy elimination	▬	▬	▬	▬	▬	
1.2	Value-added assessment	▬	▬	▬	▬	▬	
1.3	Duplication elimination	▬	▬	▬	▬	▬	
1.4	Simplification methods	▬	▬	▬	▬	▬	
1.5	Cycle-time reduction	▬	▬	▬	▬	▬	
1.6	Error proofing	▬	▬	▬	▬	▬	
1.7	Process upgrading	▬	▬	▬	▬	▬	
1.8	Simple language	▬	▬	▬	▬	▬	
1.9	Standardization	▬	▬	▬	▬	▬	
1.10	Supplier partnerships	▬	▬	▬	▬	▬	
1.11	Automation, mechanization, and information technology	▬	▬	▬	▬	▬	
1.12	Organizational restructuring	▬	▬	▬	▬	▬	
1.13	Interview sponsors and affected people (targets)		▬	▬	▬		
1.14	Prepare new simulation models		▬	▬	▬		
1.15	**Alternative Future-State Solutions**		▬	▬	▬		
1.15.1	Prepare a minimum of three alternative solutions	▬	▬	▬	▬	▬	
2	**Perform a Cost-Benefits Analysis**		▬	▬	▬		
2.1	Include human costs and benefits		▬	▬	▬		
3	**Select the Best-Value Future State Solution**					▬	
3.1	Use groups of targets to validate solutions					▬	
3.2	Create or update the Change Project Description form					▬	
3.3	Document the business case for selection of the solutions					▬	

#	Activities and Tasks	Weeks					
		9	10	11	12	13	14
4	**Obtain Executive Committee Approval**						▬
4.1	Reaffirm initiating sponsor commitment to the project						▬
5	**Approve Preliminary Implementation Plan**					▬	

5.1	Assess the organization's capacity to assimilate the specific change proposed, using one or more of the following tools as applicable:
	  Change Project Description form (detailed descriptions)
	  When to Apply Implementation Architecture
	  Landscape Survey
	  Culture Assessment
	  Predicting the Impact of Change
	  Overload Index
	  Implementation Problems Assessment
	  Change History Survey
						▬	

5.2	Update the Role Map document based on best-value solution impacts					▬	
5.3	Assess alignment of the infrastructure with desired behavioral objectives					▬	
5.4	Evaluate the level of teamwork required for successful implementation (Synergy Survey)					▬	
5.5	Identify infrastructure changes needed to reinforce the change					▬	
5.6	Identify advocates whose help will be needed during implementation					▬	
5.7	Analyze the effectiveness of prior communications					▬	
5.8	Update the communications plan					▬	
5.9	Identify the training needs of all affected targets					▬	
5.10	Develop a training plan to meet identified needs					▬	
5.11	Identify actual or potential resistance (Change Resistance Scale)					▬	
5.12	Include resistance mitigation activities in the plan					▬	
5.13	Identify actions to be taken by sponsors to maintain target commitment					▬	
5.14	Recommend members of the future-state implementation team (FIT)					▬	

#	Activities and Tasks	Weeks			
		15	16	17	18
IV	**IMPLEMENTATION, MEASUREMENTS, AND CONTROL**	■■■			
0.1	Assess the level of sustaining sponsor commitment (Sponsor Evaluation and/or Sponsor Checklist) and take corrective action where necessary	■■			
0.2	Form the future-state implementation team (FIT)	■			
0.3	Assess change knowledge of FIT members	■			
0.4	Assess change agent competency to facilitate Phase IV implementation (Change Agent Evaluation)	■			
0.5	Conduct training as needed in both technical skills and MOC skills	■			
0.6	Complete a change project description	■			
1	**Finalize the Implementation Plan**		→→→		➤

	Review the implementation plan, revise, and update:
	  Verify all prior plan activities
	  Add any new activities identified by the FIT members
	  Detail the plan to the task level
	  Assess MOC implications of any changes to the plan
	  Identify the individual responsible for each activity and task
	  Refine the timetable for completion of each activity and task and assess the cumulative impact of the change timetable
	  Update the Role Map diagram and use it to drive implementation
	  Update and implement the communications plan (Organizational Change Implementation Plan and/or Implementation Plan Evaluation)
			→→→		➤

2	**Implement the New Process**		→→→		➤
	Secure the involvement of sponsors, advocates, and target advocates		→→→		➤

	Deliver required training for all targets
	  technical or job skills
	  MOC or resilience competencies
			→→→		➤

	Implement the planned changes to the infrastructure	→→→			➤
	Communicate the future-state process specifications	→→→			➤
	Provide simulation models of new processes when feasible	→→→			➤
	Implement the planned changes to the process	→→→			➤
	Update simulation models	→→→			➤
	Provide rewards and recognition for adopting new required behaviors	→→→			➤
	Implement plans for removing excess people (sponsors and targets)	→→→			➤
	Maintain frequent contact with sponsors to prevent new "black holes"	→→→			➤

#	Activities and Tasks	Weeks			
		15	16	17	18
3	**Establish In-Process Measurements**		→———→		
	Include both in-process and outcome measurements		→———→		
4	**Establish the Feedback Systems**			→——→	
	Create focus groups to solicit feedback			→——→	
	Conduct "town meetings" for collecting feedback			→——→	
	Conduct an Implementation Problems Assessment			→——→	
5	**Monitor Results**			→——→	
	Analyze effectiveness of communications			→——→	
	Track process measurements against goals			→——→	
	Include tracking of human as well as process metrics (Landscape Survey and/or Overload Index)			→——→	
	Initiate MOC tracking			→——→	

Index